REFEREE!

REFEREE!

A Year In The Life of David Elleray

David Elleray

BLOOMSBURY

First published in Great Britain in 1998
Bloomsbury Publishing Plc, 38 Soho Square, London W1V 5DH

Copyright © 1998 by David Elleray

The moral right of the author has been asserted

PICTURE CREDITS

Allsport: pages 13, 14 *bottom*
Empics: pages 4 *bottom*, 11 (Michael Steele/Barry Bland), 12 *bottom*
(Chris Turvey)
Richard Saker: page 12 *top*
All other material supplied by the author

A CIP catalogue record for this book is available from the British
Library

ISBN 0 7475 3692 9

10 9 8 7 6 5 4 3 2 1

Typeset by Hewer Text Ltd, Edinburgh, Scotland
Printed in Great Britain by Clays Ltd, St Ives plc

Dedicated to my family, my godchildren and Druries

FOREWORD

In 1966 the football bug bit me and I began refereeing in January 1968, at the age of thirteen, having reluctantly accepted that I would never play for my school 1st XI – let alone England. When I started refereeing I set myself the target of refereeing the 1998 World Cup Final. The 1950 and 1974 World Cup Finals had been refereed by Englishmen so I was determined to repeat the 24-year cycle.

Throughout my time at Dover Grammar School, Oxford University and Harrow School refereeing has been an integral part of my life. It has complemented my work and given me a physical and mental escape from the daily stresses and strains, bringing a different dimension into my life which has both motivated and stimulated me.

I have officiated in 2195 matches – 1582 as referee, 17 as reserve referee and 596 on the line, sending off 210 players and cautioning 1592. I have officiated at Wembley 10 times, including the 1994 FA Cup Final and the 1992 FA Charity Shield. My 64 international appointments have seen me officiate throughout Europe and in recent seasons I have refereed in Brazil, Japan, Saudi Arabia and South Africa. I had the unique experience of refereeing the 1994 World Champions (Brazil) in their away victories over the 1994 African Champions (South Africa) in Johannesburg and the 1996 European Champions (Germany) in Stuttgart. In 1995 I became the first Englishman for 20 years to referee the World Club Championship – Ajax v Gremio in Tokyo.

The experience of leading the greatest players in the world onto the field in great footballing cathedrals like Wembley, Nou Camp, Bernabeu, Stadium of Light, Olympic Stadium in Tokyo and the Morumbi in Brazil brings apprehension and exhilaration in equal measure. This season's experiences include watching from a few metres as Ronaldo scored to inflict Germany's first home defeat and incurring the wrath of 100,000 fans in Sao Paulo.

I have spent thirty years of my life actively involved in football as referee. Whether it was at Wembley or on the local recreation park, whether the teams were Brazil or Harrow School's under 14s, each match has been different and challenging. Each one a privilege to take part in.

I could not have done any of this without the encouragement and support of a huge number of people: my parents and family; Alan Gausden and Duncan Jackson who started me refereeing; Bill Cleere, Norman Matthews and Ken Ridden who have guided me at important stages in my career; colleagues like Steve Lodge, Martin Bodenham, Philip Don, Dermot Gallagher and thousands of referees and assistants who have worked with me; the Referees' Association; players and managers who have encouraged and criticised me; and many at Harrow School, including my geography classes and those who have stood by me through good and tough times – particularly Peter Hunter, George Attenborough, Hugh Thompson, Howard Shaw, the Bieneman family, the Mrowiec family, the Smiths and Nick Bomford.

Above all I owe a considerable debt of gratitude to everyone in Druries where I am so proud to be House Master: Glynn Jenkins, Shirley Porter, Rita Kent, JPA, WJM, PGD, MJS, PD and most especially the boys and their parents. They have support me, tolerated my absences and taken a genuine interest in all I have done.

Amidst all the action replays, all the criticism and all the pressure, the fun and fulfilment of being a football referee is immense and I would encourage anyone who wants an active role in today's game to think seriously about taking up the whistle. I would urge all those already refereeing, especially the youngsters, to keep working and learning, for the rewards are many and the satisfaction and sense of accomplishment enormous. I hope that this diary of Season 1997/98 will give an insight into my life as a referee and my pleasure at being a master at Harrow School. If it inspires others, particularly the young, to start refereeing I shall be delighted.

David Elleray,
July 1998

July 1997

1–11 July

1 July marks the 'official' start of the new season as the changes to the laws approved by the International Board come into force on that date. This season there are various changes, the most significant relating to the goalkeeper who can no longer hold the ball for more than five to six seconds nor use his hands if he receives the ball from a throw-in from a team-mate. So there promises to be much focus on goalkeepers when the season starts.

I dislike 1 July intensely because it is the time of year when I have to start training and I am not, I'm afraid, a particularly good or enthusiastic trainer. I have always had a large reserve of what I like to call 'natural' fitness, which I maintain by a pretty sensible diet and an active lifestyle which sees me rarely sitting down. However, for psychological as well as physical reasons, I have to start training in July. Unlike some former colleagues such as Philip Don (who went to the 1994 World Cup) and John Martin (who was still refereeing in the top flight aged 53) I do not run for enjoyment. I find all forms of training very boring; it is the dull routine that makes them so monotonous and I have great trouble motivating myself. I tend to run as it is less tedious than swimming, but I need to think and focus on something else while I run so that I can take my mind off the physical exertion. In reality, once I get going I almost enjoy the sensation and I certainly feel good, physically and psychologically, when I have finished and am soaking in my bath. Because I was off to Sri Lanka in the middle of the month I had been running in the heat of the day to prepare for the weather I would experience out there. I knew I would enjoy training when I got to Sri Lanka as when I'm on holiday I use it as an excuse to explore, and I love chugging along coastal paths and country roads, taking in the scenery.

For the moment, however, I pounded round Harrow's playing fields, varying my route and sometimes taking in a few laps of the athletics track. I had to prepare for two fitness tests. All those on the National List of referees and assistant referees have to take the 'bleep test'. You have to run between two marks, 20 metres apart, arriving at each end to coincide with a beep on a tape. As time passes the interval between the beeps shortens so the running speed has to increase. You start at a slow jog and, as the test progresses, not only are you getting more and more tired, but you are having to run faster and faster. It is called 'progressive' and the discomfort certainly is. After this there are six sprint shuttles, and medical checks for blood pressure, body fat, cholesterol and haemoglobin. They've done away with the eyesight and colour blindness tests which would surprise many people. I shall have to do this test two days after I come back from Sri Lanka. Later on there will be the FIFA fitness test for international referees and assistant referees which consists of a series of sprints and a 12-minute run.

Although at this time of year there is little active work to do apart from training, there are still many other demands on my time. I had been approached by *Four Four Two* magazine to do a photo shoot with Mike Reed and former referee Roger Milford as part of a collage of football in the 1990s. I was happy enough to appear with Mike Reed, a current Premier League referee and friend and colleague, but Roger Milford was from the school of referees who like to referee for popularity and never really supported those of us trying to follow the FIFA guidelines. Directly and indirectly, people like him have caused a lot of trouble for referees and he is one of a band of officials known as 'alternative referees' because their style of refereeing is contrary to the official requirements. It is because of these 'alternative referees' that, understandably, refereeing has come to be seen as inconsistent, for they will do all they can to avoid issuing cards whereas others follow the strict directives faithfully. FIFA has deliberately removed some areas of judgement from the referees so that there are mandatory punishments, designed to protect the skilful players and achieve greater consistency among referees throughout the world. Some referees believe themselves to be above FIFA and certainly have no sense of responsibility towards their colleagues. In the 1970s and 1980s this flexible style was acceptable but the climate has changed, particularly with the World Cup in the USA in 1994; though some continued to plough their own furrow and gave the impression that referees have a choice as to whether or not to apply the mandates, they are rare.

Granada TV rang wanting to do a programme about FIFA referees. I was interested but rather unhappy that they had approached the out-of-work Joe Royle. He had been vehement in his attacks on me both in the press and at a disciplinary commission last season. *GQ Active* magazine sent a motor-bike courier to collect (and return) my whistle for their sports series 'Used and Abused' which is about sports items, like Linford Christie's running shoes, which get a hard time.

In early July I went to St Andrew's Prep School in Eastbourne as guest speaker for their prize-giving and sports day. It was quite an ordeal as Baroness Thatcher was the guest the previous year. To keep the children, aged 8 to 13, interested during my speech I took some of my referee's shirts including the first one I ever wore, the one I wore to referee the 1994 Cup Final and the ones I wore in Euro '96, South Africa and Japan. I had seven boys and girls dress up in these shirts and come on to the stage holding the letters spelling REFEREE. I used this as a mnemonic relating to how to make dreams come true. Before the speeches started, to make sure I did not talk for too long, I gave the head boy, Chris Mullens, a red card and whistle and after 10 minutes he stood up and blew the whistle, waved the red card and told me to 'Get off!' It finished everything with a laugh. The day was great fun, chatting to the boys, girls and parents about refereeing and Harrow School. Inevitably, though, there was no escape from the media, both with photos beforehand and then one of the parents, who works for the *Daily Mail*, wanting an interview. Three days later, just back from one of my runs, I was talking to her about refereeing for her series 'My Obsession' in the *Mail*'s Health section.

Just before I went off to Sri Lanka on 12 July, the appointments for the start of the season arrived. We usually receive them about six weeks before the month in which the matches are being played. These were just the August appointments and I had three matches . . . Opening day – Blackburn v Derby, then Southampton v Arsenal and on 30 August Liverpool v Newcastle. This was a fantastic appointment, given that in the last two seasons this match finished 4–3, and I had the great pleasure and thrill of refereeing last season's match, one of my personal highlights of the year. My delight at the appointment was snatched away almost at once, as the match was switched to Sunday to be shown on Sky TV and I would be unable to officiate then as that is the day before term starts and we would have long, very tedious administration meetings all morning. It was desperately frustrating, but the school are so good at giving me time away that this would have to be one of the few occasions when football has to take second place. Still, it was a disappointing start to what promises to be an excellent season.

In my mail arrived a letter from a 15-year-old in Nottingham:

Dear Mr Elleray,

Being an average footballer, the only way I could possibly set foot on the great football stadia in England is by becoming a referee. I believe you are one of the greatest referees of this era and was wondering if you could possibly send me a red or yellow card with some tips on becoming a referee. I would greatly appreciate this.

Yours hopefully,

Philip Laslett
Aged 15

PS My friend was wondering if you were a fan of Aston Villa or not?

Receiving such letters is a real pleasure – and not just because of the over-the-top compliments. It is always gratifying to have an impact on other people, particularly if you inspire them to take up refereeing. I sent him a red card and a letter telling him that, back in 1968, I too took up refereeing when I realised that I was not going to play football for England. I sent a copy of his letter to Arthur Smith at the Referees' Association and they got someone in the Nottingham area to contact him. I asked Philip to keep me posted about his refereeing career and will try to meet up with him at some stage.

12–27 July – Holiday in Sri Lanka

In the middle of July I escaped to Sri Lanka to visit friends, travel and have a good rest after the exertions of the term and the football season. One of the great advantages of Sri Lanka was that they were far more interested in cricket and hockey than football, so I was free from irate supporters. However, I was accosted at the French National Day drinks party given by the French ambassador and invited to talk to some distinguished Sri Lankan officials about football in the UK. Fortunately, the promised invitation never materialised.

I spent much of the holiday training. In Colombo I went running at about four in the afternoon when it was very hot and humid, as I thought this would be good for me. When I went up to the north I had some absolutely fantastic runs around a large lake, where the only company was the wildlife. I got into the habit of running in mid-afternoon, showering, having a swim and a sunbathe by the pool and then going for a massage and steam bath. When I ventured to southern Sri Lanka I went running on the beach with friends and this barefoot running was later to have rather serious consequences as the jarring would revive an old back problem. Towards the end of my holiday I was staying in a fabulous hotel and I ran on the beach and then trained in the gym on their running machine. I had lost several pounds, which is not easy for me as I do not carry very much spare weight, and was convinced that I would return to the UK fitter than ever before. Depressingly, however, just as I was packing to return to Colombo I felt a spasm in the base of my back which got worse over the next 24 hours. I saw a doctor who prescribed a week's rest and gave me anti-inflammatory pills and Valium to help me sleep and ignore the pain. I'd never taken Valium and did not intend to start then, but the back was really uncomfortable. Fortunately, I began doing some exercises which eased the pain sufficiently so that I did not have to postpone my flight home. It was good to get back home and be able to rest properly.

The next few days were mental rather than physical agony. The back was slowly getting better, but matters were complicated by the fact that while I was away I had been appointed to referee a UEFA Inter-Toto Cup semi-final in Germany – MSV Duisburg v Dynamo Moscow, two days after the fitness test. I knew that I would not be able to do both and spent the entire weekend worrying what to do and getting depressed every time I felt a twinge in my back. The last thing I wanted was a false start to the season, and it was all the more irritating because I had worked so hard on my fitness. At times this whole football business can really sour you off and make everything seem awful. Monday would be a vital day.

Monday 28 July

I woke at 6.30 a.m. and was unable to move for five minutes. I had slept pretty well and hardly stirred in my sleep. However, in that twilight between sleeping and waking I was terrified to move in case my back was really bad. My mind swam with all the questions in front of me. Will I be able to do the test? What if I do it and fail? I'll then be officially unable to referee for up to four weeks. What if I complete the test and then get a reaction and cannot go to Germany? What shall I do? Gingerly I moved one leg, no real pain, and then the other. It was reasonable but the dull ache was still there. I swung my body around slowly and got out of bed. Carefully, I moved across the bedroom floor and then lay, perfectly still, on the floor for five minutes to let the back come into focus and settle. Movement was relatively easy but what about twisting and turning? A long, warm bath relaxed the muscles but then I agonised as to when to take the anti-inflammatory tablets in case I did the fitness test scheduled for 10.30 a.m. Too early and they will have worn off by the time of the test, too late and the back will not be 'free' enough to manoeuvre properly.

The sensible course of action was to telephone Ken Ridden, Director of Refereeing at the FA, to get his advice. Unfortunately, he was not at home or in the FA offices but up at Lincoln running a referees' training officers' course. I managed to leave a message for him at reception and he telephoned back about 8.20 a.m. He was very decisive. I should take the extra two days' rest and prepare for the match in Germany. To take the test against doctor's advice would risk exacerbating the injury, possibly leading to a longer period of injury and absence from refereeing. Moreover, it would do my standing in UEFA no good to pull out of such an important match at this stage, or to go into the game carrying an injury which would undoubtedly be aggravated if I did the test. It was a great relief to have the decision taken out of my hands; Ken Ridden is always very good when it comes to prioritising matters.

Much more settled in my own mind, I was able to get on with other things. In the spare bedroom I laid out all the kit for the trip to Germany. I never pack the day before a match as I then have to double check the next day, just in case something has mysteriously left the bag! I have a mental list of what to take but can nearly always be relied upon to forget something, which is irritating as I like to think of myself as a perfectionist and someone who's really well organised. On my last official trip, for a World Cup match in Hungary, I suddenly remembered on the airport bus to the terminal that I had forgotten to pack any shorts.

About 9.30 a.m. I wandered down to the Harrow School sports centre to watch the test and to chat with those taking part. Jackie, from the Human Performance Centre at Lilleshall, was there to conduct the test. She sympathised with me as she had been suffering from a back complaint for 18 months and was really down about it. I did not want to tell her that I was hoping to referee on Wednesday, as she might well have wondered how I could possibly referee on Wednesday if I was unable to do a test on Monday. The truth is that it is possible to pace oneself in a match, especially a UEFA one. In most international matches the physical demands are not as great as in a Premier League game because attacks tend to build up much more slowly. The real problem is mental alertness since it is easy to drift off and lose concentration when nothing seems to be happening, only for a quick move suddenly to catch you flat-footed mentally and physically. Nor is there the pressured twisting and turning which is an integral part of the fitness test.

About 15 colleagues arrived for the test in various stages of physical fitness and morale. Almost everyone hates these tests as they are something that you can actually 'fail', unlike a match where you can have various levels of performances but there is no black and white, pass/fail line. As you cannot take the test if your blood pressure is high, it always astonishes me that a few referees turn up not having had their blood pressure checked beforehand by their doctor. Often the travel and the general stress of the test causes people's blood pressure to rise and there were two today who had to go and lie down and rest to get their blood pressure down before they could take the test. Rather unprofessional in my view. I am disappointed that, each year, a few of my colleagues are clearly overweight and do not really look like athletes. Some obviously do not take their fitness as seriously as they should, and their physique is such that they do not do our profession any good at all. Still, all this group passed without any problems.

Returning home I contacted the FA and told them that I had arranged to take the fitness test next week, at Lilleshall.

Talking to Ken Ridden's secretary I discovered that all the Premier League referees are being issued with the new electronic assistant referees' flags for the coming season. The referee wears a sensor on his arm, in his pocket, or wherever he fancies and, if the assistant flags and the referee does not see him, then the assistant can press a button which causes the sensor to vibrate and attract the referee's attention.

To round off the football part of my day I went to the mews studio of David Bailey to have my photo taken as part of a selection for *Four*

Four Two magazine. For their October issue they were running a selection of photos of the top 40 people in football. I found him at work surrounded by paintings, poring over some photos but he emerged to chat, and from the somewhat withdrawn chrysalis flowered into an amusing man devoid of any arrogance and with a great sense of humour. After studying me discreetly and not too unnervingly for some time, he asked me to put my referee's kit on. Earlier that day he had photographed Graham Kelly (unrecognisable without glasses, the reporters claimed) along with a Crystal Palace Eagle and he had also done the 'three witches', the international managers Bobby Gould (Wales), Craig Brown (Scotland) and Mick McCarthy (Republic of Ireland). David Bailey was sensational. He relaxed me, appeared genuinely interested in his subject and had me in fits of laughter. He worked patiently and made me feel special and valuable – it is easy to see why he has such a fine reputation. He claimed he only knew three sportsmen. One was a golfer called 'Lucky', although close questioning revealed that he meant 'Tiger' Woods. He knew Paul Gascoigne as he had been asked to do his wedding photos. I never discovered who the third sportsman was, as he went off on a tangent explaining that he refused to do Gazza's wedding as he never does weddings, though he made an exception for the wedding of the Kray twins. I remarked that he couldn't really refuse that one and David agreed, especially as he grew up in the East End. It was a hugely enjoyable hour. The *Four Four Two* reporters wanted to know my three favourite TV programmes for another feature. My mind went blank but eventually I suggested *University Challenge* (as I'd never quite made the team at Oxford and watch every programme hoping to prove to myself that I should have been selected), *Inspector Morse* (because I like trying to work out 'who dun it' and what the double bluffs are) and *Match of the Day* (out of professional duty really). Their only disappointment was that they had hoped to get Vinnie Jones so they could have us photographed together – now that would have been a really interesting shot!

Tuesday 29 July

Having woken early I packed the kit I need for the trip to Duisburg. One of the problems refereeing in Europe is that you have little idea what colours the teams will play in and thus you have to take every colour of referee's shirt, namely cerise, silver, yellow and blue. Fortunately, my colleagues have their own otherwise I would have been carrying shirts and shorts for them and would have resembled a travelling sports shop. For UEFA and FIFA matches I always go with two English assistants and one Reserve Referee who would take the place of anyone who became ill or injured.

We all met at Heathrow airport, being greeted by several of the security and passport people as we made our way to the BA Club Europe Lounge at Terminal One. It amazes me how many people recognise us, and even if they don't, the four of us with the England lions on our blazers always cause comment – usually we are taken to be Olympic riflemen, for some unfathomable reason.

It was a trouble-free flight, and, at only one hour's duration, mercifully short compared to my recent Sri Lankan jaunt. Fortunately, my back was holding up pretty well although I rather gingerly handled my baggage into the people carrier that greeted us. We were met by Dieter, a representative of MSV Duisburg, a nice smiling man whose most remarkable feature was a not too discreet wig. We had to wait about 20 minutes for the bags, always a worry as you have visions of being left with no kit for the match, and then a further 30 minutes for the arrival of the UEFA delegate. For every UEFA match one or two delegates are appointed. If it is a high-profile game there is a match delegate responsible for the organisation and security and a separate referee observer responsible for the match officials. They always come from a country neutral to the match officials and competing teams. On games like this one, one man does both jobs. On this occasion the UEFA delegate was Anders Mattsson, Chairman of the Finnish Football Association's Referees' Committee. He lives on the semi-independent island of Åland and turned out to be a very enjoyable companion. Beforehand you always wonder what the observer will be like, because he can make or break a trip depending on how fussy or punctilious he is. Ex-referees are usually better as they understand the problems and pressures on us, but they can also have particular bees in their bonnets which means you never quite know where you stand until it's too late.

We left Düsseldorf airport, rather too swiftly in fact, and Dieter almost crashed within 10 metres of his parking space – the first of many near misses. Another problem we had was his desire to play German pop music as loud as possible. This became one of the private jokes which sustained our morale and helped build our team spirit. We arrived at the rather modest hotel and after a relaxing sauna and needle-sharp shower we went out for dinner and a quick stroll to see the River Rhine, then retired for a fairly early night.

Wednesday 30 July

An early breakfast after a good night's sleep and then off to the stadium for the usual 10 a.m. meeting between representatives from the clubs, the police, security, and other officials. These meetings can last anything from 20 minutes to well over an hour depending upon how fussy the delegate is. This one was relatively short. I was asked to brief the clubs about treatment of injured players and the new UEFA multi-ball regulation. There now has to be a minimum of eight ball boys (or ball girls) around the pitch, behind the advertising boards, to throw another ball to the players if the match ball is kicked over the boards. This is so that the game restarts as quickly as possible and is another of FIFA's attempts to ensure as much actual playing time as possible in the 90 minutes. We had to check the colours of the teams and the delegate made sure that the advertising on the shirts and shorts was within the regulations. We inspected the pitch, and had the first of several contretemps with the TV people about the siting of cameras and microphones. They always want them to be as close as possible to the pitch and the teams' benches, whereas we have to preserve the privacy of the benches and ensure that cameras are not so close as to represent a danger to the players should they fall or run off the pitch. The major problem, however, developed over the changing rooms. As happens in many foreign grounds, when you go up the tunnel back to the dressing rooms the visitors are along a corridor on one side and the home team (and usually the referee) are on the opposite corridor. Our allotted changing rooms, though very spacious, shared showers and toilets with the home team. This was a problem. In the event of trouble during the match it would be unwise (if not dangerous) for us to be using the toilet or showering with players with whom we had had problems on the pitch. 'Referee assaulted in showers by angry players' would hardly be a welcome headline. More importantly and more realistically, foreign teams are paranoid about the referee being 'got at' by the opponents and the notion that before, during and after the match we would be sharing facilities with the home team would have had the Moscow Dynamo contingent in uproars of protest. We had to instruct the home team to find us other accommodation, which they eventually did.

We had a quiet lunch and then went back to the hotel for two hours' rest. This is always part of my routine on overseas matches not least because the travelling, socialising and generally being on show takes its toll and it is important to be fresh and alert for the stresses and strains of the game.

Although this team was one that I had worked with many times before in England and overseas, before leaving for the match I had the usual meeting with my colleagues just to double check how we would operate. Mark Warren, the senior assistant referee, is by far the best in England and had just returned from Malaysia where he officiated in the FIFA under-20 World Championships. Phil Sharp, a quiet, very athletic and thoughtful young man, was still being blooded as an international assistant and this was his fifth trip abroad, his fourth in my team. Steve Dunn, at this stage England's newest FIFA referee, was the reserve official charged with taking over if I became unfit, and with overseeing the substitutions and behaviour in the dugouts. With the match being relatively low key there was no need for the police to provide an escort.

At the stadium we were greeted in a friendly way by a number of spectators, many wanting English FA pin badges. Foreign supporters have a manic desire for pin badges and I have to carry a large stock around to give to fans, groundsmen and even the police – a pin badge can get you all sorts of things that would otherwise be impossible. Then we unpacked our kit and went to inspect the pitch and the surrounds. Firstly, we had to move one of the cameras which would have intruded upon the coaching staff and blocked Steve Dunn's view of the game. The producer approached and wanted us to kick-off at 7.17 p.m. rather than 7.15 p.m., so that they could cover the news of the floods in eastern Germany. I suspected it was really the usual desire to create more advertising time. I explained that the kick-off was officially at 7.15 p.m. and I did not have the authority to change that but, sometimes, my watch does go wrong. And, by the way, could I have a video cassette tape of the match afterwards? Of course, that could easily be arranged for the co-operative English referee. The commentator came for the usual information about my age, profession and matches involving German teams, and then it was off to both dressing rooms to inspect the studs in the players' boots. There is something of a ritual here. I went in with the other three but did not check any studs. This is a pose as, on the continent, the referee is considered far superior to the other officials and it is important that he is not seen to demean himself with ordinary tasks like inspecting players' equipment.

Returning to our dressing room we undertook our various warm-ups and preparations. I lay perfectly still on the floor to relax my back before doing a series of exercises to loosen the spine and also to warm my leg muscles. I was determined to avoid silly injuries or strains in the first five minutes of the first match of the season. No matter how well prepared you are there is nothing that enables you to be absolutely match fit until you start actually refereeing matches.

The first leg had finished 2–2 and the outcome here seemed in little doubt when Duisburg scored in the ninth and eleventh minutes. There were no disputes but the foul challenges were getting too numerous and I was aware that I could do with a yellow card to impose my authority firmly on the game. As it happened, a challenge rather worse than anything previously committed occurred and I cautioned the Moscow No.4, to ringing applause from the crowd. Close to half-time Moscow scored which set the second half up for excitement – or so we thought. During the break we talked through the match so far and were generally happy although, being perfectionists, Mark Warren and I were annoyed at giving a throw-in the wrong way just before the half ended. Steve Dunn was even more frustrated as he had been sitting at the table on the halfway line and had seen the deflection and, knowing that we had not seen it, had tried to indicate to me what had happened but I had failed to pick up his subtle signal.

The second half was a most bizarre affair. With only one goal to make up we expected the Russians to attack like mad but they did not. Even when the Germans were knocking the ball around between their defenders there was no attempt from the Moscow players to challenge for it. We later learned that they had to be at the airport for 10 p.m. and we concluded that if they had equalised and the match had gone into extra-time, and perhaps penalties, they would have missed their plane back to Moscow. Unfortunately, by not being committed they rather lost their way and their discipline went to pieces. I gave several more yellow cards and then the Dynamo Moscow No. 4 – Jury Kovtun – committed a foul tackle from behind and had to receive a second yellow card and was sent off. I knew that this would particularly upset one spectator whom I had met before the game and who had come to the match to watch this very player as a possible signing for an English club, West Ham, I believe. The scout would not have been happy at me curtailing his chance to assess the player for a full 90 minutes. Late in the half another Russian committed two offences in the space of 30 seconds and was also dismissed. The match ended in dramatic and spectacular style. The thunderstorm which had threatened for much of the game finally arrived and amid terrible rain, thunder and lightning, the Moscow goalkeeper brought down a Duisburg forward conceding a penalty and earning a yellow card. The Duisburg goalkeeper decided to take the penalty and scored, just, but if the penalty had been saved we might have had an attack on an open goal at the other end and the extra-time that the Russians appeared not to want. The Russians hurried off to get their plane while the Germans shook our hands and were very complimentary about our officiating.

Back in the dressing room we did all the paperwork. The UEFA delegate was very happy and felt that we had been entirely correct in everything we had done, although he did mention one mistake – the throw-in just before half-time. After a warm shower we went back to the hotel to fax the report to UEFA before dinner and bed.

Thursday 31 July

Fortunately it was not too early a start and we breakfasted at 8.30 a.m. but we had an anxious moment as the transport to take us to the airport was 15 minutes late and we were beginning to have visions of being stranded in Duisburg. But I was sure we would be all right as the home team had won; if they lose you sometimes do have problems getting to the airport the next day when they 'forget' to collect you!

The journey home was uneventful except for the enjoyable experience of meeting the chief steward on the BA flight who was a Chelsea fan. He recognised us immediately and we chatted about football and life at Stamford Bridge, especially 'that penalty' which Mike Reed gave in the Chelsea v Leicester FA Cup match last season. At least, for once, I wasn't mistaken for Mike. At the end of the flight he gave us four bottles of champagne with a request to make sure that we protected Mark Hughes next time we did a Chelsea match. It was another of those examples of how pleasant it can be to meet genuine fans who want to talk about football rather than just give you a hard time about a particular decision.

I arrived home to find a letter from the FA informing me that I have been appointed to referee the World Cup qualifier between Romania and Iceland on 10 September.

August 1997

Friday 1 August

This was supposed to be a non-football day when I could get ahead with my paperwork and collect my new car. It is absolutely vital that I have reliable transport to travel to matches. The last thing you need is to be stranded on a motorway when you should be kicking off in a Premier League match. About 85 per cent of the mileage I do in my cars is for football so I like a solid, dependable vehicle. Typically, the garage had not filled the tank. At the petrol station, when I approached the cash desk to pay, the attendant suddenly asked, 'Are you famous?' Dumbfounded I muttered, 'I don't think so.' He obviously was not happy with this answer and stared at me, so I volunteered that I was a referee and it was like dawn breaking on his face. He was very pleasant and it gave me rather a boost, but what a strange question to ask someone.

Worryingly, when I got back there was a message to phone Ken Ridden's secretary. It turned out that Gerald Ashby had failed his fitness test and was thinking of resigning from the list, even though it was the start of his final season. I have known Gerald well for many years and tried to phone him to talk the situation through but he was not answering calls. It was an anxious time as we could not afford to lose one of our best referees, especially with Mike Reed being out for the early part of the season after damaging his Achilles tendon in his fitness test. These tests are a menace, both psychologically and physically.

Saturday 2 August

A scorching hot day for my first domestic game of the season, David Howells's testimonial match at White Hart Lane – Spurs v Fiorentina of Italy. The north stand of White Hart Lane was being rebuilt but as usual the ground looked immaculate and the pitch was in better condition than last season when the grass had not taken too well. My two assistants were Phil Sharp, who had just been with me in Germany, and Peter Walton, who had lined to me in Euro '96 and was back from a year's secondment in South Africa working for an electricity company. I often work with the same assistants and he had been in my team for much of the 1995–6 season and it was great to see him back, along with his wife Jo. There was a buzz around the ground with the arrival of David Ginola and Les Ferdinand from Newcastle. I had a long chat with Les before kick-off, who assured me he was thrilled to be back in the capital.

It was a hugely enjoyable match and Spurs looked very good for much of the first half but Fiorentina were better organised and won relatively comfortably 2–0, in part due to a handling error by the usually reliable Ian Walker. My only trouble in the match was that the Italians seemed to have it in for David Ginola and played the 'numbers game', i.e. a different person fouled him each time. However, he withstood it well and I only issued one yellow card, to a player who had the temerity to get stroppy with David Howells, whose testimonial match it was. Fortunately, the Fiorentina team remembered me from last season when I refereed a very hard UEFA Cup second-leg match in the Czech Republic when they drew 1–1 with Sparta Prague and thus qualified for the next round. Stefan Schwarz, formerly of Arsenal, had come into the dressing room afterwards to thank me and present me with his shirt, even though I'd shown him a yellow card during the game. David Ginola and I exchanged a handshake at the end and a few words about the problems playing against or refereeing Italian teams. During the game we had talked quite a bit, as I had been keen that he should not react to being targeted by the Fiorentina players. On one or two occasions he had been ready to lash out but we had established a line of communication and he was prepared to let me take control of matters. At the end of the game he wanted to show his appreciation for the way I had protected him.

One of the nice things that afternoon was meeting Andrei Kanchelskis whom I had always got on well with when he was with Manchester United. We chatted several times during the game and he told me how sad he was to have left Old Trafford. He was glad to have got away from Everton but, although he was enjoying life in Florence with Fiorentina, he still missed Manchester a great deal. Here again was an example of how players and referees get on rather better than many would imagine. We build up respect for each other over the years and this is often reflected in the use of Christian names. Once the players call me 'David', I am no longer just any old referee but a particular person.

The only significant refereeing note was that it was the first time I used the new electronic flags. The buzzer strapped to my arm seemed uncomfortable at first but I soon forgot about it, so much so that when it was first used I was momentarily disorientated as to what was going on. Although we used it only twice, for a late offside flag and a substitution, it struck me as a great aid to communication between the referee and an assistant whose flagging the referee has missed. I felt good after the match with no ill-effects from my back, just very hot and dehydrated and I drank copious quantities of fluids before returning home happy to have got another pre-season match under my belt.

Sunday 3 August

A busy day trying to organise myself for 12 days away from home during which I would referee one Premier League match and almost a dozen youth matches, so there was a need to pack a large quantity of kit. In the afternoon I watched Peter Jones referee the FA Charity Shield between Chelsea and Manchester United. I had spent some time the previous week discussing the match with him as the opening game of the season is always a very important occasion for referees, often setting the tone for the early weeks of the season. I well remember Philip Don refereeing Blackburn v Manchester United in 1994 just after he returned from the World Cup in the USA. Philip refereed in the new 'strict' manner which made the World Cup so successful, but his eight or nine yellow cards in that Charity Shield match did not go down at all well. However, it set the standard for the season and was largely responsible for establishing the firm refereeing which has greatly benefited the Premier League since then. This year's match posed some challenges to Peter Jones in the first half but he coped very well and hit a fine balance between controlling but not over-fussing. What I was particularly pleased with was his use of the formal lecture or rollicking which is an underused management technique these days. I still worry that, too often, a referee blows for a foul and either does nothing else or shows a yellow card. I strongly believe that there is an important middle ground when, for non-mandatory offences, he can be seen to deal with the incident by talking to the player(s) concerned, establishing his authority but not over-reacting. It was not a memorable match but Peter achieved a good level of player management and there were no controversies to mar his performance.

Monday 4 August

In the morning I travelled up to Keele University to take part in the FA Premier League Youth Tournament. It is an excellent event involving Premier League teams and foreign sides, with different age groups each week. There are no winners or champions as the main purpose is for the boys to learn how to play football properly. For the last three years I have been in charge of the referees and most of the matches are controlled by Premier League officials, which has improved the level of discipline and also enhanced the festival as the boys enjoy having, as they see it, 'famous' referees in charge of their matches. I arrived at lunchtime to link up with Martin Bodenham and Jeff Winter who, like me, would reside on the campus. This year the FA had decided to invite some younger male and female referees to run the line so that they could learn from working with senior referees.

The afternoon was fairly demanding as we were required to referee matches back-to-back which, although they were only 25 minutes each way, were still physically demanding as the under-16-year-olds were fit and energetic. My first game was a real clash of cultures with Wimbledon playing Ajax from Amsterdam. I was hugely disappointed with the Ajax side who showed none of the skill or discipline that has been their hallmark. Wimbledon were, as one would expect, combative, aggressive and committed and their physical (though legitimate) approach unsettled Ajax, especially the No. 10 who was an arrogant, ill-disciplined young man whom I eventually removed from the pitch after a late tackle. That young man was to upset every referee he encountered for the rest of the week. Wimbledon emerged triumphant 2–1 but it was tough to referee and not overly enjoyable. I had an interesting chat after the match with a young Wimbledon player who was very good at dishing out the rough stuff but unwilling to take it. I explained that players who give it but cannot take it greatly irritate other players and referees and it would be worth considering toning down his aggressive reaction when he is fouled or has a decision given against him.

The second match was Liverpool v Coventry, a thrilling 3–3 draw which was fully competitive, no dissent or bad tackles and a display of all that is best about British football. Steve Heighway coaches the Liverpool teams and you could see how they are drilled into the Liverpool way of playing and acting – all very professional and impressive. Coventry battled back from 0–2 down and played their part in making it a very pleasant 50 minutes of football.

After supper I was invited to talk to the Nottingham Forest and Leeds United squads while Martin Bodenham and Jeff Winter spoke to other teams. The lads were very forthright and we had a particularly enlightening discussion about how players treat referees. They seemed very surprised to learn that players who are forever getting at the referee and giving him a hard time end up losing out on the 50–50 decisions, and are more likely to be given a yellow card than be given the benefit of the doubt. To make them understand I asked them if they would do any favours for someone, perhaps a team-mate, who was always giving them a hard time. We also focused for a while on the role of technology in the modern game and they were largely opposed to its use except, perhaps, to clear up any doubt about whether a ball had crossed the line or not for a goal.

Tuesday 5 August

Up early to referee Nottingham Forest v Aston Villa, quite a challenge having spoken to the Nottingham Forest players the night before. They had obviously taken to heart my comments about being nice to referees as they all came up and shook hands before the kick-off. It was a good match with Forest beating Villa 2–1. The only problem was a young lad from Forest who committed a couple of awful tackles so I had him taken off the field. Afterwards, the Forest coach thanked me and explained that he was having a great deal of trouble with that lad and that my actions helped him a great deal. The lad was from a tough area and unlikely to last the course with Forest, not through lack of skill but because of his attitude and lack of self-discipline.

In the afternoon we were joined by Gary Willard and Uriah Rennie, the latter new to the Premier League list and getting a lot of publicity as the first black Premier League referee. I watched them refereeing in the afternoon. Liverpool were being hugely critical of Uri, Steve Heighway commenting that they had not rated him when he had been on the Central League list of referees and that he was surprised he had been promoted to our ranks. Watching Liverpool play, I had

an interesting conversation with Rick Parry, who had been Chief
Executive of the Premier League until the end of last season, when
he moved to be the Secretary at Liverpool. He outlined some of the
youth developments his club were undertaking and also talked about
the signing of Paul Ince. 'It's funny how those tackles that used to
annoy me, I now view with a wry sense of admiration when they go in!'
he remarked. His observations about foreign players were perceptive
and when I ventured that they seemed to be much more dedicated and
professional than the average British player he concurred. He told me
about Tor Kvarme who had broken his shoulder playing for Norway.
The day after a minor op Kvarme's shoulder was sore and the doctor
asked whether the painkillers were working. The reply was, 'Yes, but
I've been to the gym as I cannot afford to miss a day's training.' I
have little doubt that the arrival of so many foreign footballers will
steadily change the attitudes of many younger British players who will
see that a quiet life, rather than nightclubs and activities which attract
the attention of the tabloids, is the professional way to approach top
level sport.

In the evening Steve Lodge arrived and we all went for a few soft
drinks at the university bar – rather a weedy set of teetotallers.
Conversation focused on the appointment by the Labour Government
of David Mellor to head a soccer task force and Ian Wright being
chosen by the FA to spearhead their campaign to promote soccer.
Why can't we choose sensible role models and thinkers rather than
self-publicists like David Mellor? Anyway, I headed to bed for an
early night in preparation for the fitness test the next morning.

Wednesday 6 August

I had taken some time to fall asleep; typical pre-test nerves when you
lie in bed wanting to get a good night's rest but are so desperate to get
to sleep that you can't. Isn't the mind a strange thing! After a quick
breakfast it was off to the Human Performance Centre at Lilleshall,
Martin Bodenham accompanying me in the car which was a kind
gesture as it is always good to have someone to talk to on these
quite stressful occasions. As it turned out the fitness test went well
although it was odd taking it on my own. The first stage was to be
weighed and have my body fat measured. Last year I had been a touch
overweight at 11st 5lb so I was delighted to discover that my careful
training and sensible diet had got me down to 10st 8lb. Allied to this

my cholesterol, which is usually pretty low, had fallen from 4.5 to 3.7. All those sacrifices of not touching chocolate or crisps had worked – and what a sacrifice it had been for I am a real chocoholic. My blood pressure was low at 112 over 85 and I have to admit that I was feeling fitter than I had felt for several years.

In the test itself I completed the bleep section with some ease but did not advance too far beyond the pass level as I was mindful that I had two games to referee tomorrow and my first Premier League match on Saturday. The sprints were fine although in the first one I was a touch slow, a product of having no one to compete against and therefore being unable to judge the speed needed. The other five had me well within the limits so, with a sigh of relief, I could shower and return to the Premier League referees' meeting at Keele ready for the season, officially fit enough to officiate. However, my joy and anticipation at the coming matches were put into perspective as I did my test in the gym where players were doing rehabilitation work following injuries. I was struck by the terrible scars on the front and back of one man's legs. It was David Busst from Coventry City who had sustained a terrible broken leg earlier at Old Trafford. To see such scars and his pain and harrowed look made me grateful for my fitness and a little guilty at complaining about my minor back pains.

Back at Keele we had the final, pre-season meeting of the majority of the Premier League referees along with Ken Ridden and Mike Foster, Premier League secretary. We talked about the issues that would face us in the early matches and spent some time discussing the new Laws, especially the time limit on goalkeepers, which no one had found a problem in the pre-season games. We resolved to remain firm and strong to protect the skilful players. Jewellery has increasingly become a real nuisance in the game as these days earrings, bracelets and necklaces as well as rings are part of men's fashion. The problem is that players are not allowed to wear anything that constitutes a danger to themselves or the opponents. Long necklaces and bracelets, which can catch someone in the eye, are a major bone of contention and for several years we have all been trying to stop players wearing them. Unfortunately, some managers cannot, or will not, take action against their players and we are reduced to sending players from the field to remove offending items – but only if we spot them, which we don't seem to do as easily as the TV cameras.

We were also determined to assist a PFA campaign to stop players gesturing to a referee that he should show a yellow card to an opponent, such obvious attempts to influence a referee should have no part in the game.

The meeting was punctuated by the usual good-natured banter and, as usual, Graham Poll – an excellent referee who has a great deal to say on many subjects – tried to monopolise the conversation but was frequently put in his place by Ken Ridden, normally a reserved and placid man, and Jeff Winter in particular. It is always interesting to see who talks and who does not at these meetings and, yet again, I was disappointed that Dermot Gallagher, one of our senior referees, made no contribution, even though he thinks a great deal about refereeing and has a wealth of experience to share.

Once the meeting was over I watched some of the afternoon matches and organised referees for next week's tournament. I was later interested to see a news item that the Referees' Association was being sponsored through production of a 'Red Card' soft drink – a result of hard work from our eminently capable president, Peter Willis, the only referee ever to have sent a player off in a Cup Final.

Thursday 7 August

The morning was spent refereeing two youth matches back to back.They were good games, with Glasgow Rangers beating Aston Villa 2–1 and Leeds defeating Arsenal 2–0, although in both the boys were showing the tiring effects of the week and some of the passing was a little wayward.

In the afternoon I travelled to see friends and have the last day's break before the start of the season.

Friday 8 August

Apart from confirming the minutes of Wednesday's meeting of Premier League referees with the League secretary, Mike Foster, there was no football today. It was a magical day of sun and Test match cricket and that slightly abandoned feeling one gets on the last day of one's holiday. Tomorrow the season would start.

Saturday 9 August

When I woke up I had conflicting feelings as I lay in that wonderful state between waking and sleeping. Part of me felt the excitement of the season beginning but another part was somewhat resentful that for the coming nine months or more my life would no longer be my own. I would be at the call of administrators, colleagues and the press juggling my time to try to train, referee and fulfil my responsibilities at Harrow School. Because I had had such a short time off since the end of the previous season, the resentment started to outweigh the excitement so I woke myself up and got ready for the day ahead. My mood was not helped when I read in the *Daily Mail* that they were planning to keep a careful watch on referees this season and their 'experts' would be giving referees marks for fitness and judgement – just the sort of focus we could do without.

On match days I eat very little so it was the usual bowl of cornflakes and a couple of cups of tea. Blackburn Rovers v Derby County was my opening match and I was greatly looking forward to it as they are two clubs with whom I have always enjoyed good relations. We have to be at the ground at least two hours before kick-off but I always aim for about three hours before, just in case something goes wrong on the way. This time I was grateful I had made such an allowance because as I sped along the M56 one of my front tyres went flat and there I was, in the heat, changing the wheel. I am a complete idiot as far as cars are concerned (one of the reason why I buy a new one so often!) and the only thing I can do with any confidence or competence is change a wheel. With the new wheel safely on, I listened to England struggle in the Test match as I travelled up the M6. Despite the delays I managed to get to Blackburn by noon.

Blackburn are always a friendly club and I was greeted by the secretary, Tom Finn, with whom I got on well when he was secretary at West Ham. He was keen that I should let him know if there was anything that needed improving as far as the match officials were concerned as he wanted his club to be the best at looking after officials. He noted that the referees' room could do with a television and fridge for soft drinks. I inspected the pitch and had a long talk with the groundsman who explained how the pitch drank water and he would have the sprinklers on until close to the kick-off. I always enjoy chatting with groundsmen and witnessing their pride in their pitches – with justification too, for the standard of playing surfaces has greatly improved over the last few seasons. It is important to have a good relationship with the groundsman because you never know when you might need his help in predicting how the weather is likely to effect the pitch. I shall never forget coming off at half-time at Swindon one day when it was getting foggy and the wise old groundsman, puffing on his pipe, telling me, 'You'll not finish this one today, son.' He was right; I abandoned the match midway through the second half when fog reduced visibility to about five yards.

Roy, who looks after the match officials, tended to my needs until the other officials, David Horlick and David Booth, arrived along with the fourth official, Alan Christie from Blackpool. We returned to the dressing room about 1.40 p.m. to attend the safety briefing from the police and the club safety officer 75 minutes before kick-off. The Premier League match observer had not arrived by the official time of 1.30 p.m. so we assumed, correctly as it turned out, that it was ex-Cup Final referee Neil Midgley, who rarely arrives on time, but when he did he had us in stitches with his usual barrage of jokes and amusing stories.

At two o'clock the managers came in with the team sheets. They each gave me a copy of their team and also one to the opposing manager. I welcomed Roy Hodgson back to England and renewed my acquaintance with Jim Smith. They are both managers that I have a lot of respect for. Jim was very good when he was head of the League Managers' Association and I had enjoyed refereeing Derby several times last season. I had come across Roy Hodgson when I refereed Switzerland v Sweden in the qualification stages of Euro '96. I reminded them both about various regulations and wished them well for the season. Jim Smith popped back a while later just to check on the arrangements for players getting drinks during the match given that it was so hot. Dealing with water in hot weather is always somewhat problematic. The ideal compromise is for bottles to be available on the touchlines for players to drink from when the game is stopped. Until recently referees were not expected to take drink during the game as the powers that be deemed it improper, but it is vital to drink otherwise not only physical performance but also decision-making can suffer. I said that I was quite happy if players went to the touchlines for water. Neil Midgley advised me not to charge around like a lunatic otherwise I'd not last the pace.

The match was largely uneventful as far as refereeing incidents were concerned. Indeed it was something of a milestone for me as it was the first Premier League match since 29 December 1993 in which I did not give a yellow card. I was impressed with the discipline of the players and even Chris Sutton (Blackburn Rovers), who is usually rather sour and difficult to referee, was cheerful and chatty. Billy

McKinlay of Blackburn called me 'Mr Elleray' all afternoon and we enjoyed some good banter. It started early on when he was a little firm in a tackle and I had a quiet word with him. 'It's all right, Mr Elleray,' he said, 'I was just letting him know I was around.' 'Quite so, Billy,' I replied. 'And I'm just letting you know that I'm around too!' He laughed and that set the tone for the afternoon. If you talk to players during the game you establish a rapport which will stand you in good stead should you need to reprimand them, or indeed stop them getting involved with opposing players. It does not take long to work out who wants to talk and who just wants to get on with their game. When a player like Chris Sutton changes his attitude you wonder whether it is because he has had a genuine change of opinion about you as a referee or whether a new manager has encouraged a more positive approach to dealing with referees.

It certainly was hot and I was grateful for all the heat training I had done in Sri Lanka. At the end the vast majority of the players shook hands, Jim Smith popped his head round the door to say thank you and the match observer announced that 'it was a piece of piss'. I've had more eloquent descriptions of my refereeing but I took it as a compliment. I wound down slowly and was pleased to have coped with the heat and also not to have had any back problems. Post match it was important to take in plenty of liquid.

Driving to stay with Steve Lodge and his family in Barnsley I listened to Radio 5's 606 which Mark Lawrenson was presenting. A Bolton fan called the show to complain that Martin Bodenham had refereed as if he had had a couple of pints of mild the night before. Well, Martin rarely drinks, and certainly wouldn't touch mild. That evening Steve and I agreed that in future we would call him 'Lord Two Pints'. There is something of a standing joke in the refereeing circle that I am known as 'Lord Elleray', mainly because I teach at Harrow; a number of colleagues refer to me as 'my Lord'. *Match of the Day* in the evening confirmed that the opening day had been devoid not only of red cards but also controversy, thank goodness.

Sunday 10 August

For the last four years I have been elected by the Premier League referees to be their official spokesman so whenever there is any controversy they contact me to let me know what is going on so that I can deal with the media accordingly. Equally, the media frequently phone me partly because of my position as spokesman and also because I am the country's senior referee. My attitude to the press is that we should talk to them so that the genuine supporter has a chance to hear the referee's point of view. It took quite a time for the FA to accept that referees should talk to the press but I believe that we have been reasonably successful in getting the referees' voice and opinion heard. I checked my answerphone but there were no calls from worried colleagues and we had indeed got away to a trouble-free first day. My only concern was that I had had no cautions in my match and would be in for a great deal of good-natured stick for being soft or 'alternative'. Steve Lodge was almost as concerned, however, having only cautioned one. We watched Sheffield United v Sunderland on Sky and were impressed with how sensible Alan Brazil's comments were about refereeing decisions. Later on in the afternoon we watched Spurs v Manchester United with 'Lord Two Pints' as the fourth official. Typically Andy Gray was wrongly critical of an excellent penalty decision from assistant referee Bill Jordan. Andy always seems to start off with the opinion that the referee or assistant is wrong and if he is convinced in his own mind that a mistake has been made it is almost impossible to get him to admit otherwise, even when the replays confirm the official's decision. He really is a menace at times.

Monday 11 August

I returned to Keele for another few days of Premier League Youth Football, this time the under-14 age group. My first match was the Singapore national school team against Arsenal, who were being coached and managed by Liam Brady. The Singapore team were most impressive in terms of commitment and skills but Arsenal worked hard and only lost 0–1. Straight afterwards I refereed a relatively simple 0–0 draw between Coventry and Sheffield Wednesday. In the evening I had a long question and answer session with the Leeds United boys and we had a good debate about that Chesterfield 'goal' in the FA Cup semi-final last season. This was a shot from a Chesterfield forward that hit the crossbar, bounced down and out into play. Neither the assistant nor I could be 100 per cent sure that the whole of the ball had crossed the whole of the line so we were not able to award a goal. Although this was possibly a turning point in the game, no one has yet produced a photo which proves conclusively that the whole of the ball did cross the line. This is a case where technology could have been a great help. A group of us then watched the Arsenal v Coventry match on Sky.

Tuesday 12 August

Early in the morning I checked with the FA about the need for a visa for my forthcoming trip to Romania and then refereed Aston Villa's 3–0 defeat of Leeds United, who were in great form. It was incredibly hot and midway through each half I stopped the game to allow the players to take in some liquid so that we had no problems with exhaustion. In the afternoon it was even hotter and I did the same in the Ajax v Nottingham Forest match which ended 0–0. It was good to see this Ajax side playing disciplined, cultured football and I was asked for my autograph at half-time by several of the Dutch spectators who recognised me from the time I refereed the 1995 World Club Championship match in Tokyo when Ajax became World Champions by beating Gremio of Brazil. Some of the Ajax players also remembered me from that match and we talked about it after the final whistle.

In the evening Martin Bodenham, Jeff Winter and I went to watch Tony Bates, who had been one of my linesmen in Euro '96, referee Walsall v Exeter. He had a very good match but we were struck by the lack of atmosphere in the ground and it made us appreciate how very spoiled we are refereeing in the Premier League in front of crowds of upwards of 20,000.

Wednesday 13 August

In the morning I refereed Leicester's 2–0 victory over Glasgow Rangers. The match was notable for the comment of the Rangers trainer when he came on to look at his goalkeeper who had hit his head on the post saving a shot. The trainer remarked that the post was likely to have received the greater damage. I had greatly enjoyed the under-14 week as the lads were more interested in playing football and less concerned with being aggressive and macho. They also really seemed to appreciate having Premier League referees around and subjected us to many questions and good-natured ribbing at mealtimes. Hopefully we had shown them that referees are human after all.

In the afternoon I drove back to Harrow to deal with the mountain of post that had accumulated while I was away. Arriving at Harrow I studied the A level results and was delighted with the vast majority of grades achieved by boys in my House and also in the two Upper Sixth geography divisions I taught. I was particularly pleased that of 13 boys in Druries, one had achieved five A grades and three had achieved three A grades. Later on in the evening Steve Lodge arrived with his wife, Susan, and his son, James, from West Ham where he had refereed their game with Spurs. They had come down to London the previous day to watch Barnsley play at Crystal Palace. Steve's match had gone pretty well although he was rather disappointed with his handling of a fracas involving a number of players.

Thursday August 14

Up early at seven to be ready for the publication of the A level results. There was that sense of pleasure for those who had done well and the pit of the stomach disappointment for those who had not got the grades they needed to secure their university places. By eight o'clock the phone was continuously ringing and the next few hours were spent congratulating, commiserating, advising and cajoling. Some who had not got the grades the universities wanted found, on contacting them, that they had still been accepted. For them it was a rollercoaster of emotions from depression to elation.

In the midst of all this the press wanted my comments on Uri Rennie's abandonment of the Derby v Wimbledon match yesterday when the floodlights had failed. Fortunately, the first to make contact were the Press Association who, I knew, would circulate whatever I had to say, and that would stop most of the other papers phoning. I was asked how long a referee has to wait before abandoning a match. The simple answer is that there are only guidelines and the referee has to take advice from all relevant people. In this case I had no doubt that the referee would have consulted with the Premier League match observer, the police, safety officer and club electrician. The police and the safety officer would have advised as to how long the spectators could be expected to remain in the stadium before becoming restless and difficult. The electrician would have given some idea of when power might be restored. The other concern would be the players who would begin to stiffen up, with the consequent genuine risk of pulled muscles and injuries if they had to wait too long. As I said to the Press Association, 'Sod's law' operated and, a few minutes after the decision to abandon the match was taken, power was restored. The referee had been very upset with the home club because, when the abandonment was agreed, he had specifically requested that, should the power be restored, the lights should not be switched on. This request was made for the spectators' safety because, if the lights came back on, some of them might turn around and try to re-enter the stadium thinking the match was about to resume. My task was to get the message across to the press that the referee had done all he could and, after a reasonable period, had taken a wise decision. With the benefit of hindsight a few more minutes would have saved the game but Uri had not known that at the time and there was clearly a lot of pressure being exerted on him by certain people. What a start to his first Premier League match.

Friday August 15

Although there was not much Premier League football on, the morning was taken up by the telephone. Initially I was busy liaising with Steve Lodge following the West Ham v Spurs match on Wednesday. Apparently, video coverage of the game had shown Spurs' Iversen making an offensive gesture to assistant referee Phil Sharp after Phil had advised Steve to caution him following a bit of a brawl. The gesture had not been spotted by any of the match officials but was mentioned in the press so I advised Steve to contact the FA and explain that it had not been seen by any of the officials. It would then be up to the FA to decide whether or not to bring a charge. Later in the morning I had two calls from television companies to record shows on Tuesday. In many ways this was a bit of a bore as I was hoping to escape for a few days before the Southampton v Arsenal match. However, it is important that the referees' viewpoint is heard. I agreed to do an interview for Vinnie Jones's Granada TV show on Tuesday morning and then go to the Sky studios in the afternoon to record the *Footballers' Football Show* – a programme similar to one I did for Radio 4 last season with Ken Palmer (cricket umpire), Ed Morrison (Rugby Union referee), Larry O'Connell (boxing referee) and Jane Harvey (tennis umpire).

The afternoon was spent dealing with various boys' A levels and their attempts to get into university or to apply to do re-takes. While the majority were organised, one or two were still struggling. I went for a run and returned to do the interview for *GQ Active* about refereeing and my whistle as part of their 'Used and Abused' sports items series.

In the evening Dermot Gallagher phoned to talk through his recent match in Europe and to discuss the coming week's football. Dermot has been a great friend for many years as we have progressed up through the League together, although for much of the time he was just one step behind me. He is a fine referee who is utterly dedicated to football, so much so that at times he is almost consumed by it. A couple of years ago he was really pushing me hard for the top spot and was refereeing out of his skin when he injured a leg in a match during Euro '96. Since then it has been a tough battle back for him and he has endured not only physical pain but also the mental agony of wondering whether he would ever referee again.

Talk drifted around to France '98 and which English referee might be selected. Apparently, money was on me because I'd received my third World Cup qualification match. FIFA moves in mysterious ways and no one can tell who will be selected.

Saturday August 16

Saturdays without football always seem strange, especially when it is the school holidays. I find myself drifting around and today was no exception. Fortunately the weather was fantastic so I spent much of the day lying in the garden reading avidly. I finished one book and began another. By about four I was feeling restless so, despite a long run yesterday and the extreme heat and humidity, I decided to go for another run. Drifting down to the athletics track I chose to try the 12-minute run and see if I could complete the required 2,700 metres. It is strange that when I try these tests on my own I fail and yet, when the real thing comes, I do somewhere between 2,950m and 3,000m. It is amazing what adrenaline can do for you. Anyway, this afternoon I pushed myself and completed the 2,700m in the allotted time with reasonable comfort. I luxuriated in a bath for an hour and a half afterwards, completing my second book of the day.

Sunday August 17

No football today, just a quiet time watching sport on TV and reading. When there's no Premier League football everything seems somewhat dry and lacking bite and interest. In the afternoon it was exceptionally hot and humid so, as a masochist but also because I believed it would help me if it was hot again next Saturday, I went for another run.

Monday August 18

I spent the morning dealing with correspondence and talking to Charlie Beauchamp who runs Lucozade sponsorship for the Premier League. He is always good at ensuring that the referees get supplies of Lucozade drinks and we arranged a delivery for our September meeting. We also discussed his progress in trying to get a watch developed which the referee would use and would also control the stadium clock. It is an area of technological development that a number of us have been pushing as it is a way of everyone, especially the crowd, knowing exactly how much time is left. It should not be beyond the wit of man to develop a system where when the referee stops his watch the stadium clock stops and everyone can see that time is being allowed. It would also put paid to the dreadful whistling that starts about five minutes before the end of every match, regardless of how many injuries, cautions, dismissals and substitutions there have been. The technical stumbling block is ensuring a unique signal between the referee's watch and the clock so that other people cannot sabotage it with their own watches.

In the evening I had a chat with Neale Barry, one of the new Premier League referees. We talked through the success of his first match and various administrative details. He struck me as very organised and professional. One of the reasons for his call was to tell me that he would miss the next Premier League referees' meeting as he has been appointed reserve referee to Peter Jones in a UEFA under-21 match in Croatia. Neale was concerned that he would miss our discussions and our analysis of incidents from early-season matches and wanted to try to get hold of the tape we would examine so that he could acquaint himself with the issues involved and the collective decisions taken. I was most impressed with his attitude, quite a contrast from some people when they become Premier League referees and think they know everything.

Tuesday August 19

A busy media day. In the morning Granada TV came to record an interview for Granada Sky's *Vinnie Jones Football Show*. Diana

Binks, the interviewer, had prepared well and the straightforward interview was completed in a single take. It was largely standard questions about how I had got into refereeing and the problems facing referees at the top level. As usual, the challenge was to say something interesting without being too controversial.

After lunch it was off to the Sky studios to record a programme for the *Footballer's Football Show* which is directed by Geoff Shreeves, who used to be the link man between referees and Sky TV on the live matches. Also appearing on the programme were Test match umpire Chris Balderstone, recently involved in the Illott v Croft pushing fracas in the Nat West semi-final, and Steve Lander the Rugby Union referee who was pushed over by a player at the end of the Pilkington Cup Final at Twickenham.

The programme debated the differences between officiating in soccer and in the other sports and discussed future developments in the game, especially use of technology. Geoff was worried that we would stick together as a sort of 'referees union' but we had a good discussion and I was impressed with the perception and professionalism of the other two guests. After the recording we went for a drink and the others showed great sympathy for the pressure that is put on Premier League referees. Chris Balderstone was sure that having ex-first class players as umpires helped a great deal in his sport. Steve said that no matter what controversy there was, he could always go into the bar after a match knowing he would get nothing more than some good-natured stick. It all compared very favourably to the abuse, hate mail and offensive phone calls that soccer referees sometimes get. In my case after the 1994 FA Cup Final I got so many abusive phone calls at regular intervals throughout the night that I still sleep with the answerphone on in my study and the bedroom phone unplugged.

After that I drove down to Sussex for a short break.

Wednesday 20 August

I spent a quiet day reading and shopping in Chichester. Returning late in the afternoon I rang through to get the messages from my answerphone and it seemed that the Sky interview had stirred up quite a lot of discussion. I returned all the calls, mostly to the tabloid newspapers, and Capital Radio's *Sports Desk*, to amplify on the technology view. My suggestion that a sin bin should replace the yellow card had provoked particular interest. My view was that for a yellow-card offence a player should be sent to a sin bin for a particular period of time, depending upon the nature and seriousness of the offence. This would mean that a player would be punished in the game in which he committed the offence so any advantage would be gained by his opponents. Currently when he is eventually suspended the opponents who benefit are not the ones who suffered from his misdemeanour. Furthermore, having a player in the sin bin might well discourage other offences and stop the sudden rash of yellow cards that can occur in some games. The *Daily Mail*'s 'Whistleblower' was more interested in the merit orders for Premier League referees and an explanation as to why Gerald Ashby (injury), Mike Reed (injury) and Mike Riley (holiday) had not yet refereed a Premier League match. Unfortunately, there was no dark conspiracy for him to reveal.

Thursday 21 August

Up early to return to Harrow to deal with the publication of the GCSE results. When I arrived home again the phone was going non-stop with boys wanting their grades. I was delighted that the results were good and Alex Ward and Eustace Santa-Barbara in Druries had achieved all A grades, the vast majority being the highest possible grading – A*. I was also delighted with the results of my GCSE geography division who had all gained an A or A*, apart from one whom I would deal with when term began. Despite 20 years' experience, it is always a slightly tense moment getting the results of a group of boys you have taught for two years and worrying if you have prepared them properly. Good results mean delight all round.

I had many calls from the press on a variety of topics; they took up much of the morning and early afternoon, a welcome distraction from yet another thoroughly depressing batting performance from England at the Oval Test. Not only was I being questioned about the sin bin and other forms of technology but also about Ian Wright and Wendy Toms – no connection, of course!

With Ian Wright hoping to equal or beat the Arsenal goal-scoring record on Saturday some papers wanted the referees' view of him as a player. 'Can we say that referees like him?', I was asked. 'I think you could say that referees admire his goal-scoring skills,' I suggested diplomatically. Others had spotted that I would be refereeing the Southampton v Arsenal match on Saturday and asked what I would do if Ian Wright equalled or broke the record and indulged in overelaborate celebrations. I pointed out that my only concern was behaviour that threatens safety or provokes crowd disturbances and, if such incidents occurred, they would be reported to the FA. This policy was adopted by the FA last season as it was felt that referees should not be seen to be killjoys, and showing a yellow card to a player who is celebrating a goal might well be provocative in itself, especially if it is the player's second yellow card. Some asked if there had ever been any trouble between me and Ian Wright. As they had not bothered to do their research I did not feel inclined to remind them of the controversy when he called me a 'little Hitler'. That was a few years ago when, suddenly, Ian launched an attack on referees in which he called Robbie Hart a 'muppet' and me a 'little Hitler'. One newspaper produced a photo of me with a Nazi cap, swastika and Hitler moustache. The FA took very little action and I soon forgot it although, unsurprisingly, the boys at Harrow are quick to remind me of the nickname now and then.

As far as Wendy Toms (the Premier League's first female official) was concerned, one or two papers had spotted that Wednesday night would be her first appearance on the line in a Premier League match and the press wanted to know how the men had greeted her appointment. I said that it was welcomed because she has proved herself by coming through the promotion system the same as everyone else. Ultimately, however, her being a woman was irrelevant because, as with Uriah Rennie the new black referee, her reputation and people's opinion of her would be based on how well she performs her duties. Asked what advice I would give her I declined to comment as her second game was on the line to me in September and I would give her any advice then.

Friday 22 August

I spent the whole day at my desk writing discussion papers for school and catching up on correspondence. I enjoyed reading Mike Knapp's article 'The Men in Black' in the *Daily Express* which looked at the robot ref of the future and quoted me very faithfully, along with the comments of other colleagues. Steve Lodge phoned to report on his recent match in Finland and the FA sent me a fax from Australia in response to reports of my interview in newspapers out there. Friends in Hong Kong faxed to say that my sin bin ideas had hit the headlines in the *South China Post*. I faxed 21st birthday greeting to a young referee in Johannesburg whom I had met when I was out there refereeing the Mandela Inauguration Trophy match between South Africa and Brazil. He regularly keeps me posted as to his progress and is desperately keen to get on to the South African international assistant referees' list, not an easy task for a white referee as soccer is essentially a black sport out there.

Saturday 23 August

Today's match was Southampton v Arsenal and, as it was the Bank Holiday weekend, I set off much earlier than usual so that I would have plenty of time if caught in traffic. I had followed England's fortunes in the Test match on the radio and it seemed that we were heading for trouble again, despite some stout resistance from Ramprakash. My two assistants, Phil Sharp and Mike Stobbart, arrived early and we wandered around the lush green pitch catching up on news of early-season matches. Phil had been on the line to Steve Lodge the previous midweek and explained the fracas and his failure to identify correctly the players involved. It had been a good learning experience for him. The match observer, Tom Bune, also arrived early and, as always, was keen to check that he was up to date with current thinking and practice among the Premier League referees. He is one of the most charming of the observers, but not an easy man to please, so you are always on your toes when he's casting his eye over you.

The pre-match security briefing was mainly concerned with the possibility of pitch invasions should Ian Wright equal or beat Arsenal's scoring record. I mentioned this to the club representatives when they brought in the team sheets at 2 p.m. and was reminded that Southampton's fans might also run on to the pitch if their team scored as they had failed to find the back of the net so far.

During the first half it was stiflingly hot, humid and airless, and the slightest exertion resulted in buckets of sweat and difficulty getting one's breath. Arsenal looked good and a stunning goal by Marc Overmars was sheer class as he cut inside the defender and shot low and hard. Steve Bould received a yellow card for a tackle from behind and Ken Monkou for a nasty, slightly high tackle on Petit. Ian Wright was trying hard to behave. We chatted now and then and I did my best to be light and cheerful with him, generally to good effect although it was clear that this goal-scoring record business was getting to him, and the rest of the Arsenal team. Indeed, for much of the match, the Arsenal forwards seemed obsessed with setting him up for goal attempts, often to the detriment of themselves and their general play. Ian steadily got frustrated and when he deliberately stood in front of a Southampton free-kick he gained a yellow card, in part because Francis Benali deliberately aimed the free-kick straight at him, knowing he would block it. Sometimes, you wonder why professionals behave as they do. Dennis Bergkamp was getting very frustrated and agitated, but scored a super goal and I drifted over to him and suggested that that was the best way to deal with his opponents. He agreed, scored another great goal and then got himself booked for reacting to a challenge with too much aggression.

Overall, it was a good game but the second half had a 15-minute period when I really had to work hard at keeping the players calm – the heat was getting to them and at times Southampton were being embarrassed. They were unlucky when David Seaman just stopped a rebound on the line and I disallowed a Southampton 'goal' for a clear push by Neil Maddison just before one of his team-mates headed into the net. You often get periods in a game when you have to work really hard for about five to ten minutes and then everything calms down again. In this one the real challenge was the amount of shirt-pulling that was going on and which I wanted to check but without disrupting the flow of the game by whistling too often. There are those who believe that we should penalise every foul and infringement, but you would never get any flow in the game and players would become hugely frustrated, as would the spectators. It is necessary to find that happy balance, but it takes fine judgement.

The players all seemed very happy and many shook hands at the final whistle, although disallowing that 'goal' meant that I got the usual abuse from the Southampton fans as I left the field. Arsène Wenger thanked me as he waited by the Arsenal dressing-room door and Tom Bune, the observer, seemed very happy, especially with my fitness and my judgement of when to intervene and when to let play continue. His only real criticism was that I perhaps should have cautioned Ian Wright for delaying a free-kick earlier than I did.

The main excitement, though, was the Test match. When we left for the kick-off Australia, needing 124, were 5 for 1 wicket. When we returned they were 94–8 and we watched with great delight on the TV in the dressing room as England won a fantastic match. Returning to my car there was the usual crowd of autograph hunters (a large number had appeared when I arrived earlier in the day); Southampton seems to have more autograph-hungry youngsters than anywhere else. There was some good-natured backchat with Arsenal supporters about my booking of Bergkamp. 'You mean, I should have sent him off,' I retorted to their amusement.

I then drove cross country to South Devon for a final break before the start of term. Needless to say, the first call on 606 was from a disgruntled Southampton fan complaining about my refereeing. Now why should I have been surprised that David Mellor picked that one first? Mellor has attacked me since I refereed the 1994 Cup Final and he blamed me for Chelsea's defeat. The problem is that he always personalises his attacks on referees and is rarely prepared to hear the referee's viewpoint. Still, I was pleased later to hear him give his tacit support for the sin bin idea I had proposed earlier in the week.

Sunday 24 August

Slept until late and then had a lazy day with my god-daughter Katie, her sisters, parents and friends on the beach. We met up for lunch in the Salcombe Yacht Club with an Old Harrovian I had taught for A level and his parents, and then went back to the beach to play with the children and referee the beach football match. All quiet in the papers so we had got through the second weekend without any major controversy. How long would it last?

Monday 25 August

Another glorious day spent on the beach away from thoughts of football and school, although as I swam at the water's edge I was introduced to one rather splendid lady who wanted to find out how to get her son into Harrow. It was a long, lazy day reading, swimming, building sandcastles and enjoying a late barbecue.

Tuesday 26 August

I reluctantly drove back to Harrow, acknowledging the end of the holidays. On the way I popped in to see my 91-year-old grandmother who, as ever, was full of football stories and defending my honour and reputation. She watches *Match of the Day* religiously and roundly berates the commentators if they are rude about me. She gets upset by criticism in the press and is my greatest supporter. Indeed, when

I did the Cup Final in 1994 she phoned the BBC to complain that they had shown Manchester United parading the Cup rather than me collecting my medal.

Back at Harrow the answerphone was full of press messages wanting my comments on Wendy Toms and her first Premier League line. There were also calls from a number of colleagues worried about the high profile being adopted by Uriah Rennie, which might threaten our unity and strength of purpose. Some colleagues were shocked to hear that he had an agent, and when I discovered from Radio 4's *Today* programme that Wendy Toms's agent had said she was too busy to deal with the press, I began to wonder what refereeing was coming to. Why do referees need agents? We're not supposed to be showbiz stars, are we?

Wednesday 27 August

I was very unimpressed to receive the tickets for the World Cup game in Romania and see that we were flying Tarom. I flew with them four years ago for a World Cup match between Romania and Czechoslovakia (as it then was) and it was the worst airline I have ever been on. We had been booked in Business Class but there was no business section and no seat allocation. The aircraft seemed old and the overhead lockers were shelves, so Joe Worrall, the referee who had been presented with a great samovar had to put it on the seat next to him. The in-flight meal consisted of a roll in Clingfilm and a sachet of coffee with a plastic cup of hot water.

I was further annoyed to have my passport returned by the FA without the visa for Romania. I had been asked to send my passport to the FA about a fortnight before the trip so that visas could be obtained, which had meant that I could not use it to pop over to Paris for a couple of days as I had planned. I had not really minded as football sometimes imposes such restrictions. However, for some reason, the visas had not been organised through the Romanian Embassy and the passports had been returned with a note saying that we could obtain them on arrival at Bucharest.

Thursday 28 August

A very hectic day with the media following the trouble in the Leicester v Arsenal match last night when Graham Barber allowed about six minutes of stoppage time during which Arsenal took the lead 3–2 and then Leicester equalised. After the final whistle he was surrounded by Arsenal players and a fracas involving some members of both teams ensued. As a consequence Ian Wright, Steve Walsh and Patrick Vieira were being reported to the Football Association along with Pat Rice for remarks made to the referee in the dressing room after the match. I had to get the details from Graham Barber so that I could deal with the media questions.

Apart from the press, I did radio interviews for Capital Sports and BBC *Newsbeat* along with a TV interview in the early evening for ITN News. My views were required on the regulations for how much stoppage time referees allow. I was keen to get across that it is stoppage time and not just injury time. Last season the Premier League referees agreed that we would stop our watches for every caution, dismissal, substitution, injury, goal celebration, time-wasting and ball lost into the crowd. We felt we should all be consistent and hoped that people were aware that the referee is required by the Laws of the Game to 'make due allowance' for time lost through stoppages. In practical terms the referee stops his watch for each such stoppage and then restarts it, finally blowing the whistle when the watch shows 45 minutes – he does not add time on. These discussions developed into questions about independent time-keeping and the possibility of the referee's watch controlling the stadium clock so everyone can see what is happening. In the end, ITN did not use me and, to my chagrin, showed an interview with David Mellor instead.

In the midst of all this I received a letter from the FA informing me that they were nominating me for the FIFA referees' list for 1998. Each country can nominate up to 10 referees and 10 assistant referees to FIFA for each calendar year. Given the controversy at Leicester which led several newspapers to be highly critical of his handling of the game, it was ironic that the letter stated that Graham Barber would be nominated as England's new FIFA referee, replacing Steve Lodge who had reached the 45 age limit. I was delighted that the two new assistant referees were Pete Walton, who lost his place when he went to South Africa to work for a year, and Andy Hogg who accompanied me last season for the Rosenburg v AC Milan Champions League match in Norway.

Friday 29 August

I was stunned to receive my assessment from the Southampton v

Arsenal match and discover that I have been downgraded because of one minor incident. The match observer felt that when Ian Wright, in the 24th minute, strolled past the ball to get into the defensive wall he had delayed the free-kick and then when he had broken from the wall by about one metre (though not delaying or blocking the free-kick) I should have given him a yellow card. The facts were that he ran past the free-kick rather than strolled and did not interfere with the kick in any way. I was very disappointed by this literal interpretation of the Laws, which creates difficulties for referees and shows a total lack of understanding of the modern game. Had I cautioned Ian Wright as this match observer required then there is little doubt it would have been seen by everyone as totally unfair and unnecessary. I would have been accused of persecuting Ian Wright and there would have been huge controversy. I decided that, for only the third time in my 12 seasons as a top-flight referee, I would challenge the assessment, and I wrote a lengthy letter to the Premier League. I also decided to take the video to next weekend's referees' meeting and see what action others would have taken.

Saturday 30 August

I was phoned early in the morning by the *Sunday Mirror* wanting my comments on a *Daily Mirror* report which quoted verbatim from Graham Barber's confidential report to the FA about the Leicester v Arsenal match. That report had only been seen by Graham, the FA, myself and Arsenal so it could only have got to the paper from one source. I was at pains to explain that there was no vendetta among referees against Ian Wright, and would love to have told them that I had just been downgraded for not giving him a yellow card last weekend. I explained that referees are under such scrutiny they have to make sure they treat all players fairly and equally and that we are accused both of being too harsh and too lenient with the superstars – which suggests that we largely get it right.

I was alarmed that a confidential report had got into the press and also disappointed by Glenn Hoddle's remarks that he did not think Ian Wright should be suspended and even if he had slapped the referee he *probably* would have stayed in the England squad. I could understand Glenn Hoddle supporting Ian and not wanting club disciplinary matters to spill over into the international scene but for the England manager to be apparently condoning a player assaulting a referee was appalling (especially as Phil Richards had been assaulted by a spectator at Notts County the previous weekend). I rang David Davies, the Public Relations Officer of the FA, about both matters.

It was a free day from refereeing. On the initial appointments list I was due to referee Liverpool v Newcastle but that had been switched to the following day when I would be busy all day at school.

Sunday 31 August

A most dreadful day. I awoke to sombre music on my radio alarm and thought that the station had got changed somehow. I then remembered that in Russia they played funereal music when a president died and I immediately thought that there had been a royal death, probably the Queen Mother had died in her sleep. Going downstairs I switched on the TV and was transfixed with horror at the news that Diana, Princess of Wales had been killed in a car crash. I had always adored her and often dreamt about her. I was stunned and could not stop watching the TV. I am not ashamed to say that I shed tears many times that morning as I shuttled between meetings and watched the terrible story unfold. In the afternoon I was helping the new matron settle into the house but she too was stunned. I kept feeling that I would switch on the TV and find that it had all been a ghastly mistake.

It was rather eerie that at seven o'clock the aircraft of the Royal Flight bringing her body back to London flew almost directly over Harrow School on its approach to Northolt airport. Some people crowded into my drive which looks straight down to the runway where the plane was landing.

The Liverpool v Newcastle match was postponed as a mark of respect and this was a fitting gesture in a terrible, terrible day of tragedy. My thoughts went to the young princes and those at Eton College and Ludgrove School who would have the burden of responsibility for caring for Prince William and Prince Harry when they eventually returned to school. It reminded me of the time a boy in a House where I was tutor lost his mother in a car crash. I have never forgotten the scream of anguish he let out when told the news.

September 1997

Monday 1 September

One of the most hectic days of the year, regardless of how well organised one has been beforehand. As House Master of Druries, one of Harrow's eleven boarding Houses, I am responsible for 60 boys aged 13–18, who spend two years in my House. I choose which boys come to Druries. They live in single or double study bedrooms on the 'boys side' and my quarters are known as 'the private side'. Being a House Master is the best job in the education world.

There were 14 new boys to welcome and cope with along with various meetings with matron and the senior boys. Everything is non-stop from 7 a.m. Dan Hepher, Head of House and Head of School, had been around for two days on various leadership courses with senior masters. He joined me along with the other three House monitors to discuss the year ahead. I wanted to ensure that they would be dedicated in their role as mentors to the new boys and would help them settle in.

Amid all the preparations for the start of term I was rung by Brian Woolnaugh of the *Sun* who wanted to discuss Arsenal and referees' views of their disciplinary record. He had some quotes from Gary Willard who had refereed them in their last match against Spurs, and I had also spoken to Graham Barber after the Leicester v Arsenal match. We all agreed that they were not as aggressive or dirty as their yellow card tally suggested. When asked for my advice I said I thought it might help Arsenal if they were to look at the video clips of all their cautions for the season and then sit down with Ken Ridden, myself or some other Premier League referee and see which of them could have been avoided. I knew, for instance, that Steve Bould had been given a yellow card for a foul tackle from behind in each of his last three matches – an offence which he should learn to eliminate from his game. I have on occasions visited football clubs to speak about refereeing in an attempt to promote better relations with the players but also to help them understand the directives referees operate under. I believed this might be especially helpful to Arsène Wenger as he was new to the English Premier League and might not fully understand the attitude of Premier League referees.

By 4.40 p.m. the boys were streaming back and football was forgotten as I welcomed them, chatted to parents, calmed mothers on the verge of tears and made a welcome speech to the new boys. I snatched a bite to eat about 9.30 p.m. and eventually saw the last set of boys at 11.15 p.m. before slumping into bed. In the background all day, however, was the grief and depression at Diana's death and the disbelief at the thought that we would never see her again. It tarnished the day for us all.

Tuesday 2 September

Busy again with meetings and guiding the new boys through their first day, showing them how to cross the road at the safe places and watching them try a variety of sports. In between all this I was being bombarded with requests for comments on Brian Woolnaugh's article that had appeared under a headline something like '*Elleray ready to help Arsenal*'. I explained my views to various papers and was interviewed live by Radio Five and again restated that referees are always ready to visit clubs to discuss disciplinary matters and help them reduce their cautions. I reiterated that we, as referees, had no vendetta against Arsenal or Ian Wright but felt that they could clean up their act quite easily by being a little more careful in their tackles and not indulging in the unsportsmanlike behaviour that, these days, brings automatic yellow cards. To top it all, in last night's Sky match – Bolton v Everton – there was one of those 'did the ball cross the line' disputes so I had RTE from Ireland and others wanting to talk about the use of video replays.

Wednesday 3 September

The last few days were so hectic that I had forgotten it was my 43rd birthday and I was initially puzzled by the amount of mail I received. However, there was no time for celebrations as teaching was starting and I was also liaising with colleagues and the Premier League to decide whether we should go ahead with the planned Premier League referees' meeting on Saturday. It was the day of Diana, Princess of Wales's funeral and many sporting events were being cancelled. I was in favour of a postponement but opinions varied and, in the end, the Premier League decided to go ahead. I felt this was fundamentally wrong but, as we are professional in our approach and our commitment, we accepted it, although with a heavy heart and some resentment. The debate over the use of video replays by referees and the Arsenal controversy raged on and I did some more interviews, one in response to Arsène Wenger's 'retaliation' in the *Evening Standard*, where he called for the introduction of full-time referees. More worrying was the attack on Graham Barber by the *Daily Mirror*, in part because he would not agree to be interviewed by them. As often happens in these situations they were bringing up the past to make a mountain out of a mole hill and were trying to use his dismissal of Tony Adams at Newcastle last season as evidence of him having a vendetta against the club.

Thursday 4 September

Good news in the post with a letter from the FA telling me that I had been appointed to referee the Champions' League match between Monaco and Bayer Leverkusen on 1 October. If my 1992 trip to Romania had been one of the strangest experiences of my international career then the trip in 1994 to Monaco had been one of the highlights. The obvious wealth evident everywhere in Monaco was in stark contrast with the poverty I had witnessed in Romania while, in those matches the fierce passion of the Romanian fans was a world away from the almost sedate Monaco supporters.

Friday 5 September

A hectic morning teaching and getting packed for the Premier League meeting in the Midlands. I finished my last lesson at 3.15 p.m. and jumped into the car to try to avoid the rush hour. Driving up the M40 I became increasingly resentful that I was not going to be able to watch the funeral and hardened in my belief that the Premier League were being unreasonable in going ahead with the meeting. At one point I very nearly turned back for Harrow, convinced I should be at school, or better still, in central London paying my respects. There are times when football makes very heavy demands on one's time and one's emotions.

Arriving at Moor Hall Hotel, where we always meet, I cooled a little until I had tea with Gary Willard and Martin Bodenham who shared my views and had also very nearly turned back themselves. I then had a long meeting with Ken Ridden to discuss the weekend's agenda. Earlier in the day I had spoken with David Davies of the FA to express my concern over Glenn Hoddle's remarks about Ian Wright. I have always found Glenn very sensible and supportive of referees, but I wanted David to make sure that such careless remarks did not occur again. It is difficult enough to recruit referees without the England manager seeming to imply that attacking referees isn't all that bad.

Although pre-dinner drinks were at 8 p.m. I was determined to watch the arrival of Diana's coffin at Kensington Palace. It was the start of an emotionally draining period for so many people and I felt keenly affected by it. During dinner we managed to persuade the Premier League officials that we wanted to start early the next morning so we could break to watch the funeral. If necessary, we would have a working lunch and go on longer in the afternoon. Towards the end of the meal Mike Foster made a presentation to Roger Dilkes to mark his retirement from the referees' list. We were amused to see that the photo showed him giving someone a yellow card because he had the reputation of being more of a talker than a disciplinarian. We also toasted Graham Barber's nomination as a FIFA referee.

Saturday 6 September

An amazing day of mixed emotions and activities. Up early for breakfast and the meeting at half past eight so we could break for the funeral. A positive start with Mike Foster announcing that, yet again, English clubs' sportsmanship and fair play in UEFA competitions have earned an additional UEFA Cup place. He felt this was in no small part due to the firm style of refereeing in the Premier League which gets the players into a disciplined frame of mind so they incur few cautions and dismissals when playing abroad. Much discussion of video clips on incidents in matches so far this season, especially relating to foul tackles and confrontations. Open honesty from all the referees, not least Jeff Winter, who should have given two more red cards at Blackburn and was man enough to put his hands up and apologise for letting his other colleagues down. Not a witch hunt but integrity and honest self-appraisal among professionals.

At 10.15 a.m. we broke to watch the funeral. It was a moving cortège and service, and the young princes were so dignified that I was proud of them and ached for their loss. I was moved to tears on several occasions, especially when Elton John sang 'Candle in the Wind' and when Earl Spencer spoke with such affection of his sister. After the minute's silence we resumed the meeting and it was bizarre how I could switch back into business mode, my emotions having been through the wringer for the previous two hours.

The meeting continued either side of lunch and I was especially touched when Gerald Ashby, on behalf of all my Premier League colleagues, presented me with some Lladrò pottery and a bottle of Moët et Chandon in appreciation for the work I was doing as their representative and spokesman.

At the end we set the date for the FIFA fitness test and Ken Ridden announced that Paul Durkin had joined me in the UEFA top group of 30 referees. This must have been a bitter blow to Dermot Gallagher who, for the last year or so, has been the acknowledged number two in England's hierarchy of referees. However, he had still not returned to full fitness and this has been noted with concern both in England and by UEFA.

I drove back to Harrow as the hearse containing Diana's body was being driven to Althorp House – and various moments of the radio commentary again brought a lump to my throat and tears to my eyes. Back at Harrow I had to prepare for the dinner I was giving to my 13 senior boys, and to catch up with any business that had taken place since I had left yesterday afternoon.

As time for dinner approached one of the new boys, who was dreadfully homesick, came to see me and I spent so long comforting him and trying to talk him through the coming days, that I had to delay the start of the dinner. The food was not ready and I had not had time to get into my dinner jacket. In the event we had a superb evening which, as always, started with a Latin grace. Several courses and plenty of wine later, I proposed the Loyal Toast and explained to the boys the protocol involved. Discussion spanned the spectrum of adolescent life and interests, and enabled me to touch on certain issues, not least drugs, and why a House Master has to be tough as it is vital to protect those who might be tempted into difficulties. I explained my overall philosophy that for any offence there are always three categories of people: those who will *always* get involved, those who *never* will and those who *might*. It is, I am convinced, my responsibility to do all I can to prevent as many of the 'mights' as possible from being tempted into trouble. We finished about 1 a.m. – the end of a quite extraordinary day.

Sunday 7 September

Everyone I spoke to seemed wrung out after the emotions of yesterday. At the chapel service in the morning we prayed for Diana and Mother Theresa, who had also died. It was a busy day with the new boys: swimming trials, photos, lunch and then their first match as Drurieans against another House – appropriately a soccer match. It gave me another insight into coaching and the emotions of a manager and although my half-time talk was hardly inspirational we converted a 1–1 score into a 4–1 victory, thanks somewhat to three penalty decisions in our favour by Alex Ward, a senior boy from my House who was refereeing. Then I gave tea to the new boys and there was lots of chat about football and films. In between times I had to pack my kit for the Romania trip and phone the others in the team to agree a meeting up time at Heathrow.

Monday 8 September

While preparing for the trip to Romania, I had another busy day attempting to cope with the demands of school, making sure that all the work for the classes I would miss had been set. I had to teach an extra period with my Upper Sixth to make up for one I missed on Wednesday and this put me under greater time pressure. I received the Coca-Cola appointments from the Football League and saw I was down for the London battle between Wimbledon and Millwall. I decided that I would be missing too much school for refereeing in the next few months so asked the FA to change my availability list with FIFA and UEFA. Originally I had closed (i.e. declared myself unavailable) the third week in October so that I could get a break during half-term. However, that would mean being appointed to a second-leg match in the next round of the European Cup competitions which would be three days away from school. To avoid that I changed it so I was available for the first leg and I would sacrifice some of my half-term holiday to referee.

The other interesting development was the news that Lancing

College's Headmaster, Chris Saunders, a friend of mine and on the FA Council, had decided to retire at the end of the academic year. It was just the sort of school I would love to become Headmaster of so I began to give thought to applying, with all the turmoil and uncertainty that such a move causes.

Late in the evening I packed my briefcase, checking I had all the FIFA World Cup documents, plenty of work to do on the plane and a supply of chocolate and biscuits in case the food was poor.

Tuesday 9 September

One of those extraordinary days when I changed from one 'profession' to another and found myself travelling halfway across Europe to do so. I attended chapel with the boys in the morning and taught the first period before taking a taxi to Heathrow. Tarom, the Romanian airline were much better organised than before. Change was evident at Bucharest airport too, where the anti-aircraft guns that used to line the runways had gone and the burnt-out wreckage of old planes had been cleared away. We were met at customs by the female interpreter and the Chairman of the Romanian Referees' Committee who took our passports away to sort out the formalities. I was somewhat alarmed when he re-appeared a few moments later without them, confidently announcing that someone had offered to queue on his behalf. Would we ever again see our passports, now in the hands of a total stranger – bearing in mind that such passports must be worth a fortune on the black market? Still, there were no problems and we were soon off to the Bucharesti Hotel where I had stayed back in 1992.

What a change! Gone were the prostitutes in the lobby and the brown and orange carpets. The brown wallpaper, with rusty bath water to match, had also been swept away and the hotel was modern, clean and well decorated. Almost a perfect Western hotel, or so I thought until I tried to have a bath and found . . . no bath plug. A quick check with my other colleagues, Mark Warren, Phil Sharp and Steve Lodge, revealed that they too had no plugs. I tried the hotel reception but to no avail, not least because the hotel clerk muttered something about my controversial refereeing of Benfica v Steaua Bucharest a few years ago. The hotel manager was charming, promised the earth and delivered nothing even though I signed an autograph for his son and gave him an England pin badge.

We were taken off for an excellent meal accompanied by Leyla, our interpreter, and the Referees' Committee Chairman. We watched the Romania v Iceland under-21 match on TV as we ate and were then entertained by some Romanian folk singers and dancers. The leading lady we soon nicknamed Sybil (of *Fawlty Towers*) as she looked and sang like her, and when she approached to choose someone to dance with and kiss on the dance floor I drew the short straw. Fortunately, photos do not exist of this event.

Wednesday 10 September

A late start with the official meeting scheduled for eleven o'clock. We met the Yugoslav FIFA delegate who I had worked with before and also Christian, the Romanian FA's Deputy General Secretary, who had been the match delegate for the Karlsruhe v Brondby match I had refereed in November 1996. The pitch at the Steaua Bucharest FC stadium was poor and the facilities still drab and unchanged since my visit in 1992. The surrounds were being dug up and we had been promised that the front two rows of seats would be filled with police and army so no one could have access to the rocks and debris that littered the perimeter. It was an easy meeting, not least because I knew the Romanian officials, and the Icelandic officials included the Chairman of their Referees' Committee who had invited me to Iceland back in April to give some lectures to their top-division referees.

We then had a tour of Bucharest and stopped outside the palace that President Ceaucescu had built for himself, supposedly the second largest building in the world, after the Pentagon. Sweeping down from it is a fine Parisian style boulevard with wide roads, fountains and trees. In Ceaucescu's time it was called the 'Triumph of Socialism Avenue', but our interpreter said that most people added the words 'over the Romanian people'.

We looked around the sports complex that holds the Nationale Bucharest team's stadium, not least because Steve Lodge would return there in three weeks to referee their UEFA Cup Winners' Cup match. After lunch it was the usual sleep, then the growing nerves and rush of adrenaline and off to the stadium, me in something of a panic because I had developed the runs and was hoping that the two Imodium tablets I had taken would do the trick. While inspecting the pitch we were approached at various stages by Dan Petrescu (Chelsea), Gheorghe Popescu (ex-Spurs and now with Galatasaray) and Ilie Dumitrescu (ex-Spurs, now playing in Mexico). There is always something of a bond on these occasions when foreign players recognise that they have English referees and want to catch up on the news. Dumitrescu was particularly happy that he had got back into the Romanian team after nine months, and was hoping that a good performance in the World Cup in France would open the door to a return to club football in Europe.

The match went well and quietly, Romania having already qualified for France and Iceland keen to preserve some national pride. Romania won 4–0. Indirectly I became part of Romanian footballing history. A free-kick led to Gheorghe Hagi scoring his 30th goal for Romania, thus equalling the national goal-scoring record, and when, in the 81st minute, the Icelandic goalkeeper floored an opponent in the box, I awarded a penalty and Hagi scored, establishing a new record. The Romanian FA promised me a mention in their history books; for once it would not be a controversial one.

After the match we had a splendid meal in the Casino Palace Hotel, dining on caviar and smoked salmon, wonderfully cooked beef and excellent Romanian wines. Everyone was happy and the Yugoslav FIFA delegate was particularly pleased with our low-key approach to the match. I had a fascinating discussion with him about the current political and economic state of his country and the troubles they were facing.

Thursday 11 September

A trouble-free journey home and I was met at the airport by taxi and back to school to teach and catch up with the post and messages that had accumulated while I was away. I faxed through my reports to FIFA and completed the other paperwork before preparing for afternoon meetings.

Friday 12 September

Lots of teaching to do to make up for the periods I had missed so in the afternoon I taught from 1.50 p.m. until 4.45 p.m. Little by way of football to deal with except to give some advice to Graham Barber who had been called to an FA disciplinary meeting following his report on the Leicester v Arsenal match. I gave him some guidance about what to say and what not to react to, and how to deal with the press. I also checked Mike Foster's minutes of the Premier League referees' meeting from last weekend.

Saturday 13 September

An extraordinary day not so much in terms of the game – Manchester United v West Ham United – but because of the people I met on my travels to and from Old Trafford. When I have a Saturday match in Liverpool, Newcastle or Manchester I often go by train as it is quicker and less stressful than driving. There is, however, the pleasure and problem of travelling with supporters and being recognised. Many is the time I've returned on the train in disguise, sitting behind a newspaper while all around me fans are fulminating about the idiot who refereed the game.

I drove to Watford Junction to catch the train to Manchester Piccadilly and, while I was waiting on the platform engaged in conversation with a Manchester United fan, David Butler came and said 'hello'. David had been Terry Venables' physio at Spurs and then with England. He was working for Terry in Europe, keeping Terry appraised of the form of various Australian players. David was off to watch two Australians play in the Oldham v Northampton match. As the train came into the station we parted and I headed for first class but it became clear that the train was totally full. Not only were there Manchester United and West Ham fans but there were also Liverpool supporters who were travelling to Manchester and then across to Merseyside because there was trouble on the direct line to Liverpool. There wasn't a spare seat so I sat on my bag in the corridor and prepared for an uncomfortable journey. It reminded me of the time some years ago when I made the same journey for a Coca-Cola semi-final at Old Trafford. John Martin was the referee and I was the reserve referee. The snow had been so bad that most trains were cancelled. We sat in the corridor all the way with a rather grand lady who was off to her daughter's silver wedding party. When it became obvious how long the journey would take this lady undid her parcels and we feasted on the sherry and cake she was taking for her daughter.

A number of supporters jokingly offered me money for penalties but none offered me their seat, even when I suggested that if I had to stand all the way I would be so tired I'd not be up with play enough to give them the penalties they wanted. After a while David Butler appeared having been equally unlucky in finding a seat and we chatted for the rest of the journey. He gave me the inside story of Terry Venables' sacking by Alan Sugar at Spurs and talked about the excitements of England's success in Euro '96. We discussed Spurs' problem with their long list of injured players and also debated England and Australia's chances of reaching the finals in France. We joked that if they both got there fate will ensure that the two countries were in the same group so that Terry could have his chance of revenge.

We arrived at Manchester Piccadilly rather later than I wanted and as I queued for a taxi I fell into conversation with a couple of fans and we agreed to share a cab. One of them explained that he was a top-flight boxing referee and we had a really enjoyable journey to Old Trafford comparing the pressures in our respective sports.

The game itself passed without much incident although prior to kick-off I was approached by someone from Sky TV who wanted to discuss the possibility of putting cameras in the goalposts and crossbars and of me wearing a mini camera in a match so that people could see the referee's view.

After the game John Goggins, the match observer who had been in charge of referees when I was a Football League referee, took me to the station where, to my horror, I discovered there was a major power problem and trains were being delayed or cancelled. I managed to get a seat on a London train and then the fun started, and continued for the next four hours both in the station and when we eventually got going. Two men, one a Manchester United supporter, the other a West Ham supporter, struck up a conversation asking if I'd been to the game. As we discussed the match's incidents, it became obvious that they did not know who I was. We debated the penalty appeal and I commented that the referee had been very close to the incident. They agreed. Indeed, I said, the referee was quite brilliantly positioned. They did not demur. All around people who had recognised me were stifling laughs as I led these two on further and further. A while later, after the conversation had ceased a youngster came and asked me for my autograph. The Manchester United supporter, Andy Slater, resplendent in a dreadful orange shirt, noticed, and as I signed my name it suddenly dawned on him who I was. Both he and his West Ham friend, Terry Moffat, realised what fools they had been made to look and the whole compartment began mercilessly taking the mickey out of them.

It turned out to be a very pleasant trip, soured only by a fat, bald, drunken West Ham supporter who came up to accuse me of being biased towards Manchester United. I am fairly used to dealing with this sort of situation but Andy Slater objected and there was a rather nasty exchange between him and the drunken fan. This lout is just the sort of idiot who has few brains and spoils the atmosphere for many people. Indeed, once he had gone the West Ham supporters around me were genuinely apologetic and embarrassed by him and hoped that I would not judge them by this one coarse individual. What struck me was the range of people who were supporting the two clubs and their genuine niceness and interest in the game.

Some of the fans were keen to know what I said to players during games. I illustrated this by telling them how, early in the second half when Manchester United were not playing especially well and were getting frustrated, Paul Scholes had had a go at me. I had turned to him and told him that just because he was playing badly he shouldn't take it out on me.

Sitting across from me were three teenage girls and their father, all in Manchester United kit. Chatting to the girls, Anna, Claire and Sarah, it emerged that the eldest had taken a shine to Ryan Giggs and had started supporting Manchester United as a result. The younger two fancied David Beckham. The upshot was that they had become fanatical football supporters and Manchester United fans in particular. Poor old dad, who hated football so much when at school that he would do anything to get out of it, was now a fervent fan himself, converted by his daughters. To me it was fantastic to see young girls interested in the sport – albeit for not strictly footballing reasons – and I was pleased that the game is now safe enough and attractive enough for them to want to go to matches. It shows that we must do all we can to ensure that the drunken fans remain a pathetic minority.

I got home much later than planned but it had been a wonderful day, enlivened by the genuine fans I had met on my travels.

Sunday 14 September

A quiet non-football day as far as refereeing, although I did see the new boys win 4–1 in their second match of the term. Alex Ward, who had controversially given three penalties last week, this time awarded only two but he did send off one of the opponents.

In the evening I was rung up by the man writing the 'Whistleblower' column in the *Daily Mail*. He wanted, and got, my opinion of David Mellor and his vitriolic attacks on referees on the 606 show. I remarked that it was a shame that Mellor was prepared to condemn referees merely on the word of one fan and that he allows his show to be characterised by the slagging off of referees. For someone supposedly charged with developing the game he scores pretty cheap points.

Monday 15 September

The main press interest today seemed to focus on my quiet chat with David Beckham on Saturday after he reacted to taunting by the West Ham fans. I was happy to explain that I was not reprimanding David but giving him a few words of advice about ignoring abuse from fans rather than reacting and getting into disciplinary trouble. David had taken the advice well and we had had a good laugh about me getting far more stick than him and him having most of the fans on his side whereas I had no one. I explained to the press that, although I thought David was coping well with the pressure, if I could help avoid a problem by giving him some fatherly advice then I should be able to do so without it being blown up out of proportion. Other reporters who tried to manufacture a story out of nothing then picked up my comments to the Press Association, but I had made it clear there was little to write about.

During the morning it became obvious that my presence would be needed at Harrow the next day and I had to withdraw from refereeing the Wimbledon v Millwall Coca-Cola match. There were meetings that I just could not miss.

Tuesday 16 September

My comments about David Beckham produced a few more enquiries but generally the press was supportive and I was able to put across the view that referees and players are not always at loggerheads and we do try to work together. One newspaper wanted to know whether the pressure on players from the fans is any worse than in the past. It is just that the types of player being targeted has changed. Ten years or more ago the targets were the black players with the awful racism that was endemic in some clubs. Thankfully, after hard work from the Professional Footballers' Association in particular, that has been largely eradicated and the targets now tend to be the young 'superstars' like Ryan Giggs, David Beckham, Robbie Fowler and Steve McManaman.

Wednesday 17 September

A day mainly free from football matters except the odd colleague phoning to see if I was all right as I had not done last night's match at Wimbledon and they had assumed I was ill or injured. This was typical of the great camaraderie that exists among many of the referees on the Premier League. Also nice was the letter I received from Mike Riley thanking me for supporting him so strongly in the *Daily Mail*.

Thursday 18 September

Much of the day was spent at a meeting of the Independent Schools' Football Association committee on which I sit as president of the Lent Term Soccer Schools organisation – schools who play rugby before Christmas and football after. We had wide-ranging discussions on forthcoming competitions but the most interesting was the debate over the impact Howard Wilkinson's proposed 'academies' would have on school, county and international schoolboy football. He was suggesting that boys accepted into these academies – and each Premier League club would have one – would not be permitted to play for anyone other than the academy. It would move England more towards the continental style of football coaching and destroy school soccer as we know it.

I returned home to the news that Ian Wright, Patrick Vieira and Steve Walsh had been found guilty by the FA, and had been warned and ordered to pay the costs of the hearing. It was a decision that came as no surprise in that the FA found the players guilty and levied a punishment that, in reality, had little impact on them. The only punishments that are effective and hurt clubs and players are suspensions – fines are a mere pinprick of discomfort. My phone was soon buzzing with the press but I told them that referees, on principle, never comment on the outcome of disciplinary hearings as we regard our job as over once we have submitted our reports and, where necessary, given evidence to the disciplinary committee. One reporter from the *Daily Express* could not understand why Graham Barber had not shown the players the yellow card and I explained that we are only permitted to show red or yellow cards during play. After the final whistle has been blown we can only report the incidents.

Friday 19 September

A bad start to the day when I received my assessment from the Manchester United match only to discover that I had again been downgraded for a minor incident, again a tendentious delay in a free-kick affair. It really bugged me for the whole day and I felt like chucking the whole thing in and telling the Premier League to employ mindless robots if they really are so concerned about such matters. I can accept criticism, indeed I am my own harshest critic, but it seemed wrong that a single, technical matter should colour the overall performance grade. Match observers are appointed by the Premier League to assess the match officials as well as assist in the general administration of matches. Most are ex-Premier League referees and thus have the experience of having refereed at the highest level. In addition, Brendan Batson from the PFA and Adrian Titcombe from the FA are on the panel. The real problem, as with referees, is achieving consistency in their reporting and grading. Some are concerned, rightly, with the overall performance and accept there will be the odd error. Others, admittedly only a few, sometimes convey the impression that they have to find something to be critical of to justify their existence. In the event I calmed down but sent a somewhat stinging letter to the Premier League asking if they thought their assessment scheme was working well when a referee could, in theory, be on the verge of being removed from the list for not booking players for technical offences.

My humour worsened further when the tickets for the Monaco match arrived and they had booked us to fly out late on Tuesday morning and back Thursday afternoon. This would mean missing a lot of teaching and I phoned to complain and to get the tickets changed. I knew there was a late Tuesday flight which would enable me to do all my teaching that day and there was also a flight back arriving at Heathrow at 10.00 a.m. which would mean I could be back in school for 11.15 a.m. and thus fulfil my teaching commitments for the day. Fortunately Colin Downey worked hard and within an hour or so had the Football Association's travel department change the tickets. I was most grateful.

Later on, BBC Radio 5 Live set up an interview over the phone with Gordon Taylor of the Professional Footballers' Association to discuss the use of the referee's watch to control the stadium clock. The press had discovered that this item was to be included in the forthcoming meeting of the Football Association's Technical Liaison Committee, which includes representatives from the FA, the Premier League, the Nationwide League, PFA, LMA and myself for the Premier League referees and assistant referees.

Late in the afternoon I had to re-record the interview I had given a few weeks earlier for Granada Sky's *Vinnie Jones Football Show*, as the equipment had been faulty first time round. Now a whole team arrived, wanting to record in my classroom rather than my study. We had a great palaver as they moved desks around to set up the shot and it was interesting to observe how different they all became once they got into a classroom. Deep-seated anxieties and memories of fierce teachers from childhood were clearly being revisited. As I usually have to do with TV I said I had a meeting at four o'clock, but they continued until 4.40 p.m., getting very apologetic that I was missing an important appointment. In fact, there was no meeting, as I revealed to them at the end, but it was the only way to avoid spending hours on a five-minute item. I returned home just in time to do the BBC Radio interview only to find that it had been cancelled because of the horrific train crash at Southall.

Saturday 20 September

No match so a busy morning teaching. Much amusement from Harrow colleagues in the mid-morning break about a short piece by Russell Kempson in *The Times* who had obviously heard about my train journey to Manchester. He recounted the story of me sitting on my kit bag in the corridor, reporting that 'Lord David', as he claimed I was known by Premier League colleagues, only got a seat at Stoke. It's amazing what they find out and what they print. I was tempted to ring him to explain that I'm known as 'Lord Elleray' but decided against it. I watched rugby in the afternoon at school. Then I entertained my Lower Sixth to dinner and we ended up chatting and drinking until about 1.30 a.m.

Sunday 21 September

The morning began with a message to call Paul Durkin following his excitements at Bolton v Manchester United where he had sent off Gary Pallister and Noel Blake. I eventually caught up with him in the evening and he discussed the dismissals and his opinion, having watched *Match of the Day*, that he had been harsh to send off Pallister. While I was keen that he should be fair to all players, I also thought that it was very important that everything was done correctly and the right procedure followed as there are always accusations that Manchester United get better treatment than other teams. My advice was that Paul should agree to see the video, if it was submitted by Manchester United to the FA in the proper way. If, on reflection, Paul thought that Pallister's actions were aggressive rather than violent then he would be within his rights to ask the FA to downgrade the red card to a yellow card.

There is no formal right of appeal over such decisions except in the case of mistaken identity. However, referees have always been prepared to view videos of incidents provided they are submitted through the FA. Our standpoint has always been that only if the video clearly shows that the referee made a mistake should the decision be changed, i.e. we must be fair to the players but also accept that our view at the time, and our judgement of the atmosphere, should be taken as correct and only changed if the video undoubtedly shows that we were wrong.

Monday 22 September

One or two colleagues phoned to complain about the 'Whistleblower' column in the *Daily Mail* that quoted comments from Steve Dunn. This seemed to go against our agreement at the Premier League meeting that we would not give this column credibility by talking to the author, although I was asked to comment as the official spokesman. However, it emerged that the quote had come from another source, as often occurs in the press, and that Steve Dunn had not flouted our collective decision.

Tuesday 23 September

No football today but I did referee. We have a huge number of inter-House sports matches at Harrow and I was called upon to referee a rugby match between Druries and another House. I enjoy refereeing rugby, not least because of the opportunity to wait and see with the advantage clause. Indeed, it was my experience of refereeing school rugby that inspired me to work with the FA to get the International Board to change the Laws of the Game so that in football these days the referee is allowed some latitude in playing advantage and, if it does not immediately accrue, penalise the original offence. It was hot and sunny and a good physical workout for me, made all the more enjoyable because Druries won convincingly 40–0. After that I watched our 1st XV in a titanic battle against Pretoria High School from South Africa. Roger Uttley runs the rugby at Harrow and there are many jokes that he and I vie to get the most publicity for the school in the newspapers. At this stage he was well in the lead as I was having a quiet season and he was in the headlines because of his appointment as England rugby manager.

Wednesday 24 September

Very little football business today but plenty to do at school with marking, correcting and trying to get ahead so that the pressures of the coming week, when I would be away for three days in Monaco, would not become too great.

Thursday 25 September

The afternoon was taken up with the medical for the FIFA fitness test. I had the standard blood pressure, eyesight and hearing tests, although why a referee needs good hearing I do not know as it would sometimes be better if he could not hear what is being shouted or said! I then had an ECG at rest, which I always rather enjoy as I can drift off and relax. My blood pressure was even lower than in the summer and suggested that the term and season were not yet putting me under any great strain.

I returned to the clinic later in the afternoon for the stamina test on the treadmill, wired up to a computer that constantly shows heart rate and pulse. The doctor always reminds me that he is used to having heart attack patients who last on the machine for no more than about 10 minutes. Every three minutes the machine gets faster and the incline up which you are running gets steeper. He mentioned that no one in the last year had beaten my 18 minutes from 1996 but I was determined to better it. I duly completed 20 minutes with no problems. While I was getting my breath back he mentioned that his son, a keen Arsenal supporter, was coming for my autograph so would I mind hanging on until he arrived. It was the least I could do.

An interesting evening as Dermot Gallagher had asked to come to see me. He arrived at 9.15 p.m. and three hours went by in a discussion about the problems Dermot was having. He had been through a tough time since his injury while refereeing in Euro '96 and was concerned about his future, his international position and his relationship with some of his Premier League colleagues. Dermot was prepared to listen, take in what I had to say and then ask for advice. I believe that we achieved much for him that evening but it did mean I was several hours behind with my marking and preparation for the next day. It turned out to be a long night and early morning.

Friday 26 September

I spent much of the morning with Philip Don, no longer a referee but a Premier League match observer. He is a headmaster in the grant-maintained sector and had a visiting Canadian headmaster who wanted to see around Harrow. Showing visitors round the School makes me realise what a wonderful collection of buildings and rich history Harrow has and how lucky I am to be a master here. Having been founded in 1572, the school has a rich variety of buildings and there is an all-pervading sense of history throughout the School. My visitors were particularly interested in discovering that Lord Byron and Lord Palmerston had been boys in Druries.

The build-up to Saturday continued and I had to get my head around the, what I deemed unfair, criticism from my last two matches. On paper I seemed to be having a poor season and yet I believed I was refereeing well. I felt under pressure as another poor performance would not help and I experienced, for the first time in many years, concern and a slight crisis of confidence. I felt on top form and I had to remind myself that I have only been criticised for technical offences. Nevertheless, I can appreciate how referees who are going through a bad patch feel. How difficult it would be if I was full-time and had no other job to escape to and therefore would be much more likely to dwell on criticism and be unable to keep it in its proper context.

In the midst of all this BBC Northwest television wanted an interview on the use of technology in football. Typical of some sections of the media, they had left about six messages on my answerphone, clearly unable to accept that I might have been out. However, the interview was done over the phone and they had the courtesy to ring back afterwards to thank me for my contribution.

Saturday 27 September

Having a game in London meant that I could teach for part of the morning, a rare Saturday match day luxury. It always amuses me that on such days I spend the morning in a suit and academic gown and the afternoon in striped kit – two of the more bizarre sets of clothes that people can wear.

As I travelled to Crystal Palace's Selhurst Park ground I began psyching myself up to referee well and prove to myself, if no one else, that I was not past my best. As I often do if a match has not gone well, I changed something in my dress or routine – whereas if things are going fine I am so superstitious I wear exactly the same clothes and maintain a rigid, unchanging routine. I had a new stopwatch that I had purchased when I was in South Africa so when I arrived at the ground I wandered off with the fourth official to buy a new battery for it. On the way back I did some shopping in Sainsbury's which is next to the Crystal Palace ground. I always enjoy going to Selhurst Park just for that reason; I like to think of it as efficient time management.

The pressure was increased somewhat as Wendy Toms was one of the assistants and there would inevitably be a lot of focus on her as the first woman on the assistant referees' list. Many people were watching her, some wanting her to succeed but others wanting her to fall on her face and show that her promotion had been a political one. The reports I had heard about her gave me no cause for concern as I was sure that she would cope well with the match, but it would be interesting.

The game went well, fortunately, and Kelvin Morton, an exacting match observer, seemed very happy. Needless to say, though, there was a 10-yards incident when I penalised a Crystal Palace defender for a back pass which the goalkeeper picked up. I gave the free-kick in the wrong place and, as Kelvin Morton admitted, it was almost impossible to get the players 10 yards back because the free kick had to be taken on the edge of the six-yard box as the offence had occurred within the goal area.

Wendy did well as did Peter Walton, the other assistant, whom I would be seeing a lot of in the coming days in Monaco and at Liverpool. One slight problem was a cameraman on the side where Wendy was operating. Fortunately, she was unaware of him until he grabbed her shoulder at the end of the match. I had wanted to move him away during the game but decided that, as she had not seen him, it was best not to draw attention to his presence and increase the pressure on her. The biggest compliment I could pay her was that, apart from the fact that she had to change in a separate room, I did not think of her as different from any other match official.

The game had required a great deal of talking on my part to keep the players sensible and co-operating. One experience mirrored something that occurred in my first match at Blackburn. Jamie Fullarton, a Scotsman playing for Crystal Palace, always addressed me as 'Sir' or 'Mr Elleray' just as Billy McKinlay had done at Blackburn. It is obvious that in Scotland the players treat the referees with great respect, or at least are more formal when swearing at them.

Steve Coppell, the Palace manager, popped in afterwards to offer his thanks and Colin Todd of Bolton later did the same. He had told the press it was time that we stopped having video replays of decisions and simply accepted that football involves human error and everyone should get on with the game and leave the refereeing to the referees. It was a refreshingly simple and sensible philosophy.

With all the boys at home for the weekend there was a chance for relaxation, a take-away Chinese and champagne with friends and the prospect of a nice long lie-in tomorrow.

Sunday 28 September

A very busy day working on this book, clearing paperwork and getting ahead so that the coming week did not pose too many problems. It is days like these which sometimes make me long for the time when I no longer referee. On what should have been a day of rest and relaxation I spent some 10 hours at my desk, broken only to watch the excitement of the Ryder Cup and the wonderful victory for Europe. In late afternoon I watched the end of the Blackburn v Coventry match with two sendings off for Peter Jones and the inevitable discussion over whether TV replays suggested that Dion Dublin had been unlucky and would, like Gary Pallister, ask for the decision to be reviewed.

Monday 29 September

Great delight in Druries as Eustace Santa-Barbara had been awarded the Fifth Form scholarship for his outstanding GCSE results.

Ken Ridden from the FA made contact to discuss improvements to the match observers' reports in the light of some difficulties that we had been experiencing with the assessment of referees. He also wanted to check my 'open' dates as he was working on the appointments for December already. He had me down to referee Liverpool v Manchester United on 6 December, always one of the most difficult matches in the English calendar as neither teams nor supporters really get on. This year the match was being built up as a clash, in the true sense of the word, between Paul Ince and Roy Keane. I was free on that date and all seemed fine until Ken mentioned that the match would kick off at 11.15 a.m. This would be complicated as the evening before I had to attend a major event at school until at least 11.30 p.m. I would have to book a hotel in the Midlands and drive part of the way up late on Friday night and complete the journey the following morning – another difficult mixing of the twin demands on my time.

The evening was taken up packing and preparing for the trip to Monaco.

Tuesday 30 September

The morning was spent teaching and finishing off the arrangements for my time away. I met up with my other colleagues, Mark Warren, Peter Walton and Graham Barber. It was a short flight to Nice where we were met by Edouard Lampel, a wonderful man in his 70s who looks after the referees for AS Monaco. He had just retired as the liaison man for all the tennis players for the Monte Carlo Open and seemed to know everyone in the Principality. Waiting with him was Paulo, in charge of AS Monaco's youth team, and the Portuguese referee delegate, Carlos Alberto Silva Valente, who was a World Cup referee in Mexico (1986) and Italy (1990). The club had chartered a helicopter to take us across to Monaco which was a 'first' for Peter, Graham and the delegate, so we promised them champagne if they survived. A short, six-minute flight took us along the coast to the Monte Carlo heliport and then we were whisked to L'Hermitage Hotel – opulence in the extreme! We were introduced to the UEFA match delegate, Hans Bangerter, a formidable man who was the first Secretary General of UEFA. He summoned us for a briefing and was clearly going to be a stickler for everything being done correctly and exactly on time.

Later we met Edouard, Carlos and Paulo and had a pre-dinner glass of champagne and some nibbles, which included '*badajuan*', a green vegetable minced and creamed inside a pastry-like envelope. It is a local delicacy and was to help me out of a slightly delicate royal situation later in the trip. We proceeded to the L'Hermitage dining room, a stunning room with an ornately decorated ceiling and a *fin de siècle* atmosphere and had one of the finest meals I have enjoyed for a long time: lobster salad and *coquilles St Jacques*, followed by strawberry, mandarin, vanilla and chocolate soufflés, all washed down with a very fine Corton Champagne 1989.

Dinner was followed by a stroll to the Casino where the manager gave us a guided tour of the opera house, which was one of the most ornate rooms I had ever seen, the public gaming rooms and the two private gambling rooms, one lined totally in tan leather. Throughout we were stunned by the architecture and the lavish furnishings, to say nothing of the gaming tables which are all made on the premises to ensure that they are not 'fixed' in any way. Leaving the Casino we bumped into Boris Becker who, needless to say, Edouard knew.

October 1997

Wednesday 1 October

After breakfast we waited for the match delegate who we were convinced would be strictly punctual but who swanned in 25 minutes late without a word. Then it was off to one of the most remarkable stadiums in the world. It was built in a part of Monte Carlo reclaimed from the sea and because land is so scarce and expensive the ground floor consists of offices and shops, the dressing rooms are on the first floor and you have to go up another flight of stairs to the pitch which is, literally, on the roof. Everything was immaculate and we had a good meeting with Herr Bangerter who wanted me to lecture the officials as to the disciplined conduct required for the match. To ensure we kicked off on time I was told that the timing would be undertaken via an atomic clock linked to a satellite so that throughout Europe all the Champions' League matches would begin at exactly the right time.

We left the stadium and went up to the rock on which the royal palace and the cathedral are built to watch the changing of the guard. Just before the start the police took us through the crowds to a specially reserved section, much to the annoyance of a group of Russians whose view we blocked. I got more abuse from them than in the entire match later on.

Our route to lunch at the Monte Carlo Country Club followed much of the Grand Prix course, where we bumped into Marco van Basten. I sat on the balcony doing the *Daily Telegraph* crossword in the warm sun, watching the stunning array of yachts before having my usual pre-match sleep.

A police escort took us to the ground where we prepared in our usual way, interrupted only by a summons to meet Prince Albert. I was surprised at his strong American accent. He immediately struck me as someone who does not lead the conversation and this is where last night's delicacy came in. I had heard that he has his own soccer team, which was named *badajuan* after this delicacy, and my mentioning this seemed to bring him to life and we chatted for a while about sport in general and whether he will again compete in the Olympics. Everything was going to plan until Mark Warren tore a calf muscle warming up and, with only 10 minutes to go on the atomic clock, Graham Barber suddenly discovered that he was going to run the line rather than sit at the desk taking notes. He and I were pretty relaxed about this sudden development, not least because Graham was a FIFA linesman before becoming a national list referee. Indeed he had lined to me in Real Madrid and in Parma as well as being one of my linesmen for the 1994 FA Cup Final. I informed the UEFA officials and asked them to get another referee to stand by just in case there was another injury.

The match passed off well and we noticed Prince Rainier had joined his son in the Royal Box. At half-time Monaco led 1–0 and I had issued four yellow cards, two apiece. The only real problem we had was that our dark blue shirts clashed with the dark green of Bayer Leverkusen, so we changed to yellow during the half-time interval. At half-time we discussed the match, and remarked how well Graham had adjusted to lining. I was concerned that the German No. 2 – Robert Kovac – was in danger of getting a second yellow card as the Monaco winger was running rings round him and he was unable to do anything other than foul him. As it turned out my fears were justified as in the 69th minute he again blocked an opponent and I sent him off. This was an historic moment in my refereeing career as it was the 200th time I had sent a player off. The match finished 4–0 to Monaco with the German defence collapsing somewhat and three spectacular goals being scored by the French team.

One nice moment had occurred before the game when we were doing the pre-match check of the stadium and pitch, and a tubby photographer came and took our photos. He introduced himself as the photographer who had sent me some photos after my last visit and then remarked that I was the only referee who had ever bothered to write and thank him for the photos he sends out after every match. It pleased me that such small courtesies are appreciated.

We dined late in a fabulous Italian restaurant on pasta in a frog and truffle sauce and sea bass washed down with champagne and fine white wine. I got to bed at 2.30 a.m.

Thursday 2 October

I was woken at 6.15 a.m. by room service for breakfast and then off to the heliport for the quick flight, as dawn broke, across to Nice and thence home to London.

I arrived home at eleven and was teaching by half past. After lunch I dealt with the mail and opened the acknowledgement from Lancing College of my application for the post of Headmaster. I faxed through my match report to UEFA and phoned the FA to warn them that poor Mark Warren, or 'hop along' as he had become known, was injured and would be unable to line to me at Liverpool next Sunday. The late afternoon and evening were spent entertaining an American university expert who came to tell us how to complete US university reference testimonials. I eventually got into bed at 11.30 p.m. feeling remarkably alert despite the lack of sleep of the previous few days.

Friday 3 October

A fascinating day. I spent most of the morning at my desk, in part filling in the referees' self-assessment form which UEFA now requires from all Champions' League referees. It is a tricky form to complete because you want to be honest but fear that if you are too brutally self-critical they may take this as indicative of a poor performance or lack of confidence, and future appointments might suffer. After teaching and lunch I was informally interviewed by one of the Harrow governors as it seemed that I was being considered as a candidate for Head Master of Harrow when the current head, Nick Bomford, retires in September 1999. The governors were meeting that afternoon to discuss the first stages of the selection procedure and it emerged that they were contemplating the unusual step of making an internal appointment.

Further teaching, then up to Oxford University for a Gaudy at Hertford College which was a reunion of all those who started in 1973, 1974 and 1975. I didn't know who would be there but it turned out there were many old friends, some of whom I had not seen for 20 years. I had been invited to make one of the speeches but had declined, wanting to enjoy a relaxing dinner with my chums. Because I had been President of both the Junior Common Room and the Middle Common Room, I was placed on the top table and spent the evening in enjoyable conversation with Lady Bodmer, Sir Michael

Jackson and an OH friend. Afterwards I was much castigated by my friends for not speaking, not least because the actual speeches had been less than entertaining. I chatted to my friends until about midnight when I departed for Harrow, my journey home spoiled by two encounters with speed cameras – my only hope was that they had run out of film otherwise I was due for two fines, having avoided any such problems for almost 20 years. I crawled into bed a little after 2.30 a.m. for another brief sleep, wondering what the governors of Harrow had decided.

Saturday 4 October

With a Sunday match, I had Saturday at school. I taught for much of that morning and then received an encouraging debriefing about the governors' meeting. It seemed they had some reservations but were generally very positive about my candidacy. The beginning of a dilemma was upon me. In the afternoon I watched the school play rugby against Tonbridge and consulted one of my referees, Michael Hepher, Chairman of Charterhouse and wise man in matters such as these. The rest of the afternoon and evening was spent at my desk and packing for tomorrow.

Sunday 5 October

A hell of a day and one which may well turn out to be significant in my future as a referee. I was up early for the long drive to Liverpool, taking over three hours with plenty of time to think. The pre-match preparations were the usual except that Ray Olivier had replaced Mark Warren in my team so needed to be inducted into the group as I had not worked with him before. In the corridor outside the dressing rooms I bumped into Paul Ince and we discussed the forthcoming England v Italy World Cup match and our individual experiences in Europe last week. Paul seemed in good form, relaxed and positive.

Before the match Martin Tyler, the Sky commentator, popped in to say 'hello' and to debate the latest footballing issues. He is one of the few commentators, along with John Motson and Barry Davies, who takes the trouble to talk to referees and keep himself up to date with interpretations of the Laws and refereeing matters.

The match began well on a green, lush pitch and the first few fouls were against Dennis Wise and Paul Ince; I knew that the three of us would have a busy afternoon. They are both players from whom you can get a good response if you talk to them all the time and try to defuse any growing frustration. After 15 minutes I cautioned Bernard Lambourde for pulling Steve McManaman back and this began a very hectic 30 minutes which saw me allow a controversial goal for Chelsea, when Liverpool thought Mark Hughes had committed a foul. There were then two goals from Liverpool, I turned down a penalty appeal for Chelsea and gave yellow cards to Paul Ince (dissent), Dennis Wise (foul) and Dan Petrescu (foul). The latter had a personal significance as it was the 1,500th caution of my refereeing career.

Perhaps the turning point of the match was my dismissal of Lambourde for his second foul on McManaman after 25 minutes. It was a senseless challenge, a block on his winger, rather like the offence I had similarly penalised in Monte Carlo in midweek, and I had no option but to send him off. As soon as Lambourde committed the offence, Ruud Gullit, the Chelsea player-manager, who was one of the substitutes, immediately stripped off his tracksuit to come on. When I went to my top pocket where I keep the red card, Lambourde grabbed my hand to stop me and for a second or two there was a gentle tug of war. It was one of the most difficult 30 minutes I have had in Premier League football for a while and I managed to upset both sets of fans.

I had felt that much of the niggling was coming from Chelsea so asked Paul Ince to have a word in his dressing room at half-time to tell the Liverpool players that they should stop reacting and leave me to sort things out. There was an undercurrent between the England players (Fowler and McManaman especially) and the Italians (Zola and Di Matteo) which had been stirred up by the tabloid press during the week as part of the build-up to the Italy v England match. Whenever there was a clash between the two nationalities there tended to be an over-reaction, implying that every challenge was a hidden attempt to injure the opponent and make them unavailable for the vital World Cup game. Fortunately, I know most of the players well and we tend to be on Christian name terms which makes communication much easier. Some players are enjoyable company on the field. I always find Jamie Redknapp good value and, as was the case with his father, you can talk to him sensibly regardless of what is happening in the game. Others are so wrapped up in their own game that I have little to do with them unless they start contesting a decision. Robbie Fowler is very much like this, he is so focused on his own performance that he is not really interested in passing the time of day, even when play is stopped. With players like Dennis Wise and Steve McManaman the more you can chat to them the better.

In the second half tempers were calmer and common sense prevailed. The game finished 4–2, the only additional disciplinary action being a yellow card for Jason McAteer for a foul tackle from behind on a Chelsea player which led to a penalty. I had turned down another appeal for a penalty from Chelsea minutes before but this one was clear-cut.

I cannot say that I particularly enjoyed the match and I reflected on the greater pressure officials feel at places like Liverpool compared with last week's match at Crystal Palace. Martin Tyler came in to say that they agreed with the penalties and non-penalties but thought that Hughes had probably fouled for the Chelsea goal. He agreed with the sending-off in the sense that I had no option. However, he felt that there were now too many mandatory offences and that too many games were ending up as 10 v 11 and the Laws should be changed to allow referees greater discretion. I pointed out that greater discretion leads to greater inconsistency and that, as all Premier League referees would have sent Lambourde off, surely the players and managers should be able to adjust. We did agree, however, that the introduction of sin bins would be a step forward so I had another supporter for my campaign. The match observer remarked afterwards that it was fortunate that there was an experienced referee in charge otherwise the players could easily have lost their composure and three or four would have been sent off. However, I did not feel that I had refereed particularly well. My decision-making had not been as sharp as I would have liked and I certainly had not felt on top form.

Leaving the dressing room I bumped into Roy Evans, the Liverpool manager, who gave me an interesting insight into what managers say to the media and what they actually think. He had told the press that my decision not to penalise Mark Hughes had been a 'diabolical non-decision'. Talking to me he admitted he had been critical but then added that 'everyone knows how difficult it is being a referee, they are only human like everyone else'. Of course that was not said in the press room and will not be the headline tomorrow.

The journey home was long and tedious with terrible traffic and it took me over four hours. I reflected that I had not really enjoyed the game and that I was tired after a long week. Did I really need the hassle of long drives home and did I really need the aggro that comes from the fans and the press? My mind concluded that I did not, and for much of the rest of the journey I pondered on whether I had reached the stage where I no longer really enjoyed what I was doing and it was time to think of retirement.

My mood had not been helped by the match observer who, after a fire and brimstone match like that, wanted to talk about one occasion when I might have cautioned or lectured Poyet for dissent. It really annoys me when, after 90 minutes of huge mental and physical endeavour, people want to nit-pick over minor isolated incidents. I believe that too many have forgotten what refereeing is like at the top level and cannot put themselves into the mind and soul of present-day referees. By the time I reached Harrow I was reasonably resolved that I should retire at the end of the season, especially if a Headmaster's position came my way.

I collapsed into bed at midnight after a thoroughly exhausting week.

Monday 6 October

I woke still tired after a short sleep, ready to face the press. When I walked into Speech Room, where the entire school meets on a Monday morning, I was confronted by a number of boys holding up the back page of the *Daily Mail* with the headline 'Elleray, you blew it!' The boys in my geography lessons were especially talkative about the match. They adore controversy so this was all just up their street and I had to make it clear that the lessons would be about geography and not wasted debating the finer points of some of my decisions.

My spirits were dealt a further blow when I learned that Matthew Raynham, an old boy of my House had died at the age of 23. He was my first Head of House and the current Head Master's first Head of School and had had a distinguished career both here and at Cambridge University. He was the first Harrovian to win a Royal Marine scholarship and was serving in the Marines when he died, after a car crash. He was a young man full of life, destined for the top. His death was a real body blow and I spent much of the rest of the day contacting other masters and his friends to break the news. I spoke with his father who was planning the funeral and we discussed various ways in which Harrow might make an appropriate contribution to the service.

All the while the phone was ringing with invitations for the *Big Breakfast* and the *Richard Littlejohn Show*, while Jeff Winter phoned to report on the injury he sustained when he was hit in the face by a missile last Tuesday at a Coca-Cola match in Carlisle. We both anticipated the usual reaction from the Football Association.

Tuesday 7 October

Not a great day. I was very low after yesterday's news and the last thing I felt like doing was the FIFA fitness test. Although our fitness is assessed on every match report, the authorities are still keen that we should pass regular fitness tests, especially at the start of the season. There is some controversy about whether these tests actually relate to the physical demands made on referees during matches but they at least provide a season by season comparison of fitness levels of the whole group as well as individuals.

I telephoned Matthew's parents, who were being very brave and positive, offering to organise the Harrow School end of the funeral arrangements. This involved contacting many of his friends and relaying the news and then getting as much information as possible about Matthew to pass on to the Head Master, who had been asked to give the eulogy at the funeral. We also discussed the possibility of the House singing one or two Harrow songs as part of the service. All this talking and organising brought home the reality of Matthew's death.

I arrived at High Wycombe for the test and was so subdued that several colleagues enquired what was wrong and offered comfort and support. In the event it was probably a very good thing to have something to take my mind off such depressing matters. Everyone passed the sprints and the 12-minute run with some ease, although a strong wind played havoc coming up the home straight. I was very pleased with my 12-minute run as I completed just over 2,900 metres, thus maintaining the standard I had set myself in previous years. In between the sprints and the long run I did a video interview for the Football Association which will be part of their recruitment drive for new referees.

After showering and changing a group of us were due to be photographed by the RNIB for an advertising campaign but they were so hopelessly disorganised that only a few could take part. I stopped and talked with Ken Ridden and was delighted to find out that I had been appointed to another Champions' League match – Sparta Prague v Galatasaray of Turkey. I was in Prague almost a year ago and it is one of the nicest cities I have ever visited. My discussions with Ken Ridden raised further dilemmas for me as he explained that he had to nominate an English referee to FIFA for possible selection for the World Cup finals. He was keen to nominate me but I was concerned about being away from Harrow for five or six weeks during the summer term. However, if I was appointed Head Master of Lancing College then there was the possibility of resigning from Harrow at Easter and going to the World Cup. The great difficulty was that the first round of interviews for Lancing was scheduled for 11 and 12 November, exactly the days when the FIFA Referees' Committee would be meeting to make their selections. I wondered if I should withdraw at this stage, or allow my name to go forward in the hope that I became available. Ken made it very clear that I was the FA's first choice and he did not want me to jeopardise my chances of going. On the other hand, it would not have been good for English refereeing if no one went, which would have been the case if I was nominated and then had to withdraw. It was yet another problem to niggle away at for the coming fortnight.

Wednesday 8 October

A day busy with funeral arrangements. I telephoned the Football League, and Jim Ashworth, the referees' officer, opened by announcing how pleased he was that he had been able to give me Ipswich v Manchester United in the next round of the Coca-Cola Cup. I had to squash his pleasure by withdrawing as Matthew Raynham's funeral had been arranged for that date. He was disappointed and said that perhaps I should forget all the other rounds and he would just pencil me in for the final. It being the only major domestic honour I have not received, I told him I would be delighted if he did. To help matters, however, I did reopen a date for the next round so that I could do a match.

Thursday 9 October

I received the assessment from the Crystal Palace v Bolton match and had been given a very high grading, which gave me great pleasure and took some of the mental pressure off me. It confirmed that I was refereeing pretty well and that I was wrong to let the nit-picking of some assessors get me down. Nevertheless, several Premier League colleagues who were also getting fed up with assessors making a meal of isolated incidents and downgrading them as a result had approached me. Therefore I arranged to meet Ken Ridden during half-term to talk about this and to thrash out my options for the World Cup. The post also brought confirmation from the Oxfordshire Police that there had been film in that blasted camera and I was liable to prosecution. Still, it served me right for being careless, I suppose.

Friday 10 October

Nothing of note in the football world but a major day in the House with House Songs. This is an evening when I entertain about 30 boys, masters and wives to supper and then we go through to the House hall where the boys sing a selection of Harrow Songs and do little sketches or mini plays portraying me and the other guests in a jocular, 'spitting image' fashion. Various individuals and groups of boys sing solos or particular verses and some of the new masters and boys have to sing the first four lines of 'Men of Harlech' as their new boys' solo.

We always finish with the Druries House Song, written over 100 years ago. The final line of the chorus is 'Druries is oldest and best, Sir!' One verse honours the two Old Drurieans who won the V.C. They do this individually and it is part of the formal assimilation of people into the House community.

We had a great evening, as I greatly enjoy cooking and entertaining. There is something creative about producing a meal for other people and I like to experiment with different dishes and wines. I collapsed into bed about 1.30 a.m.

Saturday 11 October

A great day for England and also for the credibility of refereeing. The World Cup match in Italy had been built up with passion and I had, unthinkingly, invited a dozen junior boys for supper. I offered them the chance to postpone it but they were insistent on coming so we mixed supper with frequent visits to the kitchen where the television was showing the match. It did not take me long to realise that whenever the boys offered to clear the plates they were not being helpful, merely desperate to pop out and see what the score was. Towards the end of the match we heard a great cheer from the main TV room. Thinking

England had scored we began to celebrate, only to discover that the cheering was because an Italian had been sent off. For the final eight or nine minutes a group of boys and I were crowded around the television willing the referee to blow the final whistle. It was a great relief when he did and we could then return to persecute Johan Harder, a junior boy from Denmark. We had had great debates with him about the relative merits of English and Danish football and he was looking forward to the two countries being in the same group in France.

I was also delighted that Mario van der Ende, the Dutch referee, had handled the game so well and had shown by his performance that the rubbish in the Sunday newspapers that he would be biased towards the Italians had been unfounded. Another late night but I slept well, knowing that an English qualification improved my chance of being selected and possibly provided a solution to my dilemma. If England do well in France then the English referee will probably have to come home after the group games as FIFA only keep on referees from those countries not involved in the knockout stages. Would that give me the chance I needed to hit a balance between refereeing in the World Cup and honouring my professional responsibilities at Harrow? I would have to find out the exact dates of the tournament's various stages.

Sunday 12 October

A busy day with many of the boys away on a night exercise with the School's Combined Cadet Force. It was a day at the desk.

Monday 13 October

A day of teaching and then lunch with a brigadier from the Royal Marines who was here for the general inspection of the school's CCF. I was invited to the post-inspection lunch, as I was the House Master of Rupert Lion, the boy who was head of the CCF. The Marines were keen to entice him away from the Army. After lunch I showed about 30 prospective parents around Druries and spent the rest of the afternoon and evening going through half-term reports with boys and finalising the singing arrangements for tomorrow's funeral.

Tuesday 14 October

A dreadful day when all thoughts of football were banished for the funeral of Matthew Raynham. The church in Sussex was packed and as a party of his fellow Royal Marine officers carried the coffin into the church, self-control became difficult. The first hymn, 'I Vow To Thee My Country', moved most to tears. Following this the Head Master delivered a moving eulogy, either side of which a group of boys from Druries (the House XII) sang two Harrow Songs in a poignant tribute to someone whom most had only known by reputation. The service ended with the coffin being ceremonially carried out as the organist played 'Forty Years On', the Harrow School Song. The burial in the churchyard outside was a grim but dignified affair and I was coping well until, in a far corner of the graveyard, a trumpet sounded the Last Post.

Many of Matt's friends were at the funeral and most went to pay their respects to his parents afterwards. The sombreness wore off and we recalled the fun things that Matt had done and the wonderful person he had been. I especially remembered catching him climbing back into the House on his very last night at Harrow, dressed only in a sheet, having been to a toga party down by the school lake. I had sealed all the windows except one and caught him and his friends as they climbed in in the darkness, thinking they were safe. We often used to laugh about that incident and the way I had taken no action as both he and I knew nothing wicked had really occurred and he was just being 'Matt'.

His death put so many things into perspective. I was immensely proud of the boys who had sung, many attending a funeral for the first time. They had been stunned to be placed so close to the coffin but they had paid a fitting tribute to a fine young man who had been a much admired and loved Old Druriean and Old Harrovian.

Wednesday 15 October

A quite extraordinary day which began with abuse and ended with a real challenge. Returning from teaching in the middle of the morning I was standing on the pavement in my M.A. gown talking to a colleague when a van stopped in a queue of traffic. Suddenly, the passenger opened his window and announced that I was 'a cheat' and 'the worst referee in the world' and, the ultimate, 'a f*****g doughnut'. My colleague and I were amazed but I followed my usual practice on such occasions and stood and stared rather than get involved. I do not mind abuse at matches but it comes to something when people like that think nothing of using foul language in public to people going about their daily lives.

In the afternoon we had the House cross-country relays. Druries had already won the senior and intermediate weekly competitions and we knew that other Houses, especially our main rivals, Elmfield, would be out to snatch the relay titles. It was a tense affair but some excellent running from Alexis Chrisafis, Blair Abbiss and Johan Harder ensured that we won both the senior and the intermediate races and thus the overall competition. To rub salt into our opponents' wounds we also won the senior and intermediate B team races, so enjoyed a clean sweep of trophies. It led to one of the other House Masters asking if, as well as an academic interview, I required prospective pupils to undertake the referees' bleep fitness test.

Back in the House, where the boys had proudly placed the trophies on my desk, the phone rang at 6.10 p.m. It was Sir Michael Connell, Chairman of the Governors of Harrow School. He explained that at the recent governors' meeting they had discussed the appointment of Nick Bomford's successor as Head Master and there was a strong desire that I should apply. They had decided that being an internal candidate represented no bar and they regarded me as a strong candidate. They were aware that I was applying for other schools but very much hoped that I would apply for the Harrow post. I was stunned. Suddenly something which people had suggested in semi-seriousness was becoming a stark reality.

Two dilemmas face me. Should I continue with the Lancing application? And what about the World Cup? My immediate reaction was to proceed with Lancing as it would give me good interview experience and I was by no means convinced that I should really consider the Harrow headship. As far as the World Cup was concerned, if I proceeded with the Harrow application then I would have to be available in June to attend interviews as the Chairman had indicated that he hoped and expected that I would at least make the final shortlist. My world was spinning but, fortunately, I had 30 half-term reports to go through with the boys and celebrations for the cross-country successes to organise.

I worked until nine o'clock, broke to hear a rehearsal of the House XII and Glee in preparation for the next day's competition, and then had the cross-country runners for Big Macs, Coke and beer in the boys' hall. I was reluctant to finish as I wanted to keep my mind off the Chairman's phone call and it was not until 11.30 p.m. that

I kicked the boys off to bed. I was so tired I slept soundly and did not have the inevitable questions charging around in my head.

Thursday 16 October

A busy morning teaching and trying to keep my feet on the ground. The boys were intrigued at lunch because there was a TV crew filming outside Druries. After lunch I did an interview for CSI who have a 52-minute programme every week which goes to 150 countries or more, consisting of Premier League match highlights, League tables and features – and I was to be the feature this time. Kate Berrington was the interviewer and was very professional and we did the interview in one take. She was concerned as to how I fitted everything in – but that is a question I increasingly get asked so the answer was easy: no social life. Needless to say, the phone rang during the filming and it was two women wanting to do a programme for Channel 4.

The evening represented a special triumph for the House. With me bedecked in black tie and academic gown and the boys in tails, the whole school assembled in the Speech Room, the vast semi-circular hall that resembles the Globe Theatre and can seat well over 800 people. Each of the eleven Houses enters a Glee (a part song group) and a XII (broken voices). We won the Glee which was a great triumph for my wonderful resident House tutor, Glynn Jenkins, an enthusiastic music master. The triumph was all the sweeter because Druries were hissed before they sang, in part in fun and in part because some boys in the school do not like the fact that we are so successful. We celebrated in style afterwards, having discovered that Druries had last won the competition in 1946, so we had been waiting for 51 years. A particular source of pleasure was that three brothers sang in the Glee. All were music scholars and one had just won a choral scholarship to Oxford. Their parents had come for supper and had greatly enjoyed seeing their sons sing together with such success.

Friday 17 October

A day spent catching up on work and trying to keep awake having been up to 2.30 a.m. the night before celebrating our victory. I had an interesting discussion in one of my geography periods with some senior boys who regretted that there was a group of negative boys in the school, who needed to be persuaded to strive for excellence rather than decry it in others.

I had an interview with the Head Master to apprise him of my phone call from the Chairman and also to get his views. His main reaction was that it was 'an interesting idea' and he recounted the various occasions when this had happened in other schools. He promised to think it over during half-term.

As I had to miss two of the next day's lessons to travel to Leeds, I taught my Lower Sixth from 7.45 until 8.50 p.m. to make up for it.

Saturday 18 October

A good journey up to Leeds and an interesting match with Newcastle who played particularly poorly. Elland Road is a fine stadium but a rather intimidating atmosphere. I certainly couldn't have believed beforehand that I would end up having my name chanted as a Leeds fan before the first half was completed.

One of the nicest people in football is Alan Sutton, one of the physios at Leeds United. We chatted about my blisters, and he suggested I try some Sleek tape which Lee Sharpe uses and brought from Manchester United when he was transferred. I was having more problems with stopwatches as the strap had broken and I ended up holding it together with sticking tape – it was going to be one of those days.

The game began pretty well but during the first 15 minutes I had an increasing number of complaints from both sets of players that my outfit was very similar to Newcastle's strip, a dark blue and green affair which also had a large white badge rather similar to the white Premier League badge on my shirt. It soon became clear that, as when my kit had been a problem in Monaco, I would have to change. I went across to Alan Sutton in the Leeds United dugout and asked him if he could find something suitable. Five minutes later he returned with a light blue Leeds United training top. It was certainly different, but I wondered if I should be seen wearing a top that was clearly part of the home team's strip. I walked to the Newcastle dugout and asked Kenny Dalglish if he was happy, as it was mainly his players who were complaining about the clash. In his dry, Scottish way he replied that he didn't mind what I wore as long as I stayed neutral. To great hilarity, I put on the Leeds top and returned to the field with the crowd chanting 'David Elleray's a Leeds fan'. Ironically, almost the first thing

I did in my Leeds strip was to give a yellow card to Ribeiro of Leeds. I was very conscious that I was wearing a Leeds top so when they scored I quickly turned it inside out so that the LUFC badge and logo did not show, but I was sure that someone in the press would have got a photo. By half-time Leeds were 3–0 up.

In the dressing room I got hold of a green shirt with no LUFC marking on it. Three shirts for one game – but at least I was back in the green that we had enjoyed wearing as Premier League referees in past seasons. The match finished 4–1 and was a bit of a battle in the second half with Leeds being frustrated at not increasing their lead and Newcastle battling to avoid humiliation. However, all seemed happy and when I left the ground I was besieged by Leeds fans asking for my autograph and wanting to comment on my equipment. One young lady rushed up to the car and breathlessly said, 'I never thought you'd be a Leeds fan, and certainly never dreamed you would wear one of our shirts.' I spent the evening in Barnsley with Steve Lodge and his family.

Sunday 19 October

Returned to Harrow mid-afternoon to peace and quiet as all the boys had gone away for half-term. I worked at my desk for much of the afternoon and evening to clear all the paperwork so that I could relax for the rest of the break and enjoy the forthcoming trip to Prague. Several papers mentioned the shirt changing and Alyson Rudd wrote in the *Sunday Telegraph*, '. . . certainly do not think you will ever see referee David Elleray looking as if he is at a rave. But that is how it was at Elland Road yesterday.'

Monday 20 October

Two meetings at the FA. The first was with Ken Ridden, Martin Bodenham and Dave Richardson to discuss the future of the Reebok tournament and also to try to establish a young referees' course in the Easter holiday which would help us identify good young referees who might be suitable as assistant referees in the Reebok festival and in the FA Premier Youth League. After that I had a three-hour meeting with Ken Ridden, initially to establish items for the November meeting of Premier League referees.

Over lunch we discussed the forthcoming appointments for the

World Cup in France. I clarified my situation – although clarify is probably not the right word. I had applied to be Head Master of Lancing College. The first round of interviews was scheduled for 12 and 13 November and the final round for 24 November. In the meantime I had to decide whether or not to apply to be Head Master at Harrow School. I intended to pursue the Lancing post to see what I thought of the school and whether I would want to be head there, if offered the position.

Conversely, I might not get Lancing and apply for Harrow. If that was the case would FIFA be prepared for me to be absent for part of the tournament to return to Harrow for interview? If I applied for Harrow, would it be appropriate to absent myself from the School for half a term just at the time when I would be trying to convince the governors that I was the right man to take the School into the 21st century?

My inclination was to do the honourable thing and not allow my name to go forward to be considered for selection. This would give either Dermot Gallagher or Paul Durkin the chance to go to France – or indeed, Mark Warren, if they decided to take only one official from England. If I was selected and then had to withdraw it would be unfair on England and English referees who would not have a representative in France, since it is the individual who is selected rather than each country being entitled to send a referee.

Overall, I felt that the chances of my being able to go to France were about 10 per cent and would have posed great professional dilemmas for me. Ken Ridden was of the opposite view and was clear and firm that he wanted me to allow my name to go forward. He felt that I should give myself the chance and that the FA would much prefer someone of my standing to go and were prepared to run the risk of not having a representative.

We discussed the repercussions should I be selected and then withdrew. This would inevitably focus attention on the need for full-time referees, as my withdrawal for 'professional reasons' would be used as ammunition against the so-called 'amateurs' who referee the professional game. I was also concerned that the publicity might reflect unfairly on Harrow School, who might be seen as being inflexible in not letting me have time off to go to France. That would be very unfair and I wanted to avoid it at all costs as the School has been fantastic in the way it has supported my refereeing and allowed me to travel the world almost without restriction. And to complicate matters further, because of the confidentiality surrounding the selection procedure, I would not be able to reveal that my application to be Head Master of Harrow was a major consideration.

I returned to Harrow no clearer in my mind. Indeed, I felt more confused since Ken had been so insistent that I give myself the opportunity to officiate in France.

On my way back, a middle-aged man on the station at Baker Street approached me and very politely asked me to sign his copy of the *Sun* for his son. There was a photo of me in the Leeds United shirt which he wanted me to autograph. Very courteously he asked when I was next refereeing Arsenal and when I said on Boxing Day against Leicester he asked me to be kind to the Gunners. It was really heartening to be treated with such courtesy by a stranger and it reaffirmed my faith in the ordinary fan. It did nothing to help solve my dilemma though.

Tuesday 21 October

It was quite a luxury to have an overseas appointment in the holidays so there wasn't the usual rush to get up, pack, teach and get a taxi to the airport at the last moment. At Heathrow I met up with the rest of the team – Steve Lodge (on probably his last overseas appointment before retiring from the international list at the end of 1997 having reached the grand old age of 45), Peter Walton and Philip Sharp. Passing through security we were recognised and one of the ladies asked Steve Lodge where we were off to. He said we were doing Sparta Prague versus Fenerbahce and I had to correct him and say that it was Galatasaray. 'It's a good job he's not refereeing,' the lady remarked.

We were met at Prague airport and whisked off to the VIP lounge while officials retrieved our luggage and we met up with the Icelandic UEFA match delegate. He looked about 35 but turned out to be 50 and a good basketball player.

We dined in fine style in a lovely restaurant just below the Prague Castle walls along with Rudi Bata who is the International Secretary for Sparta Prague and was the General Secretary of the Czech Football Association for many years. I had first met him in Croatia where he was the UEFA match delegate when I refereed Hadjuk Split v Legia Warsaw. Along with him was the International Secretary of the Czech Football Association and also Leo van der Kroft who was the Dutch UEFA referee observer. Leo is one of the longest-serving members of the UEFA Referees' Committee and was there to watch me. All the members of the UEFA Referees' Committee had been sent to watch referees under consideration for selection for the World Cup.

At the end of the meal we were each presented with a bottle of Sparta Prague wine. On each box was listed all the club's domestic successes. We have to be very careful when we are on UEFA and FIFA matches that we do not compromise ourselves by the hospitality received; on the other hand, we do not want to offend our hosts. We are not allowed to accept any gifts before the match unless the neutral UEFA officials who are with us directly sanction them. In this case, a bottle of wine was of no real consequence but there has been a real clampdown since a Spanish referee was offered all manner of gifts before a game in Eastern Europe during the 1996/97 season. One of the difficulties is that what is regarded as a token gift in Italy or Spain would be regarded as lavish and expensive in, say, Albania. It is always best to be guided by the UEFA officials and in many cases the referee observer accompanies us everywhere to satisfy everyone that we have not been got at.

Wednesday 22 October

After breakfast there was the usual visit to the ground for the pre-match meeting. The pitch still had a covering of frost. It was a fine ground with no running track so the crowd would be close to the field, just as in England. Then I was placed at the top table and asked to chair the referee's part of the meeting, not least because the Icelandic match delegate was somewhat overwhelmed by all the organisation and the number of people attending. He was a relatively inexperienced delegate and had never been to a Champions' League match before.

After the meeting we did some shopping in the centre of Prague and I bought some more Bohemia crystal wine glasses to add to the half dozen I got on my first overseas appointment as a linesman for Red Star Belgrade v Real Madrid in 1987.

During lunch in a beautiful, high ceilinged restaurant, Vaclav Krondl, the No. 1 FIFA referee in the Czech Republic, who was looking after us, revealed that his hopes of going to France for the World Cup had been dashed by Eastern European politics. He had recently refereed the World Cup qualification match when Bulgaria beat Russia. The Russians felt that they should have had a couple of penalties and also that a Bulgarian should have been sent off. The

FIFA referee observer had ironically been Leo van der Kroft and he had been happy but the President of the Russian Football Association had been most unhappy. Krondl claimed that he had telephoned the Czech Football Association President and told him to remove Krondl from any nomination for France and also take him off the FIFA list at the end of 1997. Krondl was desperately upset but could do little about it because, he alleged, the Czech Football Association President wanted to get on to the UEFA Executive Committee and needed the votes of Russia to be elected. So here was this fine man believing he had lost his chance to officiate in a World Cup because of politics. We sympathised but there was little we could do to lessen his disappointment so it was back to the hotel for a two-hour sleep and general preparation for the match.

The drive to the stadium certainly got the adrenaline flowing as we shot through Prague with a police escort. Returning to the dressing rooms from the pitch inspection we bumped into Gheorghe Hagi who recognised me from the Romania v Iceland match where I had 'helped' him set that national goal-scoring record. I also met Gheorghe Popescu who had played in that same match and, like Hagi, was playing for Galatasaray.

The weather was crisp and cold but perfect for football with no wind. Galatasaray were the better team for the early exchanges and the play was end to end with a few minor fouls. The first yellow card came against the Galatasaray captain after 17 minutes for a foul tackle from behind. Galatasaray then missed a clear chance to take the lead and fairly soon after that Sparta Prague scored a scrappy goal from a corner. The Turks lost their composure and I gave their No. 4 a yellow card for a foul tackle, followed almost immediately by a yellow card to a Sparta Prague player for a similar offence. It is often helpful, when you have given two yellow cards for one team, if a player from the other side then infringes and gets a yellow card as both teams feel they are being fairly treated. Unfortunately, the No. 4 of Galatasaray did not heed the warning and two minutes later he was guilty of a late tackle and was sent off for a second yellow card offence. The Turks accepted the dismissal without any protest. At half-time the score was 1–0 and there were no problems as we left the field.

The second half followed an almost similar script. I turned down a penalty appeal for Sparta Prague much to the noisy chagrin of the crowd whose whistles turned to cheers moments later when a high ball came out of the floodlights and hit me in the face. The

Galatasaray No. 11 received a yellow card for a foul and a few minutes later Sparta Prague scored to make it 2–0. Again the Turks lost their composure and the No. 11 launched himself into a dreadful tackle, taking off from about five metres and jumping two–footed at an opponent. Fortunately, I was very close and rushed in and brandished a red card straight away, having decided that this was not merely a second yellow card but a foul so bad that it merited a dismissal in its own right. This calmed the situation and I ushered the player to the touchline where Steve Lodge was trying to separate a few hot heads from both benches. The game petered out with just one more yellow card for Galatasaray and another goal for Sparta Prague.

At the final whistle players from both sides shook hands warmly and everyone seemed happy. The referees' observer was very complimentary although, as usual, he had the odd comment to make. He felt I might have given a yellow card to Hagi when he gestured to me to give a yellow card to an opponent. However, he described the instant red card in the second half as 'fantastic' and seemed very pleased with the way we had all performed. Perhaps I had taken another step towards France.

For dinner we returned to yesterday's magnificent restaurant but it was very late. Having kicked off at 8.45 p.m. the match had not finished until just after 10.30 p.m. so it was well beyond 11.30 p.m. when we sat down to eat. We were weary and returned to the hotel relatively soon although it was not much before two in the morning by the time I fell into bed.

Thursday 23 October

We got up late as the other advantage of being on half-term holiday was that there was no need for an early flight home. During breakfast Steve Lodge was at his most grumpy and we decided that he had become a real Victor Meldrew so he was called Victor for the remainder of the trip. He is a terribly fussy eater and has a very brusque manner with waiters so we enjoyed giving him a taste of his own medicine. We spent the morning sightseeing in Prague. As we disembarked an Arsenal supporter came up to say how much he had enjoyed the game last night. He was a season ticket holder at Highbury and asked that I prevail upon my colleagues to be kind to Ian Wright and just accept that he is slightly mad.

Returning home I completed the paperwork, although there was not much to do as I had already faxed my report to UEFA from the hotel in Prague. It was a truly great trip and one which had probably increased my chances of selection for France. For that I was grateful to my colleagues for their support and high-quality performances.

Friday 24 October

The phone was humming this morning following Chelsea's match last night in Tromsœ. The first half had been played on a pitch which resembled a mixture of ploughed field and skating rink, while in the second a blizzard had descended and players and officials must have had considerable difficulty seeing, let alone playing. *London Today* wanted to do an interview about the criteria referees use in deciding when to play and then when, and if, to abandon. The problem with UEFA matches is rearranging an abandoned match. The regulations require an attempt to be made the following day and this would certainly have impinged upon Chelsea's preparations for their weekend game. In addition, the UEFA match delegates have a great deal of power in these circumstances. Even though the referee is technically the only one who can decide whether to play or not, the UEFA delegate often takes over the situation and the Polish referee in Tromsœ would have been under enormous pressure to complete the game. I did not approve of the three Polish match officials officiating in black tights and gloves. With players not wearing tights it did seem rather ridiculous and certainly did not enhance their authority. However, some would argue that if they were warm they would officiate more effectively than if they were freezing cold.

Having arranged a meeting with Chrysalis sports to do a programme on 'a day in the life of a referee' and had a discussion with BBC World Service about technology and referees I could now escape from football for a few days' break in Rye, just sleeping, reading and relaxing. It would enable me to give plenty of thought to headship applications and final decisions on the World Cup.

Saturday 25–Monday 27 October

An excellent break with almost complete abstinence from football apart from *Match of the Day* and the great pleasure of watching a youth match in the glorious autumn sun on Sunday morning. It took me back to my early days as a referee, nearly 30 years ago, when I used to referee four matches each weekend: one on Saturday morning at school, and then three local league matches on Saturday afternoon, Sunday morning and Sunday afternoon. No matter what heights referees eventually reach they all come through the local parks and there was a real feeling of going back to my roots. The referee for this match was a little late on parade and I heard one or two of the spectators comment that I was on the touchline and could always do the game if the ref failed to appear.

While pottering around the bookshops of Rye I came across a book called *Football Shorts* which had a section on referees. It included a number of quotes of mine, some of them rather embarrassing when taken out of context. However, the amusing part was the error they had made in describing me as an *Eton* House Master. They also told the story that before the 1994 Cup Final I mentioned that I drink a lot of tea and hoped Wembley would have some Earl Grey available. These comments were widely reported at the time and Graham Kelly, Chief Executive of the FA, presented me with a box of Earl Grey tea bags on the Wembley terrace several hours before kick-off.

I returned to Harrow on the Monday afternoon to be confronted with controversies from the weekend. Arsène Wenger had come out with a ridiculous comment that referees only booked players like Bergkamp because they were 'trophy hunters'. Presumably he was trying to suggest that we get some sort of kick out of booking famous players when the reality is quite the reverse, since whenever a famous player is cautioned there is likely to be much more press attention. However, if we do not operate fully objectively then we stand accused of giving the top players special treatment. Matters had been compounded on Sunday when Paul Durkin sent off Petit of Arsenal for pushing him, so Monsieur Wenger was voicing yet another attack on referees.

In the pile of mail was an invitation for interview for the Lancing Head Master's post, so I had made it to the first shortlist. I also received my assessment from the Monaco match – a high mark and very complimentary so I was in a great mood for all sorts of reasons when I set off to Battersea for a preview of an art exhibition by a former pupil.

Tuesday 28 October

I avoided the telephone for much of the day as I needed to

get on with the mass of paperwork that had built up while I was away.

In the evening I did an interview with Capital Radio in response to the comments from David Unsworth and John Hartson (West Ham) about Mike Reed's refereeing last night at Leicester. They felt that he was biased against them because he was under so much pressure on his first return to Leicester since the controversial FA Cup match last season when he awarded a last minute penalty against Leicester at Chelsea, effectively knocking Leicester out of the Cup. Mike's appointment to Leicester had aroused much controversy but with only 19 referees on the Premier League list it is impossible to keep referees away from certain clubs. I remember my first visit to Stamford Bridge after the 1994 FA Cup Final – I certainly felt under very real pressure and got a white-hot reception from the Chelsea fans.

Unfortunately, Paul Durkin's dismissal of Petit on Sunday had brought referees back into focus, although I always believe that there are three or four times during a season when referee baiting hits the headlines and late October/early November is a prime time for this. This particular incident was important because it constituted a technical 'assault' on the referee as the player was alleged to have pushed Paul. One of the concerns is that whatever happens on TV one weekend happens the following weekend on the local parks, and there are enough problems already with junior referees being assaulted – sometimes violently – without it creeping into the top level of the game as well. There was some doubt as to the intention of the player and, once again, Arsène Wenger seemed more concerned with supporting his player than accepting that Petit had done anything wrong, or indeed that he needed to get some discipline into his team.

This was somewhat surprising as Wenger is a very intelligent man who clearly thinks a great deal about the game and had already been a breath of fresh air. However, he does not seem to realise that if his players have a poor disciplinary record then he is likely to lose them through suspensions and this could easily have an impact on their European and Premiership title aspirations.

Wednesday 29 October

An extraordinary day which began with an exciting phone call from Colin Downey at the FA telling me that FIFA had appointed me to referee Saudi Arabia v China in the World Cup qualifier next week. The appointment came out of the blue, not least because officials usually referee matches only within their own continent. I had never visited that part of the world and it was a wonderful opportunity, and a very high-profile match. I was walking on air for the next few hours.

The rest of the day went by dealing with the media and a huge number of requests for interviews. By the end I was booked for an early morning interview on BBC Radio 5 Live, had arranged for a reporter to accompany me to a match at West Ham, and a film crew from Chrysalis TV to film at Harrow and then accompany me to the Derby v Coventry match, and accepted an invitation to take part in *Planet 24* – a quiz show which re-creates sports incidents and then invites participants in the original event to answer a series of questions.

By early evening the boys were streaming back to School after the half-term break.

Thursday 30 October

I was up early to do a radio interview with BBC Radio 5 Live about the pressures on referees. I tried to stress that, like players, we are human and make mistakes. Moreover, controversy is an integral part of most sports and, indeed, can be one of the attractions for many people. After teaching a few periods I did the TV slot for *Planet 24*. This edition involved re-creating the Chesterfield v Middlesbrough FA Cup semi-final from last year – it seems that the 'did it cross the line?' controversy will never go away – and I was filmed as the 'mystery guest', rather like in *A Question of Sport*.

The FA phoned to say that there was trouble getting flights to Saudi Arabia and we would have to leave immediately after the match on the 2.15 a.m. flight. It meant we had no chance to see much of the country as we would be in Saudi Arabia for only 28 hours.

The rest of the day was taken up with meetings.

Friday 31 October

A morning working at my desk and doing an interview for *Football Collection* magazine. In the afternoon I spent some time interviewing Prince Amir, the son of HRH Prince Abdullah, Crown Prince of Pahang in Malaysia, who is due to come to Druries in 2000. HRH is a keen footballer and was closely involved in the summer when Malaysia hosted the FIFA Youth Championships.

November 1997

Saturday 1 November

A busy morning teaching. In the afternoon the concluding stages of the inter-House rugby competitions took place. Druries had an excellent day reaching all three finals, winning the senior and new boys finals and just losing in the intermediate (Torpid) so there was much to celebrate that evening.

Sunday 2 November

I spent the entire morning writing references for half a dozen boys who were completing their university applications. After watching the new boys convincingly win another soccer match and entertaining two Old Drurieans to tea, I set about packing my kit for the coming matches. I also began my research into customs and life in Saudi Arabia and the Muslim world so that we did not offend anyone with our behaviour. I got much of this information from Hugh O'Donnell's parents with whom I had stayed in Sri Lanka but who, before that, had been in Saudi Arabia where Colonel O'Donnell had been attached to the Saudi Arabian National Guard.

I spoke to Ken Ridden who has frequently lectured and run tournaments in the Middle East. He was able to brief me on the personalities I was likely to meet and the various footballing do's and don'ts. We also had a further discussion about the World Cup nominations and the significance of this particular appointment. Discussion then moved on to the forthcoming Premier League meeting, part of which I would be chairing in his place, as he would be abroad on a UEFA tournament.

Monday November 3

A full day and one which ended strangely. I taught the first period and then accompanied my Remove geography division into Notting Dale in London where we remained until 2.00 p.m. doing a GCSE urban fieldwork exercise.

As soon as I got back my doorbell rang and it was Huw Williams from BBC Radio 5 Live ready to accompany me for the rest of the day for a feature on 'a day in the life of a referee'. It would turn out to be quite a day! I popped down to the games fields to watch some cross-country races, back for a bowl of cereal, my only food since breakfast, and then we were off in the car to West Ham. During the journey we talked about football. Huw was recording the interview though our voices were often drowned by the noise of buses and lorries. Arriving at the ground I unpacked my kit ceremoniously explaining to him, and the listeners, that I take two sets of everything in case of wet weather or accidents. We then inspected the pitch and met up with the other officials, Phil Sharp and Peter Walton, my regular assistant referees, and Gary Willard, a Premier League referee. I have a huge amount of respect for Gary who is a fine young referee and is great company – our matches together are always punctuated with great humour. He was one of the FIFA referees I hoped would become one of my regular reserve referees on international appointments once Steve Lodge retires from the FIFA list at the end of this year. Dennis Hedges, one of the most honest and sensible Premier League match observers, arrived. He is a referees' man and always puts himself in the referee's position. Though never easy to please, he always has good advice and is not over-critical about minor matters.

We met up with Huw briefly so that he could record the safety briefing from the West Ham safety officer, John Ball, and then we began our usual build-up to the match – knowing that timings would be handled by the Sky TV people, especially John Smart, who is a really good link man, courteous and never pushy or difficult.

The match began at great speed and the first half was full of fast, entertaining football with Crystal Palace taking the game by the scruff of the neck and never allowing West Ham to settle. The home defence were having trouble with offsides and I remarked to Steve Lomas that 'your right back is murdering you' as he was playing opponents onside each time the rest of the defence were appealing, usually for a player on the opposite side of the field. Literally a minute after I had made that remark a poor clearance from the goalkeeper was sent straight back to a Crystal Palace forward who appeared offside but Phil Sharp's flag stayed down. There were no real protests and a quick look at the replay screen confirmed that a player in the right-back position – Eyal Berkovic – had played the forward onside. By half-time the pace had not abated and Crystal Palace were winning 2–0 with West Ham looking poor in patches. The game had flowed well, and with no malice or niggle between the players I had been able to play outrageous amounts of advantage and had not had to speak in anger to a player.

At half-time West Ham made two substitutions. They soon got a goal back and in the 65th minute a cracking shot levelled the score at 2–2. A few seconds later the floodlights went out.

I immediately stopped my watch, grabbed the ball and told the players to go back to the dressing rooms. In the tunnel I met the safety officer and the police who informed me that the electricians were trying to find the cause of the problem. I suggested to my assistants that they return to the dressing room to keep warm and, having put on a black training top, began a round of consultations and discussions.

I had a number of priorities, not least to take charge of the situation and ensure that everyone was kept informed of developments. In cricket when play stops for bad light the umpires are encouraged to stay on the field so that they are seen to be concerned and in control and I felt I should do the same, so I returned to the edge of the pitch. I had experienced such a situation three times before. In December 1992, when I was refereeing Wimbledon v Chelsea, the lights had gone out at Selhurst Park because someone had mis-set the time switch. In October 1993 the lights had fused in a Coca-Cola Cup match between Peterborough and Barnsley and a few weeks later the same had happened in the Champions' League match in Portugal between Porto and Werder Bremen. These three instances had taught me a great deal, not least that I should not back myself into a corner by putting a limit on how long I was prepared to wait.

I liaised with the teams and told them that I would not be making any decisions until we knew the scale of the problem. I assured them that if we did get going again I would certainly allow them several minutes on the pitch warming up so that we did not get any unnecessary injuries. The same information was given to the club officials and we also ensured that the crowd was kept informed. I did an interview with Sky in which, to the amusement of many, I stated that we were literally in the dark as to what was happening.

The lights had gone out at 9.23 p.m. with 19 minutes and 55

seconds showing on my watch. At 9.40 the two banks of lights on the North Stand came on and things looked hopeful, but three minutes later they went out again. At 9.45 p.m. the police seemed to be getting news that the problem could not be solved. I decided to go up to the police control room with the match observer to get the full picture. In the control room were the police, safety officer, electricians and Peter Storrie, West Ham's Managing Director, who is a calm, sensible and excellent man. The news from the electricians was that the contactors had failed and while they were able to restore the North Stand lights any attempt to turn on the South Stand lights resulted in the North Stand lights tripping off. There was no alternative but to abandon the match, as there was no prospect of the problem being solved for many hours. The police asked me to delay an announcement so that they could put in place a ground evacuation programme. They also wanted to alert London Underground so that additional trains could be made available for the 25,000 people who would be leaving the stadium.

I returned to convey the decision to Steve Coppell and Harry Redknapp, who are both extremely sensible men. They were clearly disappointed although Harry did admit that he had thought of fusing the lights himself at half-time when West Ham were playing so badly. Rather sadly we changed and packed up and the crowd, who had been excellent throughout the delay, left in an orderly manner. BBC Radio 5 Live asked me to do an interview and the West Ham press officer requested that I go to the press room later to talk to the reporters there. I showered and went to meet the press. I explained what had happened, and West Ham issued a technical outline of the problem. I explained that there were no rules governing how long one should wait and praised the clubs and spectators for their conduct. The evening concluded with me doing a final interview with Huw Williams and then driving home.

Tuesday 4 November

Up early to fax my report on the West Ham situation to the Premier League. I taught for much of the morning and then spent some of the afternoon in bed having developed a dreadful sore throat, possibly from standing out in the cold wind last night. The papers had been sensible and as there had been no controversy there was little that they could do other than accurately report the facts. As usual at mid-morning break I was the subject of good-humoured teasing from my colleagues: 'Elleray in the dark again' . . . and the chaplain made some comment about 'the light shining in the darkness'. By the evening my throat was really bad and I was feeling lousy so started taking large doses of Paracetamol and anything else I could lay my hands on.

Wednesday 5 November

I taught until 10.30 a.m. and then took a taxi to Heathrow, where I met my assistants, Paul Vosper, Phil Sharp and Steve Lodge.

The flight to Riyadh was very comfortable and we were well looked after by the cabin crew who were all interested in the match. A Norwegian who knew a lot about football and had been in Budapest when I refereed the World Cup qualifier between Hungary and Norway in June warned us that the queues at Riyadh would be awful. Fortunately, as we disembarked there was an announcement for us and we were met by several security officers and Abdulrachman, a Saudi Arabia FIFA referee. Our passports were taken and we walked past all the queues, straight through passport control, collected our bags and then off to the Riyadh Palace Hotel where we were left to our own devices.

Thursday 6 November

I slept very well apart from being woken at five in the morning by the faithful being called to prayer at the mosque near the hotel. I was stunned to see the roads flooded and realised that the flashing lights during the night had not been illuminations but a major storm. And I had been worrying that it would be too hot and dry. At breakfast Steve (or Victor Meldrew as we still called him) also complained about being woken. Just before breakfast I had been phoned by the Sri Lankan FIFA delegate, Joseph, the General Secretary of the Sri Lanka FA. He was a charming man and would turn out to be a good companion and a sensible, if slightly panicky, official.

Our referee's guide then took us on a brief tour of Riyadh before we arrived at the Prince Faisal Ban Fahad Bin Abdul-Aziz Stadium for the pre-match meeting. One of the first people we met was Ted Buxton, who had been one of Terry Venables' right-hand men for England. He was there in his capacity as adviser to the China team, but somewhat embarrassingly, he was wearing his England FA blazer, identical to the ones we had on. He told us that Terry Venables had heard we had the match and sent us his good wishes and hoped the ball ran well for us. It is always a source of comfort and pride to know that when we are abroad we not only have the support of English refereeing colleagues but also of others involved in the game. The arrangements reminded me very much of the meeting in Tokyo when I had refereed the World Club Cup Final in 1995. After a lengthy and effusive welcome from the General Secretary of the Saudi Arabia Football Federation, the administration was handed over to Joseph. He announced that this was an historic match for it was the very first occasion in the history of the World Cup that a European referee had officiated in a qualification match played in Asia.

We had a quick tour of the ground before going off to the King Fahd International Stadium where the match will be played. On the edge of the desert and looking like a series of Bedouin tents, it is the most fantastic stadium I have ever seen and was built in 1988 at a cost of millions. The architect and stadium manager showed us round his pride and joy. It holds 70,000 people and has parking for 37,000 cars. Tickets are sold only on the day of the match and there are enough exits to clear the ground in just under three minutes in the event of an emergency. It employs 370 people working 24 hours a day on three shifts, although after we discovered two of them asleep in one of the changing rooms, we were pretty convinced that by the time we left for lunch that number had been reduced to 368.

The Saudi Arabians had just received the electronic flags we had been using in the Premier League. They were keen that we should use them so that they could claim the record of being the first Asian country to do so. We agreed. It was certainly becoming a record-setting match.

Despite the rain there would be no problems with the pitch as there was cell structure drainage. The team changing rooms were enormous and each included a full-size gym for the pre-match warming up. The VIP area was just unbelievable – a huge room with marble floor and gold everywhere. The dressing rooms were on the opposite side to the main stand (or tribune as it is known abroad) and we would have to walk across the pitch to line up for the national anthems. On that far side of the pitch we were shown where we would be taken in the event of trouble severe enough to make it impossible to return safely to the main dressing rooms. Underneath the main stand was a dressing room and a large bedroom with four comfortable beds which, we were told, we could use to stay the night if the crowd are exceptionally hostile. They even showed us the small hospital and operating theatre in the same part of the complex. Stunned by the incredible stadium, we then sped off to see some camels – an event which provided the most embarrassing moment of the trip. Before leaving, and again on the flight, I had carefully been through all the protocol we should follow. As this is an Arab country I had assumed that my colleagues would know that the people are Muslims and do not eat pork as the pig is considered unclean. As we were being shown the camels, we enquired what uses they were put to apart from transport and were told that, among other things, they were eaten. Before I could stop him, Paul Vosper said in total innocence, 'I imagine they taste like pork, don't they?' I was stunned and, in very clipped tones, said that I very much doubted it, and changed the subject as quickly as I could. To be fair to our guide he did not bat an eyelid.

Fortunately, my throat infection had collapsed under the bombardment of pills and I was feeling well again. We left the hotel at 5.30 p.m. and by the time we arrived the stadium was full and an amazing atmosphere was developing. Both sides needed a positive result to have a chance of progressing to France.

Prior to the match we met several FIFA officials, including a Saudi prince who is on the FIFA Executive Committee and said he hoped that we would return to his country to referee in the future. I certainly shared those hopes. The administration was efficient and the officials produced a team sheet with all the details including the temperature (25°C) and humidity (67 per cent). I would certainly be warm. I cannot adequately describe how proud I felt as we led the teams out into a cacophony of noise of 70,000 Saudis, almost all in traditional Arab robes. To be not only the first Englishman but the first European referee to officiate in a World Cup match in Asia was a huge honour and responsibility and I was determined to referee out of my skin.

The formalities over, the game kicked off with the crowd performing a wonderful Mexican wave. The match itself was incredible. It was clear early on that it would be frantic as both teams were very fit, had considerable ball skills and were not interested in route 1 football but in playing their way out of trouble. After three minutes Saudi Arabia scored and the crowd went wild. Ten minutes later China equalised to almost total silence. The players were very well disciplined and there was little in the way of dissent. However, the Chinese were somewhat over-enthusiastic in their challenges and I showed three yellow cards around the 20 to 30 minute period. We then had a moment that showed I was not a 'homer'. A Chinese forward dribbled skilfully into the penalty area, went wide and the Saudi Arabia goalkeeper came charging out. I could tell from his approach that a foul was likely. Sure enough he brought the Chinese player down and I awarded a penalty, ignoring the Saudi Arabia captain's broken English 'it cannot be a penalty as the ball was going out of play'. That did not matter and I wanted to tell him that it made the goalkeeper all the more stupid for fouling. Instead, I showed the goalkeeper the yellow card for the challenge. The Chinese penalty taker hit the shot poorly and it was well saved by the keeper, to the second loudest cheer of the evening. The score remained 1–1 for the rest of the half, a thrilling half of wonderful exciting football. A scoreline of 4–4 would not have been a surprise.

At half-time I drank plenty of water. Steve Lodge reported that the FIFA delegate had been delighted that we had kicked off exactly on time. Joseph then appeared and announced that he was extremely happy with the way we were refereeing the match and made the interesting observation, 'All your decisions are exactly correct, unlike most Asian referees'. He went on to relate various incidents which, he implied, showed that some Asian referees have trouble being mentally strong enough to be neutral.

The second half was just as exciting as the first. I redeemed myself in the eyes of the Saudi Arabian crowd when I awarded Saudi Arabia a clear penalty following an ill-judged tackle by the Chinese full back. Unfortunately, for Saudi Arabia and their captain, who took the penalty, it was well saved by the Chinese goalkeeper. For the rest of the half the crowd gave the Saudi Arabia captain terrible abuse and I suspect that the royal princes and others will take a long time to forgive him. The final 15 minutes saw the Chinese goal under constant siege, broken only by lightning counterattacks on the Saudi Arabian goal. With a number of injuries, substitutions, time-wasting and a further four yellow cards I played an additional, nerve-wracking five minutes. The match ended 1–1 which meant that China were effectively eliminated and Saudi Arabia's chances of qualification had diminished.

Everyone seemed more than happy with our control of the match and we were each given a Chinese People's Republic and Saudi football shirt. Our friend from Sri Lanka was overjoyed with everything and we had a stream of people coming to thank us. Ted Buxton popped in and was very complimentary. All four of us were satisfied with the way the game had gone. Before a match I agonise a great deal and wonder what problems and challenges I will face. This is especially true when I venture beyond England, and especially beyond Europe, to countries where the approach to the game and the styles of play can be very different. The players are used to other styles of officiating so I quickly have to find a compromise between my natural style and what they are used to. The early minutes of this game were terribly important as the players weighed me up and vice versa. That the game had gone so well left a real feeling of achievement and satisfaction, a great relief after all the pre-match apprehension and tension. We changed quickly and hurried back to the hotel to get ready to leave on the 2 a.m. flight.

Friday 7 November

We set off to Riyadh airport only to discover that the plane was delayed and there was no room for us in Business Class. Wandering around the airport as we waited we were intercepted at various stages by Saudis who wanted to talk about the game and were most complimentary about the way we had handled it.

The flight from Riyadh to Zurich was dreadful: cramped in Economy, with no room to stretch which was a problem when you are beginning to stiffen up after a demanding match.

I had a taxi waiting at Heathrow but the driver standing with one of those signs with my name on it was not a football fan. He was surprised that he had been asked by several people if he was really waiting for David Elleray, the referee.

Back at Harrow I had a quick bath and change before meetings and then teaching. I was pretty tired but survived until mid-afternoon when I had a short nap, having first faxed my report to FIFA and sent off the other paperwork. The boys at lunch had been fascinated with the tales of the match and Riyadh. I taught again in the evening and then worked until getting to bed about 11.30 p.m., having been up for about 40 hours with only snatches of sleep. Who says that referees are not dedicated?

Saturday 8 November

Yet another 'free' Saturday but a welcome relief after the exertions of the last few days. I slept well and taught for most of the morning. I watched *Football Focus* at lunchtime and was interested to hear David Platt's views on Arsenal's disciplinary record and the high number of yellow cards. He laid the blame at the feet of players and managers. David's opinion was that since they had all demanded consistency from referees and that had, correctly, led to a loss of discretion the players now had to accept that consistency meant strict application of the laws. His point was supported by Graham Le Saux who was in the studio with Gary Lineker and who felt it was up to players to exert greater self-discipline and avoid silly bookings for offences like dissent. An encouraging sign that the message was, perhaps, getting through and being understood.

Sunday 9 November

The school's Remembrance Service was very moving as the Last Post brought back sad memories of Matt Raynham's funeral. It was a source of pride to me that four of the five boys making up the guard of honour for the wreath laying ceremonies were from Druries.

I watched some of the junior inter-house swimming and then set off for Highbury with George Attenborough (I had been his House tutor before I became House Master of Druries) and Bill Davis, who is a major involved with the school's CCF and an ardent Manchester United supporter. The Arsenal v Manchester United match had been billed as the match of the season thus far and, following the trouble last season between Peter Schmeichel and Ian Wright, there was a great deal of media hype. I was the reserve referee as there is always a Premier League referee as reserve on TV matches and other important games. It is a role I greatly enjoy as it gives me a chance to watch a match from a different perspective.

Before the kick-off much of my time was taken up with Tom Bune, the Premier League observer who had been so critical of one incident in my Southampton v Arsenal match earlier in the season. We had a very frank discussion about the inconsistency among the Premier League observers where some, like Tom, were marking down referees on the basis of single incidents, while others were basing their mark on the overall performance of the referee throughout the match. We also discussed the need for a slightly different attitude to physical offences as opposed to technical ones.

During the match I was standing in the tunnel between the dugouts with my full referee's kit on underneath a tracksuit. My main role was to be ready to take over should Martin Bodenham or one of the assistants become ill or injured so I had to concentrate on the game and be fully in tune with what was going on should I be called upon. My secondary role was to keep the benches under control and supervise any substitutions.

Early on there were few problems but Manchester United went 2–0 down and began to niggle a little. At one point Brian McClair, one of the reserves, said that I should have been refereeing rather than Martin, but I pointed out that would simply mean that they would be giving *me* stick rather than him. They drew back to 2–2 and Alex Ferguson began to lose that famous temper of his. After a couple of decisions which displeased him, he turned and levelled a volley of abuse at me, some of it suggesting that Martin was too old and slow to referee. Initially I ignored him but he continued and I firmly told him to shut up. This surprised him and he told me that I could not say that to him. I replied that I could and I did not intend to be subjected to criticism and swearing from him when it was nothing to do with me. He seemed somewhat startled by this and sat down in the dugout. Just beyond him Brian Kidd smiled and winked at me in a conspiratorial manner as did Gary Lewin, the Arsenal physio in the other dugout. About five minutes later Alex turned round and apologised to me for swearing.

Just before half-time there were two nasty incidents in quick succession when coins were thrown by Manchester United supporters at Nigel Winterburn and then by Arsenal fans at Peter Schmeichel. I alerted the police and Martin came over to ask for more officers at the South End of the ground. As he moved away, Alex Ferguson shouted to him that he should wear his glasses in the second half. I commented to Alex that I thought, after so many years as a manager, he would be capable of something more original than that. This brought wry smiles from the Manchester United bench.

In the second half the dugouts caused few problems and I was able to chat to Brian McClair about Manchester United's match in midweek when there had been one or two terrible tackles by Feyenoord players. A thrilling match ended 3–2 to Arsenal. The big screen showing replays came to our assistance on one occasion. Manchester United thought that the build-up to the corner from which the third goal came had seen an Arsenal player offside. I said to them that I thought the right back had played him onside. Sure enough, when the replay was shown

I was correct and this stopped all the dissent that was building up in the Manchester United dugout.

After the match I returned quickly to Harrow so that I would be back in time to watch the junior boys perform a play as part of the new boys' drama.

Monday 10 November

I awoke to find that Alex Ferguson has had a berserk attack on Martin Bodenham, calling him 'the master at seeing nothing' after his refusal to award Manchester United a penalty. He claimed Martin did not look like an athlete, but this ignored Martin's remarkable capacity to read the game and be in the right place at the right time.

In the afternoon I spoke with Ken Ridden and was pleased to learn that I had not got a game in either leg of the next round of the UEFA Cup competition. This might seem strange but I was under real pressure for time and the two legs would clash horribly with commitments at school. Ken also mentioned that he had spoken to a member of the FIFA Referees' Committee and had outlined my availability problems for France.

In the evening I went to speak at the Ealing Referees' Association. Throughout the country there are groups of referees who get together on a monthly basis to discuss all aspects of refereeing. These groups are usually based in towns and include the whole range of officials from those on the local parks through the professional leagues up to the highest levels. I really enjoy going and speaking to these 'societies' as it keeps me in touch with the grass roots. I also feel that I can make a real impact on them, and as Premier League referees we try our best to visit as many societies as we can. I spoke for about 45 minutes outlining the changes in refereeing since the World Cup in 1994 and looking ahead to the future. I then answered questions for about 45 minutes before returning to school to conduct the final rehearsals for the public speaking competition along with Judith Affleck, one of my House tutors and Head of Classics.

While we were doing this I got a surprise phone call from the bursar. He said that he did not wish to be impertinent or personal but had I considered applying for the post of Head Master of Harrow? He felt, from what he knew of me, that I would be a good candidate and that we would be able to work well together.

Tuesday 11 November

A change from my training routine of the exercise bike and the rowing machine today as I refereed two inter-House rugby matches. If I have a spell with few matches I work that much harder at my fitness which is terribly important because, at 43, it is easy to lose extra stamina and speed which are so vital. Fortunately, my job is such that I am on my feet almost all day – I even teach walking around the form room. I find jogging and swimming very tedious so use the exercise bike and rowing machine, usually while watching the six o'clock news on the television.

The first match was between my House and our traditional 'enemies', Elmfield. It was a splendid game, which we won relatively easily and was played in an excellent spirit. I really enjoy rugby when it is played with vigour but sportingly. The second match was a less satisfactory affair as both houses wanted to fool around until each realised they might win; they then tried to take it too seriously and began falling out. Nevertheless, it was a very good run out for me.

In the evening I attended both the senior and junior public speaking competitions; we did not win either but performed creditably.

Wednesday 12 November

I was up early trying to decide what was appropriate in terms of shirt and tie for the interview at Lancing College. My heart was not really in it, as I was becoming increasingly convinced I should apply for the Harrow post, but I felt that it would be good practice. In any event I enjoyed the experience and being under pressure. I came away feeling that I had performed reasonably well but I was starkly aware that all my answers were very general whereas if they had been about Harrow I could have been far more specific and positive. I travelled across to London to have lunch with my literary agent, Chris Little, who was still celebrating signing up two rising star authors. Chris is a great friend of the parents of one of my senior boys and has that ability to make even a minor author like me feel that their work is vital and worthwhile. Over lunch I handed over the latest two batches of the book and filled him in on recent developments in my life.

By the time I returned to Harrow I had pretty well decided that I would withdraw from Lancing and give everything to the Harrow post. Deep down I knew that I would not take the Lancing position if it were offered, for if I did not try for Harrow then I would regret it for the rest of my life. I sat at my computer composing a letter to Lancing and one to Sir Michael Connell, the Chairman of the Harrow Governors.

Midway through I wandered around the House, chatted to boys doing prep and finalised the last of the UCAS forms. When I returned there was a message on my answerphone to call Professor Michael Edwards, a Harrow governor. I phoned him and was startled to learn that the Harrow selection committee (or some of them) had met that morning, ironically as I was being interviewed for Lancing. They had discussed my possible application and it had been decided that Professor Edwards should talk to me about my thoughts for the future of Harrow at some stage before the governors' meeting on 28 November. We agreed to meet on 24 November, ironically again the day of the final interviews for Lancing. My discussion with Professor Edwards was most encouraging not just because he was on the selection committee but because of his views on what sort of person he felt Harrow needed and his perception of me as a candidate. I finished my letter to the Chairman, started one to Lancing and went to bed ready for the challenge.

Thursday 13 November

I taught for much of the morning and then had a meeting with the Head Master to let him know of my various decisions and to get his advice on how to word the letter to Lancing and how to proceed with the Harrow situation. What was worrying me, and worried him even more, was that word of the governors' deliberations seemed to be leaking out and gossip was becoming rife throughout the school. The only advantage was that people would seriously think about the prospect of my becoming Head Master and I would have some reaction to feed back to the governors. Moreover, the previous Head Master, Ian Beer, used to say that if you want something to take place you need to create the climate in which people are expecting it to, so that when it does happen they are already pretty resigned to it.

Nick Shryane, the bursar, had written to me with some ideas about Harrow's future and we had arranged to meet this afternoon. We had an excellent three-hour discussion about Harrow's problems and possible solutions and it was clear that we were very much on the same wavelength and could debate freely and easily. Nick outlined to me the basic principles of vision, strategic planning and management plans and that was the key I needed. By the end I really was ready to accept the challenge. This discussion was the final piece in the jigsaw for I had plenty of ideas about Harrow's future and what needed to be done but did not have the framework within which to carry them out. I returned to Druries inspired and spent the next five hours on my computer drawing together many threads of ideas in the first draft of my management framework document.

Friday 14 November

The morning was dominated by teaching and the arrival of the Chrysalis TV crew who filmed me teaching one of my A level divisions, a mixture of characters and several of the school's best sportsmen, including Tom Davis, captain of rugby. It was amusing to watch the boys' reactions, some studiously avoiding the cameras and others flexing their muscles and looking tough. After the lesson several boys were interviewed about what I was like as a teacher and what it was like to have a Premier League referee as a master. The boys threatened to destroy my reputation, but knew that I would see the film so I expected them to be kind. The crew then accompanied me to lunch, arousing great interest in the rest of the school. We pretended we were doing a promotion video for Druries, to show it off as the best House in the school.

In the evening I had a long talk with Jason Keen, a senior boy in another House, who needed some guidance about his future. We talked for several hours and it is this aspect of my job that I find especially rewarding.

Saturday 15 November

I had no match because I had asked not to be used in the first round of the FA Cup as I needed to have another Saturday morning at school fulfilling my teaching commitments. After lunch I watched various rugby matches and then, at about four o'clock, set off for Moor Hall for the Premier League referees' meeting, taking a load of marking to do at the hotel before supper.

With Ken Ridden unable to attend, Mike Foster was in charge and wanted to discuss the agenda with me. He handed over the tape of incidents for tomorrow morning so after supper, while everyone chatted and drank, I went up to the meeting room to go through the clips and prepare for the session.

Sunday 16 November

We began the meeting at nine o'clock, highly amused that Steve Lodge was looking very grey around the gills having been up late talking with Gary Willard. He claimed he had not drunk too much but we were not convinced.

Our main discussions focused, at first, on the role of the match observers, since the feeling persisted that some are too fussy about penalising minor technical errors. To improve consistency among match observers, I initiated a new grading scheme two years ago where the 1–10 mark system was replaced with five letter grades:

E – Exceptional. Only a handful of these would be awarded in a season.
I – Impressive. A performance which was well above the usual standard.
G – Good. A good high standard, exactly what would be expected in a typical match.
B – Below Par. A performance which had a number of deficiencies relating to law application, fitness, etc.
D – Disappointing. A performance which was well below expectation and included major deficiencies, usually in control or Law application.

After a useful discussion, in which Brendon Batson of the PFA (who is a Premier League match observer) made some useful points, we agreed that match observers should be instructed to use the grading system to reflect *overall* performance and not downgrade unless very serious errors occurred, or if the referee repeatedly missed technical offences.

The rest of the morning was spent looking at the video clips which, as ever, showed good and bad practice. As an introduction I asked my colleagues to focus on how we managed disciplinary action. Were we calm and dignified? Were we too low-key? Did we check that the dismissed player did not cause trouble as he left the field? Did we use the correct techniques when consulting assistants? We had an excellent session and I tried to ensure everyone made some contribution. Paul

Durkin was very much in the spotlight and we discussed with him
whether his aggressive manner and body language when using the
cards helped or exacerbated the atmosphere and the credibility of his
decision. Body language is a terribly important aspect of refereeing
as, without realising it, a referee can convey all sorts of messages
to players and the crowd about his own emotions and confidence. I
have worked hard to ensure that if I give a major decision I become
fractionally slower and more deliberate in my signals and the way I
move so that I convey the impression that I have total confidence and
belief in what I am doing. It is very important not to display anger
or irritation, and on those rare occasions when I let the fact that I
am cross show, I am disappointed in myself. Paul is one of those
referees who realises that when he sends a player off he often shows
the anger he feels at the player's behaviour. We got agreement from
John Barnwell (LMA) and Brendan Batson that we should compile
a video of bad tackles in the Premier League and enlist the support
of the managers to try to eliminate these from the game.

I left the meeting early at 12.15 p.m. to return to Harrow in time
for the first runners in the School's Long Ducker run. Each year well
over 300 boys run or swim to raise money for charity. The main
event, for the real athletes, is to swim 400 lengths or run 20 miles in
less than three hours. The run is from Harrow to Marble Arch and
back again. Other boys, the vast majority, either swim 200 lengths
or run the 10 miles from Marble Arch back to Harrow. We usually
raise somewhere in the order of £15,000 and this year the charity
was SPARKS, with Roger Uttley, the president, very prominent. I
was delighted that Ernie Wong in Druries beat the School record
for the 400 lengths and very proud of the many boys who ran well.
Before I left the Premier League referees' meeting I had suggested
that in 1998 they might like to take part and help raise money, but
there was not an enthusiastic response.

Straight after the last runner had arrived back I interviewed some
prospective parents and spent the rest of the day catching up on
marking.

Monday 17 November

This evening I refereed a match between Berkshire under-19s and
Buckinghamshire under-19s in memory of Ron Davis, who had
overseen schoolboy football in those counties for many years for

the ESFA Council. He died of cancer earlier this year and I was asked to referee this memorial game, as I had known him well. It was a most enjoyable evening and the match was played in a good spirit, except for one young man who thought he would be very 'cool' by trying to take me on. He did not get far but, disappointingly, could not accept this and was the only player who did not come and shake hands afterwards. The match was notable for three excellent goals. Afterwards Ron's widow made a moving speech of thanks.

When I arrived at the ground I was presented with a programme from a match in 1980 when I had been a linesman for the ESFA inter-county final between Berkshire and Durham at Maidenhead. Steve Inger, the Secretary of the Berks SFA, had found it and brought it for me as a souvenir, reminding me of my roots.

Tuesday 18 November

A letter arrived from Canada in the morning post. It was from a Ron Jenkins who lives in Vancouver, written in response to the interview that I did for CSI some while back.

In the letter he wrote:

> It was on a three-hour football programme where I saw your interview. What a pity I didn't get your message when I was a referee; I was most impressed with your admission that even you, a world-class referee, received adverse criticism. You weren't cornered; therefore you were under no obligation to speak so frankly. What you admitted did nothing to bolster your image as a referee, but it must have been encouraging to budding referees who inevitably would encounter the flak which every referee must face.

> So here I am, so eager to write to you, I am attempting to contact you not knowing your address, nor even the correct spelling of your name.

I was pleased to reply to him and take up the points he made elsewhere in the letter about time-keeping. However, the main message was that we all make mistakes. Obviously we strive hard to eliminate them, especially through studying videos, but if fans, players and managers would stop for a moment and accept that we are human beings and thus bound to get things wrong sometimes then perhaps referees would be better understood and accepted.

In that regard I was heartened by several letters in *Match* magazine which suggested that we are turning the corner and there is a growing understanding of referees and the pressures upon us. In the evening, according to one of the School deliverymen, I appeared as one of the questions on *Question of Sport*.

Wednesday 19 November

The papers were full of further criticism of Martin Bodenham for failing to give three 'penalties' in last night's Coca-Cola match between Derby and Newcastle. Of course, as often happens, the managers latched on to past comments and Jim Smith echoed Alex Ferguson's description of Martin as the 'master of seeing nothing'. It is strange how a referee often gets a run of similar controversies; it frequently occurs with sendings-off. A referee has a number of games with no red cards then suddenly has two or three in successive matches.

This evening I was due at Stamford Bridge for the Coca-Cola match between Chelsea and Southampton. Ever since the 1994 Cup Final I have had a very hostile reaction from some of the Chelsea fans (although not the players or management) and I always dread refereeing at Stamford Bridge as a result. I even woke up this morning half hoping I might be ill and could avoid it!

I got to the ground early and had a mixed reaction from the fans already there. Several came up to chat but another group, as I went to the dressing room, declared loudly, 'Oh no, it's Satan!' I've had some abuse in my time but never anything like that. With life somewhat busy at this stage I sat in the dressing room with a pile of essays to correct. The assistants arrived with their guests and, I hope not too rudely, I sent them off to the guest lounge for a cup of tea so I could finish my school work. Ray Ward, one of the assistants, had some messages for me from the Football League. Apparently, David Dent, Secretary of the Football League, was annoyed that in last night's match at Derby (which was shown on Sky TV) the corner flag posts had Coca-Cola flags on them. He was also concerned about the amount of jewellery the players were wearing and had instructed that I should ensure neither was a problem this evening.

I spoke to the assistant managers about the jewellery when they brought their team sheets in and they promised me there would be no problems. However, in the tunnel, as we waited to go out, I spotted that Dennis Wise was wearing a diamond stud earring and asked him to remove it. I also gave him a hard time as the boys at school had teased me after he kissed me in jest in the Liverpool v Chelsea match earlier in the season.

The game was very enjoyable with Chelsea eventually winning 2–1 after extra-time. I was pretty tired by the end, having refereed on a heavy pitch on Monday. In the 18th minute I cautioned Kevin Davies of Southampton for a late tackle on Chelsea's Frank Sinclair. I was sure that I'd dealt with the jewellery problem but as Frank was having treatment, I noticed that he had two studs in one ear and one in the other.

After the game I asked Gwyn Williams if I could take the match ball to use as an auction item for a fund-raising dinner I was speaking at later in the week. He kindly said yes and offered to take it away to get the players to sign it. Moments later he returned to say most of the players had gone but that he would take it to the training ground tomorrow and get them all to sign it, including Vialli and Zola, and have it sent up to school for me.

On my way home I had an encounter at a petrol station with someone who recognised me and wanted to chat about football. This chap was on his mobile phone and spent half the time talking to me and half the time trying to convince whoever was on the line that he really was talking to David Elleray.

Thursday 20 November

The morning post included a very interesting letter from a young referee in the Gambia. I occasionally get such letters, usually being very complimentary and then asking for kit, boots or whatever. Parts of the letter read:

> I am Ousman Jammeh aged 23. I am a referee and I do like been a referee and wanted to talk as a professional. I am established as a referee since August 1995. I wanted to grow as a FIFA referee like you. I definitely admire your officiating. I have been following your success for some years now both in the Premier League and International football.
>
> I have seen you playing in European Championship, World Cup Qualifying matches and UEFA club matches. The most impressive

one was your match in Euro '96. I like your appearance and the way you apply the rules of the law indicated by FIFA.

Elleray, you're the first ever International Referee I writes and I am definitely looking forward to your best co-operation and your immediate response towards this situation. I wish you all the best of success and happiness and may God guide you for a long way. Have a good progress staying in refereeing in peace and harmony. England is my team in International and I like English clubs in the European Club competition.

With all those compliments I could do nothing but reply immediately.

In the afternoon I went down to Sussex with George Attenborough, the School Registrar, and Judith Affleck, Head of Classics, to visit Brambletye Prep School. I had a fascinating time and spent about 40 minutes in the school theatre talking to the senior classes about football and refereeing and trying to answer some testing and perceptive questions.

In the early evening I got a call from the bursar's office to say that the Chelsea football, signed by all the players, had been delivered. It is remarkable how kind and helpful clubs can be, especially for charities or fund-raising events.

Friday 21 November

I was delighted to receive two videos this morning. One was of my interview for CSI; the other was the Saudi Arabia v China match. I acknowledged receipt of the videos and, rather cheekily, faxed Hong Kong and asked if they had any photos of the match. It is always one of the great frustrations that it is difficult to get hold of photographs of myself in action at a big match. Indeed, to ensure that I captured the Cup Final in detail back in 1994 I hired a local photographer to attend the game with the express purpose of taking action photos for me.

Mid-afternoon I set off to drive to Cambridgeshire for a speaking engagement. I was staying at Baythorne Park, the home of Julian Watson, real friend of Harrow and Druries. After a glass of champagne the hosts for the dinner arrived and took me to a restaurant near the village of Hundon, the community for whom the Sportsman's evening was being held. The local people were trying to raise enough money for a synthetic surface in the middle of the village for their youngsters to play on. Julian had got Jeffrey Archer to open the summer fête and I was the guest of honour at the dinner. They were delighted with the autographed Chelsea football that raised a good sum in the auction.

After a fine meal I addressed the assembled 60 people for about 20 minutes and then answered a series of thoughtful questions. Unfortunately, I had not been able to escape from the press and someone from the *Daily Express* had tracked me down for my views on the £1,000 fine the FA had levied on John Hartson for his remarks about Mike Reed earlier in the season. I simply repeated to the reporter what I've said before; that referees do not comment on such punishments as we regard our role as finished once we have reported the incident.

Saturday 22 November

We had an early breakfast as my host was due to go shooting with Prince Edward. A pleasant cross-country drive brought me to Derby and their splendid new ground, Pride Park. I had something of a feeling of *déjà vu* as the stadium is very similar to Middlesbrough's Cellnet Stadium. Keith Parsons, the Derby secretary, who is one of the most hospitable and welcoming of all the Premier League secretaries, met me. I had a good tour, being joined by my assistants, Mike Ryan and Mark Warren. It was Mark's first line since that injury in Monaco and it was very good to have him back in my team.

Chrysalis TV, who filmed me arriving at the ground, signing autographs and talking to fans, then unpacking my kit and inspecting the pitch, monopolised the pre-match preparations somewhat. Over a cup of tea upstairs we came upon a meeting of the Derby County Supporters Club and I had a really invigorating conversation with them about football, Derby's new ground and refereeing in general. I was very interested that they hated David Mellor and Tony Banks and wanted to know why referees like me did not go on the offensive, especially over Mellor's 606 radio programme. I have always thought it would be good to debate refereeing with David Mellor but in a studio where someone else was in charge of the switches as he gives the impression that if he does not like what someone is saying he will pull the plug on them. Gerald Ashby once appeared on his radio show and did an excellent job of explaining what referees do and what they are trying to achieve.

The game itself was very much a curate's egg. The early phases were straightforward with hardly a tackle out of place. Derby took the lead, I cautioned two Coventry players for foul tackles and then awarded Derby a straightforward penalty. The trouble began when Derby scored their third goal and Coventry claimed a handball. It was one of those clear cases where the ball hits the hand and is not intentionally handled by the player but 'Sod's Law' saw play switch to the other end and a goal result. Coventry, especially their manager Gordon Strachan, were upset.

At half-time Mr Strachan came uninvited into my dressing room to question why I had not given the handball. I explained that it was not deliberate but he was unable or unwilling to accept that explanation, and launched into an attack on my refereeing saying, 'You were obviously wrong because after that you gave us everything and it was very embarrassing.' I flippantly replied that if he interpreted every decision I gave in favour of Coventry as generosity then there was no point giving them anything in the second half. He lost his temper and tried to storm out. While accepting, in the cold light of day, that it was unwise to be flippant I was annoyed that yet another manager had come into a referee's dressing room with the sole intention of having a go and not prepared to listen to the referee's viewpoint. I decided to strike back and I leant against the door and would not let him leave until I had had my say. Of course, Strachan exaggerated the incident and claimed afterwards that he had been 'staggered and gobsmacked' by what I had said and that I had locked him in the dressing room. Given that the doors have no locks that was pretty impossible. I imagine that he was gobsmacked because a referee had answered back.

The main problem was that Strachan must have gone back into the Coventry dressing room and wound the players up. The end result was that Coventry got a goal back but a number of the players bitched like mad for the rest of the game. My irritation at the hypocrisy of some managers and players who feel that they can say what they like to referees but we cannot say anything back heightened as the game progressed. Even players like Gary McAllister whom I respect were prepared to make snide comments about my refereeing or the fact that I am a schoolmaster, but if I dared reply they got very stroppy and claimed 'You can't say things like that to me!' Darren Huckerby was fouled on the halfway line and he was shouting and screaming for me to show the yellow card before I had had time to get it out of my pocket. I remarked to him that I thought it pretty unimpressive that he was demanding that a fellow player be cautioned given that the PFA were having a campaign to stop such actions, but he resented my comments and said I was not entitled to speak to him that way. This caution for Christian Dailly was the ninth of the game, apparently the highest in a Premier League match so far this season. It had not been a nasty-tempered game but the players had tackled poorly, leaving their foot in after the ball had gone, and the nine cautions were all for fouls. The only other problem I had in the second half was that fog began swirling around the ground in waves and, on one or two occasions, visibility was momentarily very poor and I had visions of having to decide whether or not to abandon the match. I knew that Coventry, 3–1 down, would grasp any chance to go off while Derby would want to continue at all costs. Fortunately, we were able to carry on, but it reminded me of a game I abandoned at Swindon through fog. It showed Derby the problems of building their new ground near a river.

As we left the field at the end Gary Pendrey, the Coventry assistant, tried to talk to me about the amount of stoppage time allowed. Stewards and police kept him away and, having experienced problems with Mr Strachan when I had spoken to him, I decided not to say anything. As a result Pendrey went berserk and said I had no right not to answer his questions. So they wanted it both ways!

I decided not to speak to the press after the match as it would only inflame whatever Strachan had said. I left and drove off to spend the evening with friends in Oxfordshire. I was somewhat annoyed with myself for having lost my cool and had allowed my exchange at half-time to get under my skin. I should have been a little more professional, I felt.

Sunday 23 November

After a long lie in and a leisurely breakfast I strolled through the misty Oxfordshire countryside with Simon Duffy, my host. His wife Kathy is American and a wonderfully kind and charming hostess, and she provided a fantastic Thanksgiving lunch. I was able to switch off from refereeing for a while and forget the newspapers. When I eventually arrived back in Harrow, my answerphone was full of messages from the press. I decided that I would not respond to any as the Strachan controversy would die unless I stoked it, as he had not gone into much detail about our conversation. Usually, I am very pleased to give the referee's viewpoint but on this occasion I just felt that it would inflame matters, especially if I went into print about the inability of some players and managers to accept that referees have a right to defend themselves when under attack.

Monday 24 November

My morning began well with a really nice letter from a Derby fan, Owen Kinselle, who wrote:

> You have probably forgotten but I have written to you on a couple of occasions in support of referees and at a time when the media was 'having a go' at refs.
>
> After attending Derby County's match this afternoon I feel I must write to you yet again after witnessing an absolutely superb example of good refereeing and one which was without show or flamboyance but rather down to earth common sense.

He went on to criticise Martin Bodenham's handling of the Derby v Newcastle Coca-Cola match earlier in the week and continued:

> Today's game was all the more splendid after that and you really are to be congratulated for a magnificent performance. I know there were a lot of bookings but every one was deserved.
>
> Did you like our new Pride Park stadium after the rather antiquated but homely Baseball Ground? All those responsible are to be congratulated on providing us with a modern superb ground.
>
> That's enough except to re-iterate my earlier remarks. Very well done and many thanks for enabling the game to be exciting.

Amid all the praise it was that last comment which pleased me most. It is always gratifying to receive such letters but especially when they acknowledge that we can have a positive effect on the game and the fans' enjoyment, as too often people complain that we spoil games.

The morning and early afternoon were spent meeting the bursar and working on my thoughts for Harrow in preparation for the evening meeting with Professor Edwards. I had a very testing interview with him about my candidature for the Head Master's position and he gave me every opportunity to set out my thoughts on Harrow's current position and its future development.

Tuesday 25 November

To catch up on my work I rose at six and spent almost three hours marking. Returning from teaching in mid-morning I had an urgent message to phone Ken Ridden as the LMA were keen to know if I was reporting Gordon Strachan to the FA. I said that Mr Strachan and I had had a private conversation and I had no report to make and regarded the matter as closed.

In the afternoon I watched my House lose narrowly, in the last minute, to the Grove in the final of the House Seconders rugby competition and then returned to marking exam scripts and A level geography projects which filled the rest of the day and evening.

Wednesday 26 November

The highlight of the day was the inter-House CCF assault course competition. It has three components: the obstacle course, a run and shooting. We were regarded as favourites and we performed exceptionally well. We won the obstacle course section by 5 seconds, won the run by 10 seconds (but incurred a 15-second penalty) and won the shooting clearly. We were overall champions and the boys brought three silver cups to the House. They know how seriously I take the competition and when they returned from the announcement of the results (which I did not know) they decided to wind me up by pretending we had come second. I was disappointed and it showed, but they had a great laugh when they produced three silver trophies from under their coats.

In the evening, I was delighted to make a series of announcements at call-over (a roll call in the House) which showed the range of success the House had enjoyed over the past few days. Blair Abbiss had been awarded his School 1st XV Lion, and Mark Lawrence had been chosen to sing the solo at next week's Churchill Songs. Furthermore, Tom Oakley and David Noad learned this morning that they had both been awarded Army scholarships. This was a great achievement as there were some 400 applicants nationally and only 45 awards. Harrow had done exceptionally well in getting five of those 45 and I was thrilled for the boys.

Thursday 27 November

Another interesting letter arrived today, from Antigua in the West Indies:

> My name is Angernel Aaron and I am 11 years old. I am doing a project for school and would like some information on foot bill. I would like some information on refereeing and a list of the Laws. And something on fouls and how not to get one and any other important information. Please answer.
>   Yours truly
>   Angernel Aaron

How could I not reply to that?

After a House Master's meeting, Glynn Jenkins, matron and I took 45 Drurieans to see *The Mousetrap* in London. I always enjoy an evening off and an escape from football. But it was not to be a complete escape as I bumped into Brian Hill and his wife at the theatre. Brian was a top FIFA referee when I was working my way up and I had admired him greatly, even though his relaxed style of officiating was very different from mine.

I always feel somewhat guilty when I see Brian as I refereed at Wembley when the Football League took him off the Burnley v Stockport 1994 play-off final after he had criticised the League. It was a notable game not only because I showed two red cards and eight yellow cards but also because it was the 2,000th match of my career. The previous week I had refereed the FA Cup Final (my 1999th game) and I had been a touch disappointed that it had not been my landmark match. However, when the Football League phoned to ask me to replace Brian I had been thrilled that my 2,000th match would be at Wembley – the Mecca of football.

Friday 28 November

A very important day not in football terms but because the Harrow School governors convened for their two-day meeting and the topic of the next Head Master was high on the agenda. I was visited by one governor for an informal discussion in the afternoon and in the evening all the House Masters and senior masters dined with the governors.

I was sitting with Professor Mingos and the subjects ranged mainly across academic matters and sport. Afterwards, however, I went for drinks with a group of governors and masters to a colleague's house, and was grilled by one governor after another. They seemed very positive and encouraging although 'we are making you no promises' was the loudest of all the messages. I got to bed about 1.30 a.m. inspired by the growing challenge but not a little daunted.

Saturday 29 November

As part of the governors' autumn meeting the entire School assembles in Speech Room with the boys in tails for the Head of School's Contio, a report to the governors of events international, national and local, on behalf of the entire school. Contio is delivered in Latin and dates back to at least 1674, and at the front of the booklet containing the Latin and English translation, is the list of all the previous Heads of School who have delivered Contio. Daniel Hepher, my Head of House, stood on the stage in his tails, white waistcoat and white bow tie and delivered one of the best Contios in recent memory. Over six foot tall, he had the poise and presence to maintain the attention and respect of the School, and his performance was greeted with very warm applause at the end. The Chairman of the Governors, Sir Michael Connell, thanked Daniel and reminded the school of the importance of Contio and how, if Harrow could not spare 20 minutes each year to maintain a centuries-old tradition, then it would be a poorer place. He also launched a stout defence of Classics and his words had great effect, not least as he himself had delivered Contio some 39 years earlier.

I returned to my form room to teach. In a hectic day, I entertained a group of parents to lunch before the rugby matches and then some of the junior boys came for supper. Having had a late night I tried to snatch an hour's sleep in the afternoon but, as often happens, my attempts were thwarted: the fire alarm sounded and we had trouble with overheating in the boiler room which meant a weekend of no heating for me and the boys.

Sunday 30 November

Another hectic day, but no football. I entertained about 30 people to drinks after Tom Forman Hardy was confirmed by the Bishop of

London, followed by a lunch with Tom, his family and godparents. I left this early to return to chapel to attend Henry Gates' first communion as a Roman Catholic, and entertained his parents and sister afterwards. In the evening I had the triumphant assault course team for a celebration supper. Among all this I had to mark lots of papers and try to absorb the messages filtering back from the governors' meeting.

December 1997

Monday 1 December

The morning was dominated by press inquiries following comments from Gordon Strachan after Coventry's home defeat by Leicester. During the game the Leicester goalkeeper handled the ball outside the penalty area and there was some dispute as to whether Martin Bodenham should have sent him off. Some colleagues phoned and said that we should have the incident on video for our next meeting. Strachan had implied at the press conference afterwards that the decision not to send off the goalkeeper was part of a conspiracy by referees against Coventry in retaliation for his attack on me at Derby last week. I told the press that I was not going to dignify such comments with a response but, off the record, explained that it was part of a smoke screen by Strachan to divert attention from the problems he and his team were having. As I explained, any such conspiracy would never take place and, anyway, it would easily be spotted by fans, the media and the Premier League observers. One of the reasons why English referees are in such demand throughout the world is because we have a reputation for total integrity. We may not be error-free but we are certainly corruption-free.

After a morning's teaching I went to Eagle House School in Berkshire to referee their under-13 1st XI match against Sunningdale. It was an excellent game with Sunningdale being 4–0 up at half-time but Eagle House fighting back to 'win' the second half 1–0. The boys were very sporting and afterwards I presented them all with Premier League badges and gave 'Man of the Match' awards to Fred Milne of Sunningdale (who is due to come to Harrow) and Tom Evans of Eagle House. After tea I gave a short talk about refereeing in the Premier League and answered questions from a group of about 50 boys. Their knowledge of, and fascination with, football was quite incredible and I had a really enjoyable afternoon. Back at Harrow I discovered that news of the governors' approach to me had become pretty widespread knowledge and many colleagues were expressing support for my appointment and were going to write to the Chairman in that vein. So in the end a really good day.

Tuesday 2 December

One of the less pleasant sides of refereeing arose this morning when Jeff Winter contacted me about an abusive letter he had received from a fan. Whilst referees accept the abuse at matches – some fans get great enjoyment from shouting at the referee – the abusive phone calls and hate mail are a step too far. It was an attack on his refereeing of Liverpool v Barnsley at the weekend. It finished, sickeningly, with:

> You should be struck off. You are a known Manchester United fan, and would do anything to help the Scum. I hope you and your entire family are killed in an horrific accident you bastard the more horrific the better and then I can read with joy about your death.

Apart from the offensive and sick nature of the letter, the most annoying aspect was that it was sent to Jeff c/o the FA. I have been battling for several years to try to get the FA to open all mail that is sent to them for referees and only pass on that which is worth receiving. They have a moral duty to protect referees from this upsetting and offensive material.

Wednesday 3 December

The second attempt at the West Ham v Crystal Palace match. After a dreadful drive through central London I arrived at Upton Park to teasing about the lights and whether I had brought my torch or miner's hat. In reply I enquired whether they had paid the electricity bill this time so we would not be cut off. The assistant referees were the same but Martin Bodenham was the reserve referee and Roy Capey the match observer. In the event it was another entertaining match with West Ham running out 4–1 winners and Crystal Palace's performance being described as 'rubbish' by Steve Coppell. As with the first game there was not a great deal to referee and I only had one yellow card. Just before half-time I collided with Steve Lomas of West Ham as he tried to run into position. It was a very good body check on my part and I was pleased he did not knock me over. Now Steve is usually one of those players who talks about every decision and keeps a referee on his toes. In the second half he hardly said a word and towards the end I asked him if he was all right. He answered that he was keeping away from me after the forearm smash I'd given him in the first half. What he had not realised was that I had hit him with the arm which had the electronic receiver for the flags strapped on it and by the next day I had a huge bruise the shape of the receiver.

Thursday 4 December

The FA phoned to see if I would like to accept an invitation to go to Egypt to referee their National League play-off match at the end of the next week. Unfortunately, it clashed with the end of term at Harrow when I would have to be at school for the carol service, Christmas dinner and Songs. It was a great pity, as I would have loved to have gone to Egypt, despite the recent problem with terrorists at Luxor.

In the same conversation Ken Ridden informed me that I had been appointed to referee the first leg of the UEFA Super Cup Final between the Champions' League winners (Borussia Dortmund) and the Cup Winners' Cup winners (Barcelona) in Spain in early January. Having refereed in the Nou Camp for Barcelona's quarter-final last year I was delighted to get another chance to visit one of the best grounds in the world. It was also a prestigious appointment and I would become the first English referee to officiate in the Super Cup Final for 21 years. As Steve Lodge had retired I would have another reserve referee and the FA had, happily, chosen Gary Willard.

Ken also told me that he had informed FIFA of my availability problems for the World Cup but they would not be announcing the panel until 2 February – if the news could be kept quiet until then. He also mentioned that Sandor Puhl, who refereed the World Cup Final in 1994, had been told by UEFA that he would receive no more appointments from them for the rest of the season following a series of difficulties culminating in his refereeing of the Feyenoord v Manchester United match in the Champions' League. In that game there was a horrendous challenge on Denis Irwin which went unpunished but, even worse, when Puhl viewed it on the video he declared that he did not think it merited any significant punishment and certainly no more than a yellow card. With almost the whole of football agreed that it was a dreadful tackle deserving a red card, UEFA called Puhl's judgement into question and suspended him. It came as no surprise for, regardless of how good a referee he is, his off the field behaviour and demeanour leave a great deal to be desired and he is a very poor role model for other referees.

Friday 5 December

A major day in the Harrow School calendar with Churchill Songs. In 1940, in the darkest days of the Second World War, Winston Churchill's private secretary, Jock Colville (an Old Harrovian) was taking some papers up to him in the flat at No. 10 Downing Street. Colville heard Churchill singing a Harrow Song lustily. He organised for Churchill to visit his old school, as Harrow had not been evacuated from London. The whole school assembled in the main hall and sang songs to Churchill and a number of the War Cabinet. This so impressed him and cheered him up he returned to Harrow annually until he died. Consequently, each year we have Churchill Songs when a distinguished speaker addresses the school and Harrow Songs are sung. This year it was Sir Robin Butler, Cabinet Secretary and head of the Home Civil Service who is an old boy of Harrow and my House, Druries.

I had invited various friends for drinks beforehand including Lord Patten (formerly John Patten, the Education Secretary) who had been my tutor when I was in Oxford.   After songs I entertained the Head of School's parents to dinner along with another colleague, Peter Hunter, and Ann Longley, formerly Headmistress of Roedean School and now a Harrow governor.

Dinner was not too lengthy as I knew I had to drive north for tomorrow's match at Anfield. Returning to the House to collect my bags I found an urgent message on my answerphone which involved spending the next hour sorting out a problem in the House. Consequently, I did not leave Harrow until 10.20 p.m. and did not arrive at my hotel in Walsall until just after midnight. As I drove up the motorway I again questioned whether I really needed such a busy schedule at this stage in my life, and cursed Sky TV for organising an 11.15 a.m. kick-off.

Saturday 6 December

I awoke at 6 a.m. after barely five hours' sleep and bathed and dressed before Mark Warren picked me up at 7 a.m. for the drive to Anfield. The stress before a Liverpool v Manchester United game is always great for the two sets of supporters really do not like each other and there is fierce rivalry between the players. As we travelled north my mind went back over the previous two seasons when I had refereed this fixture, but each time at Old Trafford. The most memorable was in 1995 when the match had been Eric Cantona's comeback after suspension following his flying kick at a fan at Crystal Palace. I had rather foolishly allowed myself to be interviewed by a newspaper before the game and had said some things which were taken out of context and not helped me. We made good time and arrived at 8.25 a.m., and I had a snooze on the way.

Peter Walton, the other assistant, arrived soon after us and quickly the three of us fell asleep in the dressing room, only waking up when Steve Lodge arrived. It is strange how getting up in the dark and travelling to a match so early has that effect on people but I felt as if I had no energy whatsoever.

However, walking out on to the field at 11.10 a.m. woke us all up and the rush of adrenaline was immense for this is one of the biggest fixtures in the Premier League calendar. The early exchanges were strong and I showed yellow cards in the 9th, 10th and 11th minutes for fouls by Johnsen, Butt (Manchester United) and Carragher respectively. Jason McAteer of Liverpool told me that I should not be so strong as it was just Liverpool v Manchester United but I replied that that was exactly why I was being strong. Anyway, this had the desired effect as the rest of the game was played in a very good spirit and I only had one more card, for Jamie Redknapp, four minutes from the end. At half-time it was 0–0 and there had been a lot of good football but lots of player mistakes as well. After half-time Manchester United scored and then Liverpool equalised when I judged that Butt and Neville had fouled Michael Owen in the penalty area. The Manchester United players protested a little but it was rather muted compared to what they can produce so I was happy with the decision. It had the effect of lifting the Liverpool crowd and also the Manchester United players who scored two more goals and coasted home. Perhaps the best was the third one, a fantastic free-kick by David Beckham. The sheer quality of Manchester United's play shone through and at one point their fans sang 'Outclassed by the Champions' addressed to the Liverpool team, and there was no denying that. Everyone seemed happy and we left the field to warm handshakes from all the players. I had been able to talk them through the game and avoid controversy – not easy when Liverpool play Manchester United.

In the dressing room afterwards Arthur Jones, the Premier League match observer, seemed happy and also felt that the three cautions early in the first half had done the trick and had enabled me to play lots of advantage and help the game flow. Martin Tyler came in for his usual chat and was complimentary and we had an interesting discussion about the positive effect of strong refereeing on the standard of play in the Premier League. As we were leaving the ground we learned that Alex Ferguson had agreed with the penalty – a rarity that! – and had praised our officiating, and the Liverpool staff (Roy Evans, Ronnie Moran and Joe Corrigan) wished us well for the Christmas period, so we seemed to have emerged unscathed.

Driving home I listened to the thrilling 29–29 draw in the Rugby Union international between England and the All Blacks, taking a particular interest as Roger Uttley from Harrow was part of the management team. I marvelled at how my mood had changed from the rather resentful one last night as I flogged north. But now, in the after-glow of an excellent match I again realised what a big part of my life refereeing is and how I shall miss it when I retire. As far as other results were concerned I was interested in Coventry's 3–0 defeat by Aston Villa and the news that they had had two players sent off. Now that would give Gordon Strachan more cause to suspect a referees' conspiracy.

Sunday 7 December

A very satisfactory feeling today as the match yesterday went well and what little comment there was in the newspapers was complimentary. Patrick Barclay in the *Sunday Telegraph* described me as refereeing with 'wise zeal'. It seemed an odd phrase but it is one that I was happy with. I reflected that matters had been helped by my having refereed both clubs many times in the past, and already this season.

I have an excellent relationship with the vast majority of the Manchester United and Liverpool players as we have got to know each other well over the years. Ironically, some of the players I get on best with are those that I have sent off in the past, with the main exception of Roy Keane, whom I have sent off twice and who, quite understandably, seems scarcely able to bring himself to speak to me.

Another interesting reaction was that I did not feel too tired after the exertions, but that merely emphasises how morale has a large effect on feelings of well-being. If there had been much controversy and I had thought that I had refereed badly then I am sure I would feel low and tired. I was glad to be facing a break from football for a while which would allow me to cope with the pressures and tiredness which are the inevitable companions of the end of term.

Monday 8 December

At Monday morning school assembly I congratulated Roger Uttley on the great rugby result for England. Roger mentioned that he and the rest of the England team had watched Liverpool v Manchester United as part of their pre-match relaxation. Several colleagues were quick to point out how Harrow was very closely involved in the two sporting highlights of the weekend.

In the afternoon Druries won the quarter-finals of the House and Torpid rugby matches. The end of term academic reports were starting to filter through so I could begin the task of writing my detailed report on each of the 56 boys in my House.

Tuesday 9 December

Lessons started early today as a large number of the boys were going to Twickenham to watch the Varsity rugby match. This gave me the afternoon free to get on with my reports and clear the paperwork on my desk. In the evening I was in the boys' side of the House sorting out sketches for the end of term festivities. When I returned there was a message on my answerphone. Apparently, I was the subject of a question on *University Challenge*. The 'starter question for 10' asked which school I taught at and one of the teams knew the answer. It was useful publicity for Harrow, as I later pointed out to the Head Master.

Wednesday 10 December

A busy day finalising senior boys' geography project work for their A level and also watching the rugby semi-finals. We were defeated easily by Bradbys in the House semi but the Torpids played well to win their semi-final. In the evening I went to the CCF annual dinner.

The dress was either black tie or uniform and medals (miniatures) and I was tempted to wear my FA Cup Final gold medal.

Thursday 11 December

I taught all morning and worked at my desk in the afternoon. I declined an invitation from *Planet 24* to appear on a *Referees v Managers Christmas Quiz* being filmed on Sunday, as I would be too busy with reports. In the evening I took almost all the House, plus 14 boys from other Houses, to the first night of the new James Bond film. This was a reward for the House for doing so well in all competitions this term, and a way of keeping them occupied and out of trouble. I ordered 60 Big Mac meals in McDonald's on the way and we took over the top floor after the film. Some of the boys were full of the awful things that people in the cinema audience had been saying when they recognised me. They get a perverse pleasure in my being the subject of abuse.

Friday 12 December

The last full day of term. In the afternoon we lost heavily to Elmfield in the final of the Torpids rugby and there was a thrilling House final (Cock House match, as it is called) between the Head Master's House and Bradbys, generally regarded as one of the best games for a long time. There was a sporting moment when Will Matthews, the Head Master's House captain, offered the draw to the Bradbys captain when the scores drew level at 39–39 before Will's side could take a conversion. The offer was declined but the sportsmanship was rewarded as they went on to win 48–39.

We then had the carol service which included two Drurieans, Daniel Hepher and Sam Stevens, reading lessons. At eight o'clock the entire school and guests – almost 1,000 people – assembled in the dining hall for a full Christmas dinner with crackers and party hats. Bagpipes escorted the Christmas pudding around the hall. We then returned to Druries for House Songs. Each year-group put on a small play, usually a parody of the masters or other members of the House, interspersed with us all singing various Harrow Songs. After that the House watched videos until late and I entertained the senior boys and guests. The last left at about four in the morning and I fell into bed at 4.15 a.m. only to get up three hours later.

Saturday 13 December

Considering I had only three hours' sleep I was remarkably alert as I went round the House checking everything was tidy before having the final call-over of the term and sending the boys off to various corners of the world. It is always strange that at 9 a.m. the House is full of bustle and noise and by 11 a.m. everything is quiet. It takes a while to adjust so I went out to lunch. I returned home, had a quick nap and then went out to supper with friends before getting to bed early, forsaking *Match of the Day* for some much needed sleep.

Sunday 14 December

Up early and at the computer to carry on with the House reports. In each one I try to deal with the academic work and extra-curricular activities and then give a general review of how the boy is developing, his relationships with others and things for him to think about.

Lunchtime was a drinks party at Roger Uttley's house intended primarily for the rugby masters. It was a good excuse to escape from the reports, but I soon returned to my desk as I try to be the first House Master to finish, not least because they are a great burden which it is wonderful to get rid of. I worked all afternoon and then had supper with a colleague friend.

Monday 15 December

The morning was spent with more reports and the general paperwork which takes up the beginning of the holidays – newsletters to parents, bills, accounts, letters and the Christmas cards, which I had not yet started. There was a nice letter in the *Daily Telegraph* about my refereeing along with a less than flattering caricature drawing. The letter said:

> Sir,
>
> Watching the Liverpool v Manchester United match last weekend so expertly and calmly refereed by David Elleray, I couldn't help wondering what he was being paid in comparison with those he was controlling.

At lunchtime I went into London for a meeting at the FA to discuss the proposed Channel Four documentary looking at Premier League referees. The producers were very keen, but Ken Ridden and Mike Foster of the Premier League were most reluctant, as they feared that there was a real danger of the referees involved being stitched up, as is the case with so many of these 'fly on the wall' documentary programmes. I was disappointed to learn from Ken that Gary Willard was no longer my reserve referee for the match in Barcelona, but delighted to be taking Peter Jones, who is one of the nicest officials in the Premier League. Ken told me that I had been appointed to the Barnsley v Bolton third-round FA Cup tie which pleased me greatly as I had not been to Barnsley for a long while and certainly not since they made the major ground improvements. With Steve Lodge appointed to Chelsea v Manchester United it meant that I could stay with the Lodge family the day before my match and they could then come down and stay with me before Steve's game on the Sunday.

Tuesday 16 December

Reports were finally finished – *jubilate*! To celebrate, Hugh Thompson and I entertained a former House Master and his wife, David and Shirley Parry, to dinner. I returned home to find a message on my answerphone saying that I had featured on *Question of Sport* again. This time the footage of me changing shirts at Leeds earlier in the season had been used as a 'What happened next?' question.

I was delighted to receive my assessment from the match observer of the Liverpool v Manchester United match, who gave me an 'E' grading which is the highest category – the first time it had been given to a Premier League referee this season. It is the grade for an 'exceptional' performance and no more than half a dozen are awarded each year, usually for top-quality performances in high-profile matches in which the referee is under a lot of pressure. The FA also sent me the Manchester United club report at the end of which was the comment, 'A first-class performance by a referee on top of his game.' Fortunately, they do not send us the club reports when we have upset them.

Wednesday 17 December

The cleaning ladies finished sorting out the House today and I had them through at lunchtime for nibbles and drinks. I then gave lunch to Matthew Swift, one of my House tutors, and had a long meeting with the bursar to review the term's work and progress. In the evening I entertained various colleagues to drinks and we had a takeaway Chinese meal. While driving to get the food I listened to the commentary on the Newcastle v Derby match, which Keith Burge was refereeing. Alan Jones, a self-confessed referee-hater, was commentating along with Mark Lawrenson and they were eulogising Keith's refereeing, a surprising state of affairs. Anyway, normal service was resumed when Keith sent off a Derby player – he suddenly went from being 'outstandingly good and sensible' to making the 'worst refereeing decision' they had seen for a long time.

Thursday 18 December

A little shopping and a final few hours at the desk, mainly writing Christmas cards. I was due to go to the Football Writers Association Christmas drinks party but could not because I had to be at Harrow for a function and also because the Head Master and his wife were coming for supper. The evening function was a get-together of the staff who had been appointed to start the new Harrow International School in Thailand. Some of the Harrow masters had been asked to go along and it was an enjoyable evening meeting old friends, not least the new Head Master, Stuart Morris. They invited me to go and referee their first school football match. I also chatted to one master who was already working in Thailand and who saw so much Premier League football on TV that he felt he knew me very well.

Friday 19 December

A busy day in London. It started with a meeting at Bloomsbury, the publishers of this book, to review progress and to meet those people who would be responsible for the marketing and sales of the book. We discussed the jacket cover, which I did not especially like, but I could understand its attractiveness in terms of marketing. The notion of having the front red and the back yellow as in red and yellow cards was a good one. What I did not like was the photo which, with my hair sticking up and a glow around me, made it look as if I'd plugged myself into the electricity socket. I suggested adding an exclamation mark at the end of the title so that it reads *Referee!* (as if someone was shouting it). I then went across London to the FA for another meeting with Ken Ridden to discuss the agenda for the forthcoming meeting of FIFA officials, Premier League officials and match observers. We agreed that Ken would announce at the FIFA meeting in early January that I would not be available for selection for the World Cup. We also discussed what video clips we might use for the forthcoming meetings.

In the evening I dined with Judith Affleck and other colleagues and friends, retiring about one in the morning to ensure that I have some energy left for the match tomorrow.

Saturday 20 December

A good drive to Villa Park, a ground I always enjoy. Phil Sharp and Pete Walton were my assistants and I arrived at the same time as Pete who I had been teasing for most of the season as he seemed slightly over-weight; his wife had joined me in my campaign. Pete usually likes to eat before a match and when the road to the car park was blocked by a van delivering meat pies I had plenty of ammunition to attack Pete with. The match observer was Dennis Hedges, who had been with me when I abandoned the game at West Ham, and he was concerned that he was a jinx as he had had trouble at other matches recently. While we were having tea Keith Wiseman, Chairman of the FA, arrived and we had a long chat about the Christmas programme. We also exchanged reminiscences of Saudi Arabia as he had just been out there for part of the Confederation Cup and had succeeded in getting Saudi Arabia to come to Wembley to play England as part of the World Cup warm-up programme. Keith is always a down-to-earth man who has time for everyone and is an excellent communicator on behalf of the FA.

Pre-match Doug Ellis, the Aston Villa chairman, popped in to the dressing room for a chat. He asked how things were at Harrow and what the fees were. An odd question, it seemed to me, but it transpired that in their recent match in Romania against Steaua Bucharest, Aston Villa had visited an orphanage and been very moved by the plight of the children. Doug had raised money to help the orphanage and was considering sponsoring a boy to come to England to go to school. He thought that he would send the boy to Repton where his grandson had been but I was happy to suggest Harrow as an alternative. The generosity of Doug and the players was another example of how the good that football does is often ignored by the headline writers.

The match was a poor one with a lot of player errors and very few fouls. For the second time this season I had no yellow cards, indeed there were only 10 fouls in each half. Rapport was good with the players, especially Matt Le Tissier, Jason Dodd, Francis Benali, Ken Monkou, Kevin Richardson and Matthew Oakley of Southampton, and Gareth Southgate, Steve Staunton and Ian Taylor of Villa.

The only contentious moment was towards the end with the score at 1–1 when I gave a free-kick to Southampton. Matt Le Tissier took it quickly but several yards on from where the incident had occurred. I had gone to the place were the foul had been committed and thus had to order a retake. Unfortunately, I had briefly turned as if to give the goal and this confused the players. When I explained that I had turned because I thought the ball had gone for a goal-kick they understood – well some of them did. The game finished without trouble and most players shook hands. Le Tissier waited for me at the dressing room to enquire politely what had happened, and I was happy to explain.

Leaving the ground I was stopped by the press for an explanation, but it took some time for them to follow the niceties of the Laws. I explained that the free-kick had been taken from the wrong place as everyone realised. However, had it gone for a goal-kick, Southampton would not have had the kick again because they had tried to benefit from taking it from the wrong place so they had infringed the Laws and I would give the advantage to Villa and restart with a goal-kick. The fact that a 'goal' had resulted meant Southampton had benefited, so the kick had to be retaken. It was, I said, rather like a player taking the throw-in from the wrong place but throwing the ball to the opponents. You wouldn't stop play and order the throw to be retaken; you would allow the advantage to the opponents and let them keep possession. I then did an interview with Tony Gubba for *Match of the Day*. Interestingly, several reporters thought I had played a few seconds short in each half; I probably had – it was such an awful game and there had been no stoppages.

That evening I had dinner with Peter Brandwood and his family in a wonderful restaurant near Walsall, aptly named the Old School House. They assured me it was not a football place, but as we finished our meal a group which included several Villa fans collared me and we had a most enjoyable review of the afternoon's match before I drove home through the fog.

Sunday 21 December

I awoke to find a message on my answerphone from Jeff Winter who had had a stormy match between Leicester and Everton. He had cautioned eight players and there had been a controversial penalty, although once people had seen the video of the incident it became clear that he had been correct. Jeff was after advice for his report to the FA about Martin O'Neill, the Leicester manager, who had behaved appallingly after the match both in terms of language used and gestures made. Jeff wanted to mention in his report that O'Neill had been about to throw a water bottle at the match officials but was restrained by a steward. I suggested to him that he should be careful with his report as it would be difficult to justify what he *thought* was going to happen and that he might be better to stick to facts rather than supposition. I spent the rest of the morning shopping for the last few Christmas presents and then had lunch with Holly, Anna, Lucy and Emma – four of my god-daughters who are a great source of joy to me.

I also have two other god-daughters, Katie and my niece Sarah, as well as two god-sons, Barnaby and Michael.

I looked through the *Match of the Day* video of yesterday's game to check what actually happened with that free-kick. Tony Gubba had started by describing me as 'probably the most famous schoolmaster in the country', but my handling of that particular incident did not bring me any pleasure. I had created a controversy from almost nothing. It was not good refereeing and it disappointed me. Perhaps a recent comment in the *Guardian* that I have 'a Branson balloon-sized ego' had some validity and I was getting a little too overconfident, especially in the latter stages of a match that has been relatively easy to control.

In the afternoon I worked at my desk and took a short nap before going to the chaplain's house to celebrate his birthday with his wife and a few friends. It developed into a long night and I got to bed about 2.30 a.m. It is so nice, with term ended, to have a bit of a social life.

Monday 22 December

The final morning of letter writing, interrupted by news from Oxford University. Two Drurieans had been successful and two had not. Rupert Lion had been offered a place (subject to gaining three A grades at A level) at St Edmund Hall and St Hugh's had accepted Nicolai Roterman, who was unsuccessful last year.

The press had a busy morning wanting comments about Kenny

Dalglish's attack on Peter Jones's refereeing of the Newcastle v Manchester United match yesterday. The victory for Manchester United effectively put Newcastle out of the championship race and there had been seven bookings and Kenny was clearly looking to deflect blame from himself and his team. I reiterated to the press my view that managers should follow the LMA agreement that they should not criticise referees in public, but there is little chance of that, as we can see from the papers every week.

The other press issue was diving and feigning injury, which George Graham of Leeds had raised over the weekend. I outlined that the Premier League referees had agreed to caution a player if he dived when there was no contact. When there is some contact, the referee's task of judging the severity of the offence is made that much more difficult. There is also a knock-on effect that often leads to confrontation. A player who exaggerates a foul is supported by his team-mates who are also conned and think the referee should act strongly. The opponents protest against the over-reaction, as they see it, and there is the poor referee in the middle of it all. It really is a problem that the LMA and PFA should sort out – can they really condone and accept fellow professionals trying to get each other into trouble?

Each season there is one issue which seems to dominate refereeing concerns. A few years ago it was the illegal use of the elbow, as shown at its worst by Fashanu's clash with Gary Mabbutt; this season diving and over-reaction to tackles were taking over as the issues of the season.

I slept for most of the afternoon and spent the evening wrapping presents and watching Wimbledon v Arsenal. What an irony that the lights went out and the match had to be abandoned just after half-time. One relieved man would have been Paul Alcock who was the reserve official. He is a good Premier League referee but he was going to have to run the line for the second half after one of the assistants had a nose bleed and could not continue. This being the third time a Premier League match had been abandoned this season through floodlight failure, the Premier League were going to have to act strongly and decisively as players and fans cannot accept that, with millions of pounds in the game, there are no reserve generators to cope with such situations. But the problem is that failure in the power supply may not be the cause of the trouble; at West Ham it was the circuits burning out, so a spare generator would have been of no use.

Tuesday 23 December

I was disturbed at my desk by a reporter from the *Daily Mirror* wanting to know my views on the Arsenal v Leicester match due for Boxing Day. He was trying to see if there was a story, after the game at Filbert Street earlier in the season, when Graham Barber had difficulties over the amount of stoppage time he allowed at the end, and there was a clash between Ian Wright and Steve Walsh. I did my best to say that I expected no trouble and hoped that the Christmas spirit would prevail. The press were also full of debate following last night's abandonment at Selhurst Park and there were strong demands for the Premier League to require clubs to invest in back-up generators.

Of somewhat embarrassing interest was a piece in the 'Peterborough' section of the *Daily Telegraph* which ran:

> *On the ball*
> *Is Harrow, the north London boarding school, set to become a footballing centre of excellence after years of rugby? As the current Head Master prepares to retire, the staff room, I gather, feels that smart money goes on David Elleray, a Harrow House Master and leading football referee.*
>
> *Elleray – a cult figure among soccer fans, who holds the record for the quickest red card ever issued in a League game (four seconds after kick-off, to Vinnie Jones) – is also an enthusiastic proponent of soccer at Harrow and reintroduced it after a 50-year absence. He would, I am told, make a strict and courageous head.*

The last thing I needed at this stage was for such speculation to appear in the national press; the only consolation was that it was a reasonably flattering piece. The puzzle was who was the mole leaking information to the press, and especially to the *Daily Telegraph*, as this was the third time 'inside information' about Harrow had appeared in that column.

In the afternoon I was queuing at a till in Marks & Spencer when the man behind me dropped several £20 notes. I made some remark about giving money away for Christmas and he suggested I might like it as a bribe. As we waited we discussed football and he was still shocked by the Chelsea v Leeds match he had attended some 10 days ago. It was just like the rough houses of the 1960s, he commented. By the time I returned home there was already a fax from an Old Druriean commenting on the piece in the *Daily Telegraph*.

Wednesday 24 December

Final preparations for Christmas. I spent four hours wrapping up the last of the presents and then delivering some of them to my various godchildren. As I have done since I was confirmed, I went to midnight mass. I find the service and taking communion a very important part of Christmas and it gives me time to think about what has been and what might be, and to give thanks for the many happy times I have had and all the luck that has come my way.

Thursday 25 December

Up early to drive across to Essex for Christmas with my parents, sister, brother-in-law and niece and nephew. My mother's illness over Christmas in previous years makes it a somewhat anxious time, but this was a wonderfully relaxing day with everyone on good form, no tension and none of the family rows that can blight family Christmases. I had a generous number of presents but a not too generous Christmas lunch and only one glass of wine because of the match tomorrow. At least, unlike the footballers, I was not summoned to training.

My mind strayed back a number of years to when I was due to referee Oldham v Liverpool on Boxing Day. The weather was bad and at five o'clock on Christmas afternoon I got a phone call from Oldham wanting a pitch inspection at ten the next morning. I regarded this as totally unreasonable as there had been several days of heavy frost and I also knew that Oldham had had two local Football League referees in to inspect the pitch. They had told Oldham there was no chance of playing and had also phoned me to let me know the state of affairs. Oldham, however, were desperate to play the game as it was due to go out live on Sky and they wanted the revenue. Sky were equally eager to have an early pitch inspection so they could switch to another match if necessary. I therefore had the choice of leaving Harrow and driving the 280 miles to Oldham that evening or getting up early the next morning. I decided on the latter and rose at five o'clock on Boxing Day to drive north through ice, frost and fog and arrive at

Oldham at 9.50 a.m. The pitch was three-quarters frozen and once I had got a few Oldham apprentices to kick a ball about and watched them slip and fall at every turn, I called the game off and journeyed home. I was exceedingly angry but nothing was done about it except that, since then, the Premier League has tended to keep referees more 'local' at Christmas. At least tomorrow I was only going to Highbury and their undersoil heating would guarantee few problems.

Friday 26 December

A beautiful, mild sunny morning. A very easy drive to Highbury with little traffic on the road. Phil Sharp and Mark Warren were already there and Philip Don, the Premier League match observer, soon arrived. Everywhere was rather quiet but by the time of kick-off there were just over 38,000 people in the stadium. I had left tickets for my father, my brother-in-law Billy and my nephew David. While my father often comes to my London matches, Billy and David rarely do as they are fervent supporters of Dagenham and Redbridge. Billy is a local league referee and seemed to be taking to it very well indeed.

The quality of football was poor for most of the match but the players were in good spirits and there were no signs of the problems that had marred the game at Filbert Street earlier in the season. Ian Wright was chatty and Steve Walsh in excellent form, excellent that is until he scored a quite spectacular own goal from about 25 yards out to make the score 2–0 to Arsenal. For the next five minutes he completely lost it and I was talking to him, desperately trying to calm him down as the red mist had descended and he was charging into tackles in a manner that threatened to get him sent off. Leicester then pulled one back after an attempted dribble by David Seaman. The final 10 minutes were full of action and I had visions of Leicester equalising in the stoppage time which was necessary. In the event it finished 2–1 and all the players were cheerful at the end.

Ian Wright is a much more temperamental player than someone like Steve Bould (though he also moans occasionally) or David Seaman, who give no trouble and get on with their game almost regardless of what is happening. Ian had been in good form and there was none of the aggression which appears when he is not playing well.

Martin O'Neill, however, was not happy and harangued me and Phil Sharp as we left the field. He thought there should have been a penalty for some shirt tugging on Emile Heskey in the closing minutes.

I had seen the incident and felt that they were both pulling each other's shirts (a common occurrence these days). Although Martin was not as out of control as he obviously had been with Jeff Winter last weekend, he was not happy and I hurried to the dressing room hoping to avoid a confrontation. About 10 minutes later there was a knock on the door and it was Martin asking for a word. I was about to suggest he came back later (when he might be calmer) when he simply said that he had come to apologise for he had spoken to Emile Heskey who had not thought it was a penalty, and he felt it only right to come and apologise. I gave him great credit for having the honesty to do that. Most managers believe they are right, and even if they discover they are wrong they rarely say so. For Martin to come and apologise spoke volumes for his integrity, and while not excusing some of his lapses of control, one can not but have respect for him.

After the match I had dinner with Philip Don, his wife Judith and son Tim, who hopes to be in the Olympic triathlon team in Australia in 2000: Philip and I have been close friends for many years as we were on the Football League line together, we both got promoted to the Football League and FIFA referees' lists at the same time and had a fierce but friendly rivalry until he had to retire after the 1994 World Cup, because of pressure of work at his school where he is Head Master. We recalled over supper how we had both run the line at Highbury on Boxing Day about 12 years ago when the hospitality was so awful the only way we could get a cup of tea before the match was to go outside to a hot dog stand. Things are much better there now, not least because of the interest and impact of David Dein.

Saturday 27 December

A quick visit to the sales convinced me it was not a day for shopping. I wrote the reports on the three yellow cards from yesterday's match and reflected on my refereeing of the game. It had not been easy as the football was poor and I was keen not to intervene too much and spoil what little pattern to play there was. I did not make any major mistakes but I was aware of one or two small decisions I had got wrong and I had just not felt totally at my best. Perhaps I was not mentally as sharp as usual. Almost no one would have noticed that I was below par, indeed as there was no controversy and I did very little, I would have generally been regarded as having had a good game under the old adage that 'a good referee is one you don't notice',

my academic gown for a formal Harrow photograph: the boys pose with
e straw hats which are worn to lessons.

The stunning King Fahd International Stadium rises out of the desert on the edge of Riyadh.

Inspecting the pitch with Paul Vosper and Steve Lodge before the Saudi Arabia v China World Cup qualifier.

Keeping a close eye as Saudi Arabia attack China during the match.

Phil Sharp, Peter Jones and Mark Warren line up with me before the Barcelona v Borussia Dortmund UEFA Super Cup Final. Peter Jones is evidently having trouble with his shorts.

The elegant female translator entertains us to a post-match meal under the watchful eye of the UEFA observer.

The riot police ensure I am protected from the 100,000 fans as I leave the field at the Morumbi Stadium in São Paulo.

Hamann (Germany) gets a yellow card playing Brazil – once I can get the pencil out of my sock.

razil captain Dunga gets the yellow-red card treatment. In this 'friendship' atch I showed two red and six yellow cards.

A GAZETA esportiva

FRANCE 98
COUPE DU MONDE

AGÊNCIA

OLHA LÁ, HEIN, MISTER ELLEARY!

Depois que o juiz argentino Javier Castrilli arruinou a Portuguesa no último domingo, todos os olhos estarão voltados hoje para o inglês David Elleary, que apitará São Paulo x Corinthians, na primeira partida da decisão do Campeonato Paulista

Match-day newspaper headlines in São Paulo read, 'Watch it, Mr Elleary!'

miling faces from current Harrow boys and Old Drurieans at the Founders' ay football match.

roudly standing with the Druries Platoon who, as inter-house CCF Champions, on the Ansell Bowl.

Umpiring the Torpid Seconders Harrow Football Final: Druries v Head Master's.

Note the large ball and the umpire's stick – there is no whistle.

At the end the victorious Drurieans watch the losers trudge away.

Relaxing with my four godchildren (from left to right): Emma, Anna, Holly and Lucy.

Watching the inter-house cross-country run with other House Masters, whose grim expressions indicate another victory for Druries.

Refereeing at Elland Road in a Leeds United blue training top because my referee's shirt clashed with Newcastle's away strip.

Dan Petrescu (Chelsea) is clearly unhappy with one of my decisions at Anfield; Gullit, Hughes, and Poyet are equally unconvinced.

The lights have gone out at West Ham and I make my way back to the dressing rooms after the game is abandoned.

Bad but instinctive refereeing as I resort to a little shirt-pulling to restrain Abou.

What do I do here? Separate Calderwood and Hartson, or leave them to Peter Walton and deal with Harry Redknapp?

Abou and I make rather different points to each other.

The old green Premier League shirts come out again for Sheffield Wednesday v Newcastle. The owls are obviously unimpressed.

David Batty receives his marching orders on the last day of the season.

Druries House photo: Daniel Hepher on my left wears the traditional Head of School white tie and tails.

Posing in full Speech Day regalia with Jason Keen.

but by my high professional standards I was very disappointed with my performance. Referees are usually their own fiercest critics and I certainly was unhappy.

There was an interesting article in yesterday's *Daily Telegraph* by Bob Wilson, the former Arsenal goalkeeper, who still spends a lot of time at Highbury and is not slow to shout at referees post-match if Arsenal have been hard done by. He was contributing to the 'third eye' debate and said that

> What the referee needs is another set of eyes on the field of play – a former player, someone with empathy for the game from within . . . Every professional footballer would agree that refereeing is the most thankless of tasks . . . But professionals who sit, meet and eat together interpret the game differently to the gang of four applying the laws on a match day . . . At the moment correct decisions are being left to chance. Managers in the game all agree. We have the technology.

Bob's views were simplistic and attractive but did not address the practical issues and the fundamental impact continually stopping the game to review decisions would have on the flow and the excitement. My main disagreement with him was that most of those playing or managing the modern game do not want video evidence and replays except on those occasions when they feel hard done by. In general, they accept that referees are part of the game as much as the weather and the state of the pitch. Still, this is a debate that will not go away, not least because it is fuelled continually by the TV companies, who see great financial advantages in supplying detailed coverage of all matches. And ex-pros looking for a role in the game see themselves as the final adjudicators.

Sunday 28 December

A quiet day at my desk with a break in the afternoon to watch Newcastle v Liverpool on Sky TV. This has been a fantastic fixture for the last couple of years and I had the real privilege of refereeing the second of the 4–3 matches last season, one of the very best games of my Premier League career. This, too, turned out to be a great game, extremely well refereed by Gerald Ashby. Unfortunately, he seemed to get no credit for the part he played. It is always somewhat galling that if the referee is seen to make a mistake then it is the focus of all the post-match comment and he is often accused of 'ruining the game'. When, however, a referee performs his duties well and contributes to the flow and excitement of the match he rarely gets any praise.

I had a very pleasant supper with the parents of four of my god-daughters Mel and Viv – which gave me a chance to unwind and forget about football.

Monday 29 December

A quiet day doing lots of letter writing and reviewing yesterday's matches. Poor Dermot Gallagher was getting a lot of stick from George Graham for being slack in his control, adding to the concern this season that Dermot has become one of the referees who is not being strict enough. Graham Barber was also under fire after his match at Barnsley, but I phoned Steve Lodge who was at the game and he told me he was impressed with Graham's fitness and control. Graham received his new FIFA badges just before Christmas and has the potential to be one of the best referees in the country.

Tuesday 30 December

Spent the entire day at my desk, working on a submission to the Harrow governors and writing letters and sending faxes to friends.

Wednesday 31 December

An interesting mail bag this morning, including two items forwarded by the FA: a letter from a young man in Wales collecting autographs of famous people, and a Christmas card from a football fan declaring that I was the best referee in the Premier League. It was the first anonymous Christmas card I have ever had and certainly made a change from some of the hate mail I get. There was also a letter from an Old Harrovian I used to teach who is now at university and wanted to become a referee.

After lunch I drove down to Brighton to have tea with Martin Bodenham and his parents and then spend New Year's Eve, as I often do, quietly with a lady friend of mine. We are not really the party types so tend to stay at home and eat smoked salmon and drink champagne.

For a change there were no matches on New Year's Day so I did not have to worry about getting up early tomorrow. I did not make any New Year's resolutions, as I prefer to make them during the year because I have a better chance of keeping short-term resolutions than year-long ones.

January 1998

Thursday 1 January

I awoke to a wonderful view of the sea, choppy and powerful in the wind and the clear morning sun. A lazy breakfast and then a difficult drive in the strong winds up to stay with friends in North Wales.

Friday 2 January

Two interesting snippets in the newspapers today. The first announced that I had been selected to referee the UEFA Super Cup match between Barcelona and Borussia Dortmund although for some reason the report suggested that I was doing both legs. I was amused by the headline in the *Sun*, which read, 'Ell's in heaven'. The other news item was in the *Daily Express* which said that it was expected that Paul Durkin would get the Premiership's vote to be the English referee in the World Cup Finals in the summer. Where had they got that from, as only two or three people knew that I was not available?

In mid-afternoon I drove across the Pennines to Barnsley to stay with Steve Lodge and his family before the Cup-tie with Bolton, so that I would be on site should an early morning inspection be needed because of the dreadful storms. I arrived in time to watch the end of the Celtic v Rangers match on TV – Hugh Dallas was very impressive and likely to be Scotland's referee in France.

Saturday 3 January

I woke up to heavy rain, dark skies and high winds. As I lay in the bath the phone went. Barnsley were requesting an early pitch inspection, so I went to the ground with Steve. There was a certain amount of water lying on the surface and the forecast had proved dreadfully inaccurate. The Met Office had said the overnight rain would stop by nine in the morning but here we were, at eleven, with the heavens still chucking it down. There was nothing to do but to say that the pitch was playable and hope that there would not be too much more rain. The forecast did not help: 'rain will clear, it will be blustery with showers and probably thunder.'

Responsibility for deciding whether a pitch is playable or not lies solely with the referee. He can consult whoever he likes but in the end it is his decision. Sometimes it can be helpful to ask the managers what they think but their opinion is usually determined by whether they have all their players available, free from injury or suspensions, and their assessment of the strength of their side and the opponents.

I returned to the ground about 12.30 p.m. and the pitch was drying out in the gale. Keith Hackett, the FA match observer, arrived and agreed we could do nothing but pray. In the end it was fine, although as we walked out just before three o'clock we were greeted with strong winds and hail. On my way down the tunnel Peter Beardsley came across, shook hands and congratulated me on the UEFA Super Cup appointment. On the field several other players also offered congratulations and I am sure that this helped me somewhat later in the game when matters got lively.

It was an excellent cup-tie between two strong, competitive teams on a muddy pitch in awful weather, in front of a vociferous crowd. Exactly what English football is all about. There were many talking points before I blew the final whistle with Barnsley victorious 1–0. I had issued six yellow cards, the first after three minutes, and the game had been tough without being violent. Fortunately, the players were prepared to listen and I worked hard off the ball talking to them and trying to keep them calm and positive. Barnsley's goal came in the first half from a quickly taken free-kick which, unlike the one I had disallowed for Matt Le Tissier, had been taken from the correct place.

In the second half we had three flare-ups which tested my refereeing experience to the limit. The first was behind my back and I turned round to see the end of the incident with Alan Thompson (Bolton) and Darren Sheridan (Barnsley) wrestling on the ground. I had no idea what had happened but felt I had to be seen to be in control and take action so I gave them both yellow cards for 'unsporting behaviour', i.e. the wrestling I *had* seen. A while later there was another minor tussle and I summoned the two captains, Neil Redfearn and Gudni Bergsson, and told them to get a grip of their players before I started sending people off.

Both Gudni and Neil are players I have a lot of respect for and can talk easily to and they responded very well indeed. I rarely call on captains to do this sort of thing but it had the desired effect and, again, I was anxious to be seen to be taking control of matters. Referees probably do not use captains enough to help control the players – often because the captains are the worst offenders and spend more time berating the referee than helping him.

The final flashpoint hit the headlines. About two minutes before the end of the match, with Barnsley hanging on desperately to their 1–0 lead, the ball went into the Barnsley dugout. Neil Cox of Bolton went to retrieve it but a Barnsley official, I think it was the physio, held on to the ball and would not release it and a wrestle for the ball began. Immediately, officials and subs from the Bolton bench charged across to get involved, rapidly followed by a large number of stewards and police, all of whom obstructed my view of what was happening. I thus stood with my arms folded until sanity was restored and then felt I had to act although I had seen nothing that would enable me to take disciplinary action against anyone. One person stood out – Eric Winstanley, the Barnsley coach, who had been in the thick of it. I went to the dugout and asked the Barnsley manager Danny Wilson, to send Eric to the dressing rooms so that he was out of the way when the final whistle went and would not be a magnet for further trouble. Eric protested but Danny could see the sense of what I was asking and despatched him. Everyone calmed down and the final minutes passed without incident.

At the final whistle I expected further ructions but virtually all the players came up and shook hands and trudged off. Keith Hackett had come down to stand at the top of the tunnel in case there was trouble and was amazed to find the players coming off laughing and joking with each other.

As I changed, the police commander came into my dressing room with the safety officer to find out if I or my assistants, John Holbrook and Phil Joslin, had seen anything or were reporting anyone. I said I was not and they informed us that they had arrested a steward for allegedly striking Jamie Pollock of Bolton. The police were conducting further investigations and promised to send me their final report. The press were clamouring for a statement from me so I asked them to nominate one representative and I gave him a brief interview saying that it had been a fine, typical Northern cup-tie and I would not be reporting anyone following the fracas.

It gave me plenty to think about as I drove south through the wind, snow and rain back to Harrow where a thunderstorm had set off my burglar alarm and caused the central heating to malfunction. On the way I listened to Radio Five's 606 programme. One lady phoned and made a berserk attack on poor Mike Reed who, since the Chelsea v Leicester FA Cup-tie last season, has become the real whipping boy for referees. The Lodge family followed me down to stay the night before Steve refereed Chelsea v Manchester United the following day.

Sunday 4 January

I awoke from the howling gales of the night to find a message from Chelsea on my answerphone. When I returned their call, they asked to speak to Steve urgently and I told them I would have great pleasure getting him out of the bath as he had done the same to me yesterday. They were keen for him to get to Stamford Bridge early as the weather forecast was terrible.

In the event the match was played and it was a cracker – 5–3 to Manchester United and eight yellow cards. Steve, if he had been pedantic, could have sent off Irwin and Leboeuf but he refereed exceptionally well and contributed to a thrilling game. He had been concerned beforehand as it was the one tie that all referees wanted and yet no one wanted. In other words, it was a great game to get (Chelsea and Manchester United were joint favourites for the Cup) but so high profile that any real controversy would reverberate for days. The only controversial incident was a well-worked free-kick by Beckham for the second Manchester United goal before which TV, almost by accident, spotted that Sheringham had pulled a Chelsea player away from the end of the defence wall just where Beckham curled the ball to score. It was impossible for Steve to have seen it and no one commented at the time but it simply highlighted how cameras everywhere spot everything and referees sometimes have no chance.

Monday 5 January

I was inundated by the press. When they started phoning I thought it would be about the fracas at Barnsley but it was about Steve Dunn who had blown the final whistle in the Wimbledon v Wrexham match just as a Wimbledon player was heading the ball into the net. The result was 0–0 and this incident brought back memories of the 1974 World Cup when Clive Thomas from Wales blew for time as Brazil scored against Sweden. That decision cost Thomas his international career and since then referees usually blow for the end of each half when the ball is in a neutral area, usually high in the air around the centre circle.

BBC sent a radio car which put its huge aerial up in my drive so I could do interviews for the *PM* programme and Radio 5. I did a phone interview for Capital Radio and it was ironic that two of the interviews were recorded but broadcast later as if 'live'! Sky Sports came and did an interview too.

My main points were that the referee is the sole judge of time and once he has made due allowances for stoppages he is duty bound to blow up and, unlike in Rugby Union, does not have to wait until the ball is out of play. Thomas had been on the bandwagon recalling his incident and asking everyone to support Steve Dunn, which was pretty ironic given that Thomas had spent the last 10 years criticising referees for refereeing to the letter of the Laws and not using the common sense he claimed he used to use. This in itself was ironic given that he had been so fussy as a referee that he had been known as 'Clive the Book' for much of his career.

I used the incident to further my campaign to have the referee's watch controlling the stadium clock. If everyone knew how much time was left, in this case, the players might have taken the corner rather quicker. What I did point out was that Steve Dunn had no right to allow more time than was due and, if he had done, he would have cheated Wrexham out of the replay. None the less, while supporting Steve to the hilt, I, and many Premier League colleagues, felt that he would have been wise to have blown in a less dangerous situation.

Tuesday 6 January

I had an early telephone conversation with Ken Ridden to finalise the details of the meeting scheduled for later in the morning and to update him on general Premier League developments while he was away abroad over the New Year period. I travelled in to the FA and there I telephoned Mike Reed to clarify the situation with his dismissal of Nigel Martin, the Leeds goalkeeper, in the FA Cup-tie on Saturday against Oxford. Mike had given a penalty and sent off Martin when he had made only the slightest contact. It was one of those situations where the punishment seemed to outweigh the seriousness of the crime, but people forget that to stop a probable goal-scoring opportunity is an offence against the fundamental purpose of the game – scoring goals. Press comment suggested that Mike would review the video and he confirmed that he would if Leeds sent it via the FA.

The rest of the morning was spent at the annual meeting of FIFA referees and assistant referees. The new international officials were welcomed – namely Graham Barber (referee), Peter Walton and Andy Hogg (assistants), and Wendy Toms, who was making history by becoming the first lady FIFA assistant in England. In one sense it was welcome back for Graham Barber and Peter Walton. Graham had once been a FIFA linesman (as they were called then) and was thus following Steve Dunn in gaining promotion to the referees' list. Peter Walton had been on the list, indeed he had been in my team for Euro '96, but had been off for a year while he worked in South Africa.

The meeting was, as usual, mainly administrative but towards the end Ken Ridden announced that I had indicated to him that I would be unable to accept the nomination for selection for the World Cup Finals in France as I would be unavailable. He kindly emphasised that I would have been selected but had stood down to ensure that England did have someone to represent them in France. A number of people seemed genuinely stunned by the news. After the meeting we had our photos taken on the steps of Lancaster Gate, the Football Association's headquarters, and then most of us went to Whites Hotel for lunch.

I felt somewhat low as I returned to the Hill, reflecting that now the news of the World Cup had been announced there was no going back. I had set myself the target of refereeing the 1998 or 2002 World Cup Final back in 1968 when I started refereeing. The 1998 Final had now gone and the lowering of the FIFA retirement age from 50 to 45 meant that I would be too old by 2002. Nevertheless, the game has been wonderful to me and I have no real cause for complaint, just a touch of regret. Before returning to Harrow I did have enough time to give Steve Dunn some gentle ribbing about all the hassle he caused by blowing the whistle when he did at Wimbledon. I was also interested to learn that Alex Ferguson was unhappy with the referee appointed for the Chelsea v Manchester United match later in the season. Having thought that four players should have been sent off in Sunday's FA Cup-tie he was demanding a strong referee and trying to insist that I should be appointed to the match. He admitted to the

FA that he had had his arguments with me but believed I was strong and fair and that was what that game would need. Understandably and correctly, it was made clear to him that the appointment would not be changed.

There was much to do before the boys returned from their holidays and in preparation for the match in Barcelona. I packed my bag for Barcelona and spent some time setting work for the lessons I would miss.

Wednesday 7 January

Early morning call-over was followed by the Masters' Room meeting and Speech Room where the Head Master formally starts the term. From there it was straight to Heathrow with just enough time to meet up with Mark Warren, Phil Sharp and Peter Jones and do some shopping. As we passed through the terminal in our FA blazers we were inevitably recognised and various officials and passengers came up to chat about football. It was an excellent flight to Barcelona and on arrival we were told that our hotel had been changed and we were upgraded to the Rey Juan Carlos, very close to the Nou Camp stadium.

We were taken sightseeing before dinner and teamed up with the UEFA referees' observer from Sweden, Lars Bjorck, and the UEFA match delegate from Poland, Michael Listkiewicz. Lars I knew as he is a member of both the UEFA and FIFA Referees' Committees but he was clearly unaware that I would be declining any invitation to go to France. I had worked with Michael back in 1984 when I had been the fourth official at Wembley for the World Cup match between England and Finland and Michael had been one of the linesmen. I gave him a copy of the teams and match officials from the programme of that match. After visiting the cathedral, we had dinner in a splendid restaurant in the harbour. The walls were full of photos of the owner with various sportsmen and women, and at the end of the meal he asked to have his photo taken with us so that it too could go on the wall.

Thursday 8 January

The morning followed the usual routine of visiting the stadium, inspecting the pitch and dressing rooms (stunning in size and quality) and then having the official organisation meeting. One of the unique aspects of the Nou Camp stadium, which few people see, is the small shrine which is just off the tunnel leading to the pitch. It contains a statue of the Black Madonna and is the only major ground I have visited where religion is so obviously catered for. After the meeting we were each presented with a Barcelona pennant with our name and the details of the match on it. Later on we were to receive a similar one from Borussia Dortmund and I have to confess that unique gifts like this are very special. We went to the club shop to do some souvenir shopping and met a large number of German fans, all of whom insisted on having their photos taken (individually) with us. They were in high spirits and we chatted and signed autographs. After an excellent lunch and a visit to the castle to admire the stunning view of the city we returned to the hotel to rest.

When we arrived at the stadium we bumped into Hristo Stoitchkov who greeted me like a long-lost friend, which was surprising because, when I had refereed at Barcelona in the quarter-finals back in March 1997, he had been a very difficult customer. On the way to the pitch for the start of the match I met Van Gaal, the Barcelona manager, who said how pleased he was that UEFA had appointed me to the match. I had met him before in Tokyo where I refereed the World Club Championship when he was manager of Ajax of Amsterdam, who won the trophy that night.

The match went well and there were few incidents, indeed the players were pretty relaxed and it was played rather in the spirit of the FA Charity Shield. There were few talking points. Just before half-time I awarded a free-kick to Borussia and they took it without my blowing the whistle, which is the usual practice in England. However, abroad they expect the whistle and Barcelona were somewhat upset. As I walked off at half-time Ruud Hesp, the Barcelona goalkeeper, left the field with me and I apologised but he said that they did not mind as they prefer English referees who are not always blowing the whistle like the Spanish referees. I gave three yellow cards in the match, two for fouls where I played the advantage and then went back and gave the card once the game had stopped. This is a technique which can work well for referees as the team offended against can enjoy possession and continue the attack while the offender does not get away scot-free. The only risk is that there may be retaliation either by the fouled player or a team-mate so a referee can only officiate like this if there is a clear advantage and the temperature of the game is not too high. I remember allowing such a situation in the World Club Championship match in Tokyo. On that occasion the Brazilian who committed the foul was already on a yellow card, so after I had allowed the shot on goal I had to send him off. The main talking point of this match was in the 60th minute when I disallowed a goal for offside against Borussia and the play immediately switched to the other end where a foul resulted in a penalty to Barcelona. They scored and with no further goals the match finished 2–0.

The disallowed goal was interesting in several respects. A shot had gone in with a German player standing offside. If a goal had directly resulted from the shot then we would not have penalised the player who was in the offside position, but the keeper saved the original shot and the offside player netted the rebound. This change in the law occurred several years ago and had once caused Mark Warren and me great problems in Sweden. On that occasion it resulted in the home team, IFK Gothenburg, not qualifying for the group stages of the Champions' League and was one of many controversial incidents in a match which saw me send off two home players, the home team coach, issue eight cautions and have to stay in the ground for two hours after the final whistle before having 10 police escort us back to our hotel. Ironically Lars Bjorck had been at that match and had defended us in the Swedish papers the next day. Replays of that incident had been used by the Swedish FA to illustrate the new law to referees, coaches and players which is why Mark Warren is so famous in Sweden.

After the match everyone seemed very happy and Ivan De La Pena of Barcelona came to my dressing room to exchange shirts with me – the first time a player has asked me to do that. As the match had kicked off at nine o'clock it was late by the time we returned to the hotel to have dinner with various officials, but we drank champagne and had excellent food. The Barcelona President made a fine speech and I thanked him and everyone else for their hospitality. We retired late, pleased with Lars Bjorck's confirmation that he was very happy with our control of the match.

Friday 9 January

We got up early to catch our flight home. As soon as we arrived at the airport, various Spaniards came to chat and told us that the papers had reported favourably on our officiating. A good flight home was rounded off when the steward gave us each a number of bottles of champagne. At Heathrow there was a long delay as we waited for the bags and while we were waiting a lady from the baggage information desk came up and asked me to sign their team photo.

The drive back to Harrow was testing as the taxi driver was a Chelsea supporter who wanted to bend my ear about various refereeing decisions, but was one of those who is not really interested in anyone else's point of view and just wants to have a go. I got to Harrow at 12.12 p.m. and eight minutes later was in the classroom teaching. In the afternoon I watched the Yearlings (first years) play Harrow Football against Elmfield (2–1 victory) and then unpacked the Barcelona bag and packed my kit for tomorrow's match, Sheffield Wednesday v Newcastle. The rest of the day was spent catching up on administration. I had also received three sets of assessments from matches, all good reports, and Keith Hackett's from the Barnsley match was extremely complimentary.

Saturday 10 January

I was up early and travelled north with David Clayton, the head of security at Harrow and a keen Sheffield Wednesday supporter. We chatted about School and football all the way, and met up with my assistants, Phil Sharp and Peter Walton, while Steve Lodge and family also came to watch the match. Keith Hackett was again the match observer.

Pre-match the main issue was what kit to wear. Newcastle's black and white stripes would clash with Sheffield Wednesday's blue and white so they were again going to wear their dark away strip. Earlier in the month I had advised them to bring white shorts and socks so they would not clash with the match officials' black ones but it was clear that our dark shirts would cause a problem, as they had done at Leeds, so we decided to put on the old green shirts we used to wear. I always liked wearing the green as these were the first shirts to break the English tradition that referees only wear black and white. There was lots of teasing about whether I had the right shirt with me – as if the trouble at Leeds had been my fault. Kenny Dalglish came in to check and joked that when I had taken my shirt off at Elland Road it had caused 1,000 people to walk out of the ground. I countered that I was merely auditioning for a role in the next *Full Monty*.

It was an interesting match. The first half was very tame and the only real incident was when I turned down a penalty for Sheffield Wednesday after a forward fell dramatically in the area. It might have been a penalty but these exaggerated reactions make it difficult for referees to be sure and we are less inclined to give penalties these days as we do not want to be conned. Newcastle were frustrated at playing poorly and the second half was very tough; I issued six yellow cards. There was a strange reaction when I cautioned Paulo Di Canio for failing to retreat at a free-kick. As I took the card out he shrugged and came to me to shake hands and apologise. The crowd who were just about to give me real abuse for booking their favourite player were stunned and merely applauded politely.

After the match Mike Lowe, a former top referee who looks after the match officials, provided the usual pie and chips and then I travelled home. David Clayton was delighted with the result although somewhat perplexed that Ron Atkinson had been so pleased with the way Sheffield Wednesday had played.

I was looking forward to a quiet evening and an early night but that was not to be as some of my senior boys decided to go out late. I tracked three down quickly but two others had gone into London without permission, and although I tried to get them on their mobile phone there was no reply. I eventually phoned their parents at 12.30 a.m. to make them aware of the situation and explain that the boys were in serious trouble and would be in grave danger of being expelled when they returned. I got to bed at 2.30 a.m.

Sunday 11 January

I awoke at five in the morning and the boys were still not back. I set off for Heathrow airport to collect two boys from Hilton College, South Africa, who were coming to Harrow for a term. Mark Roe-Scott, the boy coming to Druries, arrived safely and, as we turned into the gates of the House, the two missing boys were getting out of a taxi after their night away.

The rest of the day was spent helping Mark settle in and dealing with the two boys, the Head Master and the boys' parents. Harrow is close to London – the wicked city – and boys who go into town without permission risk being asked to leave. The two concerned were very upset at their foolishness, not least because they knew that if they had asked permission they would have been allowed to go to meet their friends. By the end of the day the Head Master decided to send them home pending a decision about their future. It was a grim day and everyone in the House felt sorry for them but cross that they had been so stupid.

Monday 12 January

After much discussion it was decided that the two boys would be allowed to return after a short rustication (suspension) because to expel them would gravely endanger their A levels. They were told that they would be drug-tested and would be subject to a very strict regime for the rest of term. They would lose their exeat weekends and all social privileges, and spend each weekend confined to the House having to report in every hour.

I was drained by the whole process and in the afternoon went to take a House Harrow Football practice just to get away from the phone and run around in the fresh air. In the evening I spoke at length to the House about what had happened and why we have strict rules about going out of the House at night or going into London. After incidents like this the boys always listen carefully and can understand and accept rules and regulations because they have so much more relevance. There was general relief that the boys had not been expelled, but plenty of anger about their behaviour as well.

Tuesday 13 January

An interesting day with the arrival of two letters following the Barnsley v Bolton FA Cup-tie. The first was from Michael Spinks, the Club Secretary, outlining the results of the internal investigation into the fracas just before the end of the match. The other was from the police following their investigation. Both informed me that they had tightened procedures but no one had been disciplined. The police superintendent's letter concluded with 'I thank you for your assistance and hope to see you again, if not this season, next. I am still hopeful that Premier League football will stay at Oakwell.' Michael Spinks remarked that 'We all thought you had a good game and controlled with professionalism what you rightly described as a "good old-fashioned cup-tie between two Northern clubs". I wish you continued success with your work.'

I had a number of phone calls from people wanting interviews or help with articles. I had to turn down a chance to speak at

Charterhouse School and also an invitation to the Old Harrovians AFC dinner. *Punch* magazine wanted to arrange a 'Head to Head' debate between Ian Wright and me in an attempt to broaden the market for their magazine. A reporter from the BBC *Grand Prix* magazine rang for my views on the Michael Schumacher–Jacques Villeneuve incident at the end of the Grand Prix season. She was producing an article giving the views of referees and umpires from other sports.

Gerald Ashby phoned to express his regret that I had decided to declare myself unavailable for the World Cup in France. It was typical of Gerald that he should take the time and trouble to phone and I was touched by his kind words.

Wednesday 14 January

Requests from the media continued, leading me to wonder if we had hit a dull phase when there was no real news. Someone wanted help with an article on the Laws of the Game and a reporter from Radio Ireland phoned to book an appointment for an interview for a documentary to be broadcast on their *Weekend Sport* programme. The appointments for the fourth round of the FA Cup arrived and I was very pleased to find that I had been appointed to Huddersfield v Wimbledon. A fax arrived from *Shoot* magazine wanting to do an interview about refereeing in their 'How to Be A . . .' series. I spoke to my father and brother-in-law to arrange for them to come to Spurs on Saturday and my brother-in-law took great delight in telling me that one of the tabloid newspapers had described me as 'spineless' last week when I said I was not reporting anyone following the Barnsley fracas. Unfortunately, there are a couple of newspapers who attack me whatever I do, so on such occasions as these I am spineless, but if I had reported someone then they would have described me as pedantic and petty. These days I tend to confine myself to reading *The Times* and the *Daily Telegraph*.

Thursday 15 January

The morning post brought the appointments for the Coca-Cola semi-finals and one or two surprises. Gerald Ashby had been appointed to the second leg of the Liverpool v Middlesbrough match, which was a shock as many of us had expected him to referee the final in this his last year as a referee. I had been appointed to the potentially explosive first leg of the Arsenal v Chelsea tie, which was not one which filled me with great joy. Having refereed Chelsea earlier in the competition I was not expecting to see them again and did not relish another opportunity to upset their fans and endure 90 minutes of abuse. One pleasing note was that Rob Harris would be my reserve referee which was excellent as he was a regular linesman with me in England and abroad before being promoted to the referees' list. Much of the day was taken with meetings and teaching.

Friday 16 January

A busy morning taking the two boys for drugs tests when they returned after their rustication. I was keen that they should be welcomed back into the House and not feel they were condemned for ever. In the afternoon there were House Harrow Football matches and then some more teaching.

I was startled in the late evening to receive a phone call from a reporter from the *News of the World* wanting to know if I could confirm that Paul Durkin had been selected for the World Cup. Apparently there was a rumour going around the press boxes, and the majority of reporters were stunned by the news as they thought I was 'the best referee in Britain' and could not believe that Paul Durkin would be selected ahead of me. The reporter actually lives near Harrow School and I have known him for many years. He ventured that my job would prevent me from going. Off the record I gave him the outline of what had happened and asked him not to publish anything until I had time to consult with the FA about an announcement. However, knowing what the press are like, I felt sure there might be something in Sunday's edition. By chance the reporter was coming to the school's career convention on Sunday to talk about journalism, so I would be able to discuss it with him then. It amazed me how quickly rumours start to spread. I had an interesting chat with him about why one or two of the tabloid newspapers seemed to have it in for me. He was not aware of anything orchestrated in the press box and thought it might just be a stereotypical anti-schoolmaster reaction.

Saturday 17 January

Having a London derby – Spurs v West Ham – meant that I could teach all morning. I left Harrow at 11.45 a.m. and arrived at White Hart Lane 45 minutes later after a very good journey. On the way to the dressing rooms I bumped into Bertie Vogts, the German manager, whom I had upset during Euro '96 when I cautioned ten players in the opening group match between Germany and the Czech Republic.

When the team sheets were brought in by the managers at two o'clock I was somewhat surprised that Christian Gross came himself as he had a reputation for not appearing before a match. Perhaps it was a reflection of how important the game was to Spurs, as they were becoming desperate for points to avoid relegation worries.

The match had a quiet start and there were only two incidents of note in the first 40 minutes. David Ginola hugely exaggerated falling over when David Unsworth made the slightest contact. Having been conned into blowing, I realised that I could not penalise Unsworth, so I gave the free-kick against Ginola; he was fortunate that there had been some contact otherwise I would have cautioned him. A while later John Moncur was late in a tackle but I was able to let the Spurs attack continue and went back and showed him the yellow card once play stopped.

The major talking point of the match, and for some time after, occurred in the 41st minute when Peter Walton drew my attention to an off-the-ball incident involving Samassi Abou of West Ham and Ramon Vega of Spurs. Peter had seen Vega and Abou pushing each other and then Abou kicking Vega. I had not seen any of this as the ball was in the other half of the field at the time. When I called Abou over and showed him the red card the problems started. He refused to leave the field and began wagging his finger in my face and disagreeing, in French, with the decision. Twice he grabbed hold of me, once he pulled down my left arm which was pointing to the tunnel then, as I moved away, he tried to turn me back to face him. I was quite cross and somewhat alarmed and forcibly gestured that he should go off the field, saying 'Off' loudly, but he would not go.

I had never been faced with this situation before and was somewhat at a loss as to what to do. I could not manhandle him off the pitch, no players were coming to usher him off and I did not want to call the police or stewards on to the field to escort him off. Fortunately, or so I thought, Harry Redknapp had appeared at the touchline and, although he may well have been on his way to complain about Vega's exaggerated reaction to the foul, he seemed to me the obvious man to deal with things, so I gestured for him to come on to the field and remove Abou. After all, we were only a few metres from the touchline.

Unfortunately, the trouble then escalated. I went back to ask Peter Walton what action I should take against Vega and the next thing I knew there was a scuffle going on involving Redknapp, Colin Calderwood (Spurs) and then John Hartson (West Ham). As I calmed them down I was aware of trouble in the West Ham section of the crowd which was fairly close to where this incident was taking place. I managed to restore order quickly and Frank Lampard and Lama, the reserve West Ham goalkeeper (who is French), took Abou towards the tunnel. I showed Vega the yellow card for his initial involvement in the incident and restarted with a Spurs goal-kick as I had completely forgotten where the ball had been when I stopped play (in fact it should have been a drop ball in the middle of the West Ham half).

Almost immediately, John Hartson steamed into Vega in revenge and I had to make a very quick decision as to whether it was to be a red or yellow card, but settled for the latter. However, for the second time in three matches, I called the captains together. I told them in no uncertain terms that I would tolerate no more violence or stupidity and unless they got a grip of their players I would be throwing cards around for the rest of the match. As tempers were hot I allowed no stoppage time and then at half-time allowed an extended interval in the hope that everyone would be quieter for the second half.

My thoughts went back to another game at White Hart Lane in 1990 when Spurs had played Luton and by half-time I had sent off two Spurs players – Nayim and Pat van den Hauwe, the latter for one of the worst fouls I have ever seen on a soccer pitch in England. On that occasion I had sat in the dressing room and not wanted to go out for the second half, and feelings like that crept back again. I had never before been confronted with a player refusing to leave the field and was racking my brains to see if there was anything I had done (or not done) which had caused the problems.

As I went out after half-time I still had some self-doubts but John Hartson told me that they had discovered that Abou had kicked Vega and I had been correct to send him off. That helped and the rest of the game was very quiet, with just one yellow card for Steve Potts of West Ham for a late tackle on Andy Sinton. I worked hard talking to the players and was pleased with their response, although I still sensed there was something bubbling under the surface and was keen to ensure that hostilities did not break out again.

When I blew the final whistle, with the score still 1–0, most players came to shake hands and you would scarcely have known that there had been such trouble in the first half. The police reported few problems apart from some scuffles when Abou refused to leave the field. Knowing that the incidents would cause much media comment I wrote an outline report and immediately faxed it to the FA from White Hart Lane. The press were clamouring for me to comment, so I invited them to nominate one person to come with a tape recorder and I would be as helpful as I could, bearing in mind that, as disciplinary action might follow, much of what occurred was now *sub judice*.

John Dillon from the *People* came to my dressing room and was delighted that a referee was prepared to talk to him. 'Compared to a few years ago this is paradise,' he exclaimed. I tried to keep matters as factual as possible and decided in my own mind that Harry Redknapp's actions had been with the intention of being helpful. I explained why Abou had been dismissed and also that I had not seen the scuffle which followed Redknapp coming on to the field so had invited the FA to look at the video tape. It would be for them to decide what action to take. After John Dillon left I asked to see Harry Redknapp and told him what I was reporting and that I did not intend to make any accusation against him. Harry apologised for the scuffle and agreed readily that Abou deserved to be sent off though he was very angry with Vega for his over-reaction to being fouled.

As I emerged on to the car park I was stopped by a number of pressmen, including Henry Winter from the *Daily Telegraph*, who I have always found to be a thoughtful and intelligent reporter. For the next ten minutes or so I talked about wider issues and particularly players diving and over-reacting to being fouled. It emerged that Steve Lodge had run into controversy at Coventry: Williams had made the slightest contact with Dennis Bergkamp who had gone down dramatically leaving Steve no option but to dismiss Williams for denying an obvious goal-scoring opportunity. The view I expressed to the press was that this is a growing problem in the English game. With the arrival of so many overseas players and coaches, there were now many continental influences in our game – many of them positive, but this was a negative one. But I was keen to stress that the problem was not confined to foreign players.

In the evening I watched *Match of the Day* with interest and was horrified to see that, when Steve Lodge sent Patrick Vieira off for foul language he had, like Abou, refused to leave the field until he was ushered away by Gary Lewin, the Arsenal physio. What was more outrageous was another attack on referees by Gordon Strachan. Not only did he describe Steve Lodge as 'a disgrace' but he also deliberately and publicly accused the Premier League referees of giving Coventry nothing since his row with me at Derby. Surely the FA would now have to take action against him.

Sunday 18 January

Not surprisingly the press was full of Strachan's comments but there was little sympathy for him. Indeed Steve and I came out of our matches reasonably unscathed and the attention was focused much more on the antics of the players. I completed my detailed disciplinary reports and faxed them to the FA. There were one or two press calls but nothing much. I spoke to Steve Lodge in the late morning and we agreed that there had been contact between Williams and Bergkamp and that he was right to have dismissed Williams. If Bergkamp made a meal of things then that was not a matter for Steve as it was subsequent to the actual foul which had prevented the goal-scoring opportunity.

This incident demonstrated how trouble is often caused by players not referees, and yet the criticism is aimed at the referee. The business of diving and over-reacting is a real problem as it makes the referee's task much more difficult. It can also cause trouble between teams as one side thinks that their team-mate has been badly fouled and the referee should act strongly, while the other side is convinced that the player who was fouled is over-reacting or even diving. This unhappy situation is one that can only be tackled by a joint venture by the LMA, PFA and FA.

In the afternoon I watched the Torpid five-a-side competition in the school sports hall. Many of the boys were eager to discuss the Coventry v Arsenal match. However, all this paled into insignificance for Mark Roe-Scott, the boy from South Africa, who was still on cloud nine after meeting Prince William yesterday, when he came with the Eton team for a water polo match at Harrow. The Prince was at prep school with Aubrey Duffy who is looking after Mark and had introduced them.

Monday 19 January

One of those hectic days when I taught until 10.45 a.m. and then dashed into London for a Premier League meeting. The referees met in the morning and in the afternoon we were joined by the Premier League match observers. The morning session was largely taken up looking at videos and in particular clips of incidents where players committed sending-off offences. They were not always dismissed and the referees were questioned carefully as to why they did not apply the ultimate sanction. It was disappointing that one or two referees were not prepared to admit their mistakes while others, like Steve Lodge, were honest enough to hold up their hands and say they had been wrong. In the afternoon we spent some time persuading the match observers to accept my proposals for a reworking of their assessment forms and grading so that they focused on *overall* performance as well as the major incidents in the match.

After the meeting I was taken aside by Sky TV to do a quick interview about Strachan's remarks and the so-called crisis between managers and referees. A quick Tube journey got me back to Harrow in time for a cup of tea and an attempt to deal with 14 press messages on my answerphone before going to a geography department meeting. I taught and then leapt into a taxi to go to the Sky studios for an interview with Mark Saggers and Steve Curry from the *Sunday Telegraph*. It was interesting to meet Steve Curry who has always been one of my sternest critics. He made a virulent attack on me when I cautioned 10 players in the Germany v Czech Republic game in Euro '96 but now he was staggered when I told him that while he and the British press were criticising me for being too strict, UEFA were telling me that I had not been strict enough. It gave him an interesting insight into the pressures on referees. Just before the interview began news came through that, as I already knew, Steve Lodge had rightly decided to stick by his decision to dismiss Williams for the foul on Bergkamp.

By the time I got back to Harrow I was pretty shattered having had hardly a moment's rest. But I still did not get an early night as I discovered two of my seniors illegally drinking. It was rather a tame affair – a wine and cheese birthday celebration – but they had broken the strict rules about alcohol and were given three weeks' hard labour in the school kitchens starting at 6.30 a.m.

Tuesday 20 January

A busy morning teaching and something of a tailing off in interest from the media. I telephoned Ken Ridden to tell him that I would not be able to attend the UEFA top referees' course in Majorca in

early February through school commitments. Although this meant
that I would not be considered by UEFA for any of the matches in
the latter stages of the UEFA club competitions, I had reached a stage
where my application to become Head Master had to take priority
and, in all honesty, I could not afford to be away from Harrow for
five days especially over a weekend. Any incident during that time
would reflect badly on me at this crucial stage in the appointment
process. I was, however, delighted to learn from Ken Ridden that
I had been appointed to referee the Oxford v Cambridge Varsity
match at the end of March. The afternoon was spent watching the
House enjoying more success on the Harrow Football fields but I
returned to the House to discover that two seniors had been caught
smoking. Like the drinkers, they received the standard three weeks'
early morning hard labour in the school kitchens.

In the early evening I was contacted by a reporter who wanted me
to do a rerun of a match from the 1960s but with the present strict
refereeing style in force. We agreed it was an interesting notion but,
as it would take most of an afternoon, we settled for a date in the
Easter holidays.

One alarming piece of news was that a Football League referee
had been charged with alleged bribery after an FA Cup match. It
seemed that there was little substance to the allegations but the FA had
charged him all the same. As usual they were quick to charge a referee
and yet still had not shown any sign of dealing with Mr Strachan after
his attack on the integrity of the Premier League referees.

Wednesday 21 January

The day started badly with a summons for jury service and got
worse as I was inundated with press enquiries on two issues. First
I was interviewed on BBC Radio 5 Live by Sybil Ruscoe to answer
various points made by Gordon Strachan. He had tried to reduce the
impact of his remarks by writing a letter of apology to Steve Lodge,
but he was merely playing semantics: he changed from saying that
Steve was a disgrace to saying that some of his decisions had been
disgraceful. When he said there was need for greater co-operation and
discussion between managers and referees I had to laugh as Coventry
City were one of the clubs who had failed to send any representative
at all to the meetings between Premier League managers and referees
last season.

After that I sat in a radio car in the drive doing two interviews about suggestions that the Premier League were thinking of experimenting with a referee's watch controlling the stadium clock. This was excellent news and had been an area my colleagues and I had been advocating for over a year. I was so overwhelmed with media requests that it was interfering with my Harrow responsibilities so I asked Gerald Ashby to do the interview with the *Guardian* about professional or full-time referees.

Thursday 22 January

I thought this would be a quiet day, but no such luck. In mid-morning I did an in-depth interview with Jim Lawton of the *Daily Express*. I had been in two minds about this, having done an interview with him about 18 months ago which led to his newspaper attacking me for giving interviews in the 'hallowed halls of Harrow'. Since then the *Daily Express* had always been rather negative about me and Harrow which seemed surprising as I had been so co-operative. Anyway, Jim had been supportive in his account of the Spurs v West Ham match and I felt that I could trust him to report faithfully what I said. My theme was that players, managers and referees needed to get together to tackle the problem of diving and over-exaggerated reactions to fouls that is harming the game.

Before lunch I had a meeting with the admissions officer of Harvard University in Boston. Much of the afternoon was spent in my annual review of the House with Nick Bomford, the Head Master. As soon as I left that meeting I was contacted about an article in the medical journal the *Lancet*, which claimed research had shown that Spanish linesmen had a slight eye defect. Apparently the eye cannot change focus quickly enough to be able to judge the movement of players in a split second so assistant referees are liable to make mistakes because their eyes literally deceive them. Of course with only small samples it was hardly scientific proof but that would not stop the press having a field day and I gave a couple of radio interviews responding to the article.

Friday 23 January

The day turned into a complete mad house as the press decided that the study of Spanish officials was excellent news since there was now scientific proof for the cry 'You're blind, referee!' I recorded an interview for the BBC World Service and then ITN came to Harrow to do an interview. Immediately after lunch I recorded an interview for Sky News and one for the BBC, while I was watching the House play Harrow Football. There were many calls from other press and radio people but I just did not have the time to fit them all in and do my teaching. It was extraordinary how so many people wanted a comment and could not understand that I have a job to do. In the interviews, to defuse some of the controversy I began by sympathising with my Spanish colleagues. That usually led the interviewers to claim that what was true for Spanish referees must be true for all referees. I countered that if that was true then, as referees are not genetically different from anyone else, it must also be true for spectators. So, when the spectators see something the referee does that appears to them to be wrong, it is probably their eyesight that is letting them down and the referee is actually right.

It was something of a relief to escape to Harrow's Speech Room for the singing and organ prizes and I was delighted that Drurieans carried off half of them.

Saturday 24 January

I was up early and had an excellent journey along the M1 to Huddersfield for their FA Cup match with Wimbledon. I was hugely impressed with their stadium whose design reminded me very much of the stadium in Split (Croatia) where I refereed towards the end of the Bosnia crisis, when Hadjuk Split played Legia Warsaw. A tour of the ground and its facilities impressed me even more. On a wall in the spacious referees' dressing room there were several posters with apt philosophical quotes.

One of my assistants was Eddie Green who was in his last season as a Premier League assistant and was thrilled to be sent to a northern match beyond his usual range of grounds. The FA match observer was Peter Willis, a towering man in every sense of the word, and a magnificent president of the Referees' Association, the national 'union' of referees at all levels in the game. He had seen my interview on BBC and had many questions about Harrow Football, not least why we appeared to play with an old battered ball. During the pre-match inspection of the pitch and ground we bumped into a recently qualified Class Three referee from Dorset who was keen to have his photo taken with us. We chatted about local football and I was pleased to learn that he had battled through his first few games and was beginning to enjoy the experience.

At the toss-up comments about dodgy eyesight came thick and fast from Robbie Earle, the Wimbledon captain. I remarked that anyone who mentioned my eyes would be booked. The game began strangely with Wimbledon sustaining three injuries in the early minutes, Robbie Earle and Ceri Hughes being substituted in the first nine minutes. Seeing Ceri Hughes again reminded me of that match at Spurs when I had sent off three players, one of them Ceri, who at that time was a Luton player. In the Huddersfield team were two old stagers, Dave Phillips and Barry Horne. I have always got on extremely well with David since his days at Nottingham Forest and throughout the match we were able to chat away like old friends. Barry Horne and I had had our troubles in the past, not least at Newcastle when he was one of two Everton players I dismissed (as well as showing eight yellow cards) but he had either forgiven me or forgotten and we also talked throughout the game. It was a relatively poor match notable only for the partisan home crowd, who were upset when I refused to award them a penalty when a ball was driven at point-blank range at a Wimbledon defender and hit him on the hand. To penalise for handball the referee has to be certain that the player *deliberately* handled the ball and this was certainly not the case.

The most notable aspect of the match from my point of view was that, like several Wimbledon players, I seemed to have trouble with the pitch. In the first half my right knee began to ache and at half-time I warned the senior assistant, Peter Walton, that I was struggling a little and he might have to take over. In the second half the knee cleared up but the problem transferred to the ankle which was really painful by the end of the match.

After the game I showered and a reporter for the *Sunday Times* popped in to arrange an interview later in the week. As I left the ground I was greeted by a large group of Huddersfield supporters, and as they had lost 1–0 and I had turned down appeals for a penalty I was expecting the usual abuse. I was wrong, and they stopped and chatted about football for several minutes while I signed autographs. One young man even remarked that it was the first time he had ever asked for a referee's autograph. They seemed genuinely delighted that a referee had taken time to talk to them and it once again reminded me that there are thousands of decent people who go to football matches all over the country every weekend.

Sunday 25 January

I awoke with a very sore ankle which gave me shooting pains if I twisted or put any weight on it. I had had this trouble on and off for many years after I injured it playing tennis while at school. Steve Lodge phoned to discuss an article in the *Sunday Express* announcing that I would not be going to the World Cup. I spent the day working at my desk with the FA Cup matches on TV in the background. My main concern was my ankle and whether I would be fit for the Arsenal v Chelsea Coca-Cola semi-final on Wednesday. I am usually a quick healer so I was not unduly concerned. Among my correspondence was a letter from a French journalist wanting details from the UEFA Super Cup match in Barcelona.

Monday 26 January

Another of those hectic days teaching and then rushing into London for a meeting of the Technical Committee at the FA. This committee consists of the chairmen of the major FA committees, representatives from the Football League and Premier League plus Graham Kelly, Jimmy Armfield, Gordon Taylor (PFA) and Ken Ridden. I am on it as an international referee. The committee meets to discuss issues of general interest to the game and it was disappointing, yet again, that no one from the LMA was present.

This time we considered proposals to deal with controversies over stoppage time, with a split between those who want to relay information to the spectators and people like Jimmy Armfield who like to leave some mystery and suspense in the game. We talked about managers' post-match comments and everyone deplored the damage ill-considered and critical remarks do to the game. The best discussion was centred on the continental influence on the game and especially the recent controversies over diving and exaggerated reactions. At the end of the meeting I had a talk with Graham Taylor and discussed meeting him again to put out a joint statement deploring the actions of players who dive or over-react in an attempt to win free-kicks and penalties or to have opponents cautioned or sent off. If we could do that it would send out a powerful message.

After the meeting I was chatting with Jim Ashworth of the Football League and learned from him that they had intended to appoint me to the Coca-Cola Final. However, with one semi-final being a London derby and the other a match between Liverpool and Middlesbrough they had decided that, unlike the FA, they could not have a London referee take a final involving a London club against a Northern club. I had not expected to be in the running for the final this year. We had our money on Gerald Ashby until he was appointed to one of the semi-finals, so I was surprised by Jim's comments. While I understood and accepted his reasoning, I was a little disappointed.

I rushed back to Harrow to watch the House play Harrow Football, see some prospective parents, teach and catch up with the paperwork on my desk. Unfortunately, while running for the Tube I slightly turned my ankle and the shooting pains returned which is a worry.

Tuesday 27 January

I woke up to find my ankle so painful that I almost had to hop downstairs to make a cup of tea and get the newspaper. This posed a real dilemma as I did not want to withdraw from tomorrow's match but it would be totally unprofessional to go to the game less than 100 per cent fit. The reserve referee was Rob Harris, who had become a close friend, having been a regular linesman with me in the Premier League and abroad until he was promoted to the referees' list of the Football League. It was a great honour for him to be on the semi-final and it would be totally unfair if I had had to come off during the match and leave him to referee at a level he had never experienced before. I telephoned Jim Ashworth, the referees' officer at the FL, and we decided that I should withdraw. Under normal circumstances I might have left it until the morning of the match but we both felt that it was such a major fixture that whoever was to referee deserved time to adjust to the appointment and should not be landed with the game at a few hours' notice. I hate pulling out of matches and felt low for the rest of the day.

My spirits were partially lifted when Martin Bodenham phoned later in the morning to tell me he had picked up the game. This being his last season, he was delighted, even though he refereed the final last year.

The lunchtime post brought a letter from Liverpool. The envelope simply had David Elleray (Premier League Referee) Harrow on it so the post office had done well to deliver it. I was about to throw it away as letters addressed this way usually contain abuse, but on the back the writer had written 'Law Question'.

The gist of the letter was most interesting and highlighted an anomaly in the Laws of the Game. If a player is sent off and the match goes to penalties what happens if each side has taken 10 kicks and one team has no eleventh man? Do they lose by default? The answer is no and, worse than that, while the other team have to have their penalty taken by their eleventh (and presumably worst) penalty taker, the team who had a player sent off can use their best player for a second time. I replied explaining all this but made a note to raise the subject with the FA.

The afternoon was spent watching the House enjoy further success in the Harrow Football, unbeaten at all levels thus far. In the evening I taught for an hour and a half to make up for the lessons I missed yesterday, still very disappointed at the prospect of missing tomorrow's match.

Wednesday 28 January

I awoke with my ankle still sore so I was happy that I had made the right decision even though a nagging regret remained that I would not referee what promised to be a fantastic match. It occurred to me that I had been appointed to Coca-Cola Cup semi-finals for the last four years and each one had been jinxed in one way or another. In 1995 I was due to referee Sheffield Wednesday v Manchester United and the game had to be postponed on the day of the match because of snow. The pitch was fine but the roads were so terrible that I would have been unable to get up the M1 and, the police having closed the M62, everyone from Manchester would also have been unable to travel.

In 1996 I was appointed to Leeds United v Birmingham but did not do the game as it clashed with a Premier League match. The Premier League were having something of a power struggle with the Football League and refused to release me from the QPR v Arsenal match. Last year I was appointed for the Stockport County v Middlesbrough first leg and had to postpone the match because of torrential rain which flooded the pitch. The following week the weather was just as bad but we managed to play. Even this season I had missed two earlier matches because of extraneous matters and the draw had robbed me of the final.

I interviewed an impressive young man from Singapore who wanted to join Harrow for his A levels. As it was Chinese New Year he arrived bearing small gifts. He spoke enthusiastically about his music and water polo, and also turned out to be a really keen football fan. He had seen the TV interview I did last term when the boys were questioned about me after being filmed doing a geography test.

In the afternoon I tried some light exercise on my ankle and responded to a couple of magazine inquiries, including one from *Maxime* magazine who wanted to know if there was any Law in football I wanted to change. This enabled me to talk about the sin bin and I hoped that I might get that debate going again.

I started to watch Arsenal v Chelsea but had that awful empty feeling inside, a sense of loss that I was not doing the game. In a bizarre way I felt almost physically ill (a sort of withdrawal at the loss of adrenaline that I would be feeling if I was doing the game) and was unable to watch. I spent the rest of the evening working hard, talking to boys in the House and at my desk trying to ignore the fact that I was missing a vital match. Who says we are part-time amateurs with no dedication or love of the game?

Thursday 29 January

I was delighted to read in the papers that last night's game went well for Martin and there was no controversy. I was again on a busy schedule of teaching and then went into the FA for a meeting. This time it was the Independent Schools FA and we were trying to resolve disputes about the Cup competition and the choice of venue for the final. Martin Bodenham and Peter Jones had refereed Boodle and Dunthorne Independent Schools semi-finals. I always get Premier League officials for the semi-final as it adds to the occasion and ensures the matches are played almost without trouble or dispute. Premier League referees always enjoy these occasions as they are sporting but competitive and a break from the pressures of the professional game.

In the afternoon news came through that the FA had finally charged Gordon Strachan, although I learned that some at the FA had wanted to sweep the matter under the carpet.

Friday 30 January

After a busy morning teaching I watched some more (successful)

Harrow Football. Again I was bombarded with phone calls from the press wanting interviews about all manner of aspects of refereeing. Often they had been put on to me by the FA, who seem to think that they can use me as one of their press officers but without the slightest thanks or sign of appreciation for the work done. I tested my ankle and was pleased that it was almost completely back to normal, although with no games for a few weeks I would not have to put it to the test. However, I would have to up my training regime to counteract the lack of matches.

I was irritated to read in the newspapers that Peter Leaver, chief executive of the Premier League, suggested at a UEFA meeting that football should experiment with two referees (one in each half). It was disappointing that he was raising such issues without anyone from the Premier League asking the referees what they thought. As usual there had been no attempt to get the opinion of the very people who would be affected by these changes. One of the great misconceptions is that referees have an input into the Laws of the game so that whenever there is a change people assume it has been brought about by the referees themselves. Rather like policemen, we simply implement the law, and often we are as perplexed as everyone else is.

Saturday 31 January

The first of what promised to be a number of Saturdays off as my next scheduled match, Leeds v Blackburn on 14 February had been postponed because both teams had reached the next round of the FA Cup. In some ways it was a relief for that date is Old Boys' Day (called Founder's Day) at Harrow and I would be at School all day meeting Old Drurieans and umpiring Harrow Football.

About five o'clock while I was preparing Chinese food for a dinner for my Fifth Form to celebrate Chinese New Year, I had a call from the Press Association wanting my comments on the attack on an assistant referee at Portsmouth. I had not heard of the incident but it transpired that a spectator from Sheffield United had attacked the assistant and knocked him unconscious. He had regained consciousness after five minutes and had been taken to hospital and a man had been arrested. It sounded horrific and I had to curb my anger and give a restrained reaction.

The rest of the evening was spent entertaining and then waiting for the senior boys in my house to return from the Sixth Form Ball. One poor chap, Mark Whitson, had taken a painkiller for an ankle injury and this had caused a reaction with the wine and he had to come back early and miss most of the fun. I was enthralled by their tales of the evening, although their stories had to be taken with a pinch of salt.

February 1998

Sunday 1 February

The day was dominated by dealings with the media following the horrific attack on Edward Martin in yesterday's match at Portsmouth. As well as talking to the newspapers I went into the BBC studios to do an interview for BBC *News 24*.

Last season a fan had run on to the pitch at Everton to try to get at referee Paul Danson, and a few weeks later I had to intercept a Stockport fan who came on to the field to threaten Emerson of Middlesbrough in the Coca-Cola semi-final. Up until these incidents, the usual attitude of the police and the stewards was that they thought it undignified for them to pursue anyone coming on to the field and that they would simply arrest them when they tried to return to the terraces. These two incidents had led me and others to highlight the dangers to the FA and there had been something of a change in attitude from many clubs and police officers. For much of this season the police or the safety officer in Premier League matches had assured match officials that they would be protected by police or stewards if someone ran on in a threatening manner. Clearly such protection had not been forthcoming at Portsmouth and I did my best, without sensationalising the incident, to highlight the responsibility of clubs to ensure the safety of match officials, and also players and managers. Our concern was that one day the assailant might have a knife and we could have an incident like the one that shocked the tennis world when Monica Seles was knifed.

There was no doubt in my mind that the responsibility lay with the club and that it was vital that the FA took a lead – but would they? Many years ago referee Norman Burtenshaw was knocked down at the end of a match at Millwall and the FA were so lenient that there was a real threat of a referees' strike – the only time such action has been contemplated by English officials.

One bonus was my journey to the BBC studios with an Italian taxi driver who supported Inter Milan and Tottenham. His remarks about Spurs were crisp and entertaining. He said, 'They are a club owned by an incompetent, with a reject as general manager, a nobody as coach and a load of has-beens as players.'

Monday 2 February

The debate over the assault at Portsmouth continued and I was alarmed by a report in the *Daily Mail* which alleged, among other things, that there had been a similar incident when the two clubs played a few weeks ago in the FA Cup and an intruder had got close to one of the assistants. There was a photo to support the allegation and incredulity that, despite the trouble in that match, there had been few police on duty at Portsmouth on Saturday. The article highlighted a disturbing tendency of clubs to employ stewards at £12–£20 rather than pay the higher costs of having policemen.

I was very concerned when the Press Association phoned me in mid-morning and said that the indications were that everyone was trying to play this down as a one-off. I was very angry and gave a long interview, fleshing out many of the points I had made yesterday. I explained that a Premier League referee (Graham Poll) had been confronted in a car park well over an hour after a match two years ago at Middlesbrough and, as a result, we now had security escorts to our vehicles after every game. It annoyed me that, as usual, people were looking for easy options, so I posed the question, 'What if it had been a player or manager who had been knocked unconscious?' I also let it be known that I had expressed the concerns of referees to the FA a year ago and that this was not an isolated incident but part of a growing trend. I mentioned some of the problems we increasingly get away from matches in terms of insults in the streets, hate mail and abusive phone calls.

I escaped from the press in the afternoon to watch the new boys win their Harrow Football semi-final 5–0 against West Acre. In the evening I had dinner in London with close friends. When I arrived home there was a message on my answerphone from Edward Martin, the assistant assaulted at Portsmouth, saying that he was well and thanking me for all the support I was giving him and other refereeing colleagues by speaking out in the media.

Tuesday 3 February

A tough start to the day. Although I had heard the news on the radio yesterday, it was only when I saw in print that Paul Durkin has been selected for the World Cup in France that I knew my chances of going really were at an end. I felt empty and sick.

Ever since I turned down the chance to go to the FIFA Youth Championships in Australia in 1992 I had always secretly doubted whether I could be away from Harrow for that length of time, even if I was good enough to be selected. In 1994 when Philip Don went to the USA, I carefully logged at School all the things I would have missed and had done the same for the following three summers.

I was absolutely delighted that Mark Warren had been selected as an assistant. He will have received the news on his way to Burkina Faso for the African Championships. I wrote to congratulate Paul Durkin and stressed that, despite the circumstances of his selection, he was going on merit because FIFA judged him good enough.

I spent the afternoon watching Harrow Football semi-finals with mixed success. The House team lost 1–0 even though they were the better side. Unfortunately, the House had enjoyed so much success that every other House raises its game when it plays Druries. I also sensed that we had lost the hunger to win and expected things to happen rather than making them happen. Ironically the other favourites, Elmfield, lost their semi-final, although rather unluckily on the toss of a coin. We debated whether there should be a penalty shootout but at least with the toss of a coin no individual makes the mistake that eliminates his team. We did, however, win the two junior semi-finals against our traditional rivals, Elmfield, so having qualified for three of the four finals there was general satisfaction in the junior part of the House if not the senior.

Wednesday 4 February

Having taught until 10.30 a.m. I rushed into London on the Tube for a meeting at the FA with Ken Ridden. We spent much of the time organising the programme for the forthcoming weekend seminar for junior referees. Matters would be slightly complicated, as in the middle of the weekend I would have to return to London to referee the Varsity match.

We also dealt with two other topics. Ken was keen that UEFA and FIFA should have details of why I was not available to go to the UEFA top referees' course at the end of the week and we agreed a statement.

I was also concerned, but not surprised, to learn that some within the FA had been unhappy that I had been talking so freely to the press about the incident at Portsmouth and the need for safety to be reviewed. I made it clear that I felt I had a duty as the official spokesman for the Premier League referees to speak out, especially when some in the game were trying to give the impression that there was no problem.

I hurried back to Harrow for a meeting with the Social Services who regularly inspect the School, and then spent the afternoon marking and teaching. In the evening I drove into London to have dinner with parents of three boys in the House; Debbie had cooked a stunning meal and the conversation flowed, much of it a fascinating debate about dyslexia and how schools should treat those with the problem.

Thursday 5 February

I taught for most of the morning and caught up with one or two media people wanting to set up interviews about the attack at Portsmouth. With no appointments in the Premier League for the next few weeks I had an opportunity to be free from the match build-up pressure which, at this mid-point in the season, was quite welcome. I certainly believe that everyone in the game could do with a fortnight's break not only to allow the body to have a rest but also to relieve the enormous mental stress that players, managers and match officials are under – a window allowing a few days of socialising without having to train every day or be careful about what one eats.

Over the last few years the pressure on Premier League referees in particular has grown enormously and I increasingly have periods when the strain is too much and I want to have a break, perhaps a permanent one. Becoming full-time would not improve the situation. While it might make things easier in terms of time-management, the pressure would be ever-present, with no escape. Players sometimes hit a bad patch and that is rarely the case with referees at present as they have other distractions which help relieve the mental stress. None the less, there is little doubt that officiating at the highest level makes enormous demands on the mental toughness and resilience of referees and too little attention is paid to helping them cope with this. I know that I am nearing the stage when I will feel that I no longer want the relentless strain of refereeing – a strain exacerbated by being on the international list which has seen me referee every month for the last three years.

Steve Lodge phoned to say that he had done an interview with Yorkshire TV where he had put a lot of the blame of the spate of attacks on match officials on the media, who spend much of their coverage of referees attacking them for being incompetent. Interestingly, a senior member of the FA told me that he thought the real blame lay with the managers whose touchline and post-match histrionics and outbursts provoke the lunatic fringe among the fans into such actions.

Friday 6 February

After a busy morning teaching I spent the afternoon interviewing a boy hoping to get a place in Druries for September.

In the early evening I did a live interview with Talk Radio, again focusing on the attack at Portsmouth. I then spent some time appointing Peter Jones, Peter Walton and Phil Sharp to officiate the Independent Schools FA Cup Final at Northampton.

About 10.45 p.m. I went to celebrate with Mel and Vivien Mrowiec as he had just been told he was becoming a House Master. I was delighted for him and for Harrow as he will do an excellent job.

Saturday 7 February

A busy morning teaching with a hollow feeling in my stomach in place of the tingle of nerves usually present on match days. While I was enjoying not having to get up early, to drive to a game and suffer all the stresses and strains, I knew that at three o'clock I would miss the adrenaline rush like an alcoholic missing a drink. Instead, I drove to Oxfordshire to lunch with one of the boys who left Druries last year and was about to go on his travels around the world. I had grown to know him and his mother well, not least because his father died before he came to Harrow and while he was at the school I became something of a surrogate father to him, especially during a particularly turbulent three months of adolescence. At that time, when he was falling out with everyone, he never fell out with me. I am always very conscious that my role as House Master is somewhat different for those boys who for whatever reason have no father.

I had seven Lower Sixth boys for supper – a great evening, with Alex Ward and Sam Stevens in particularly good form. We discussed all manner of topics, initially whether we should go to war with Saddam Hussein. They, of course, remembered little of the Gulf War and it was so good to get a 'young' perspective on many matters. They were interested to know whether I was going to be the next Head Master as they had heard rumours. In typical fashion, their main motive was selfish: concern about who would take over as House Master and whether I would stay on to see them through their A levels. Those with stamina went on chatting until just before one in the morning.

Sunday 8 February

A busy day for me in the House – there's never a Sunday off during term time. I managed some early morning administration before Marcus Littlejohns and his mother came to see me to discuss his A levels and his parents' move from Syria to Houston. After that I literally ran down to the music schools to hear the House ensemble play three excellent compositions in the House competition. Eustace Santa-Barbara conducted the major piece, revealing another of the many talents which had already made him a contender for Head of School next year.

After lunch I watched the new boys in the Shell five a-side. Although very enthusiastic they were unable to score and were eliminated, amid mutterings about dodgy refereeing. I returned to my study to find a splendid silver trophy on my desk – we had won the music competition. Again I was delighted for the boys and particularly for Dr Glynn Jenkins, my tireless House tutor, who works so hard for the boys in many area, but especially music. Rehearsals for the House play – *Amadeus* – meant that we would have to delay celebrations until after half-term.

Monday 9 February

An interesting letter arrived from SPARKS, the charity who were the beneficiaries of our Long Ducker run last term. They were organising a fund-raising event at Chelsea in April in conjunction with the *Daily*

Telegraph. One of the money-raising schemes was for people to bet on whether I showed two red cards, two yellow cards, or one of each. SPARKS were keen that I should attend, and as Roger Uttley was a vice-president I could hardly say no. I also had an approach from a group of businessmen who, frustrated at not getting tickets for the World Cup, were setting up evenings to watch the matches over dinner and were inviting top players and others to come and speak. The father of a boy in another House wrote to ask if I would be willing to take part.

I had a number of media inquiries about two issues that had blown up over the weekend. Paul Durkin, in response to his appointment to the World Cup, had inadvisably launched an attack on players and managers and their comments and criticisms of referees. I was anxious not to build this up into a public slanging match and was disappointed that Paul had spoken out in this way, especially as he had been advised earlier in the week to keep his head down and just enjoy the glory of his appointment.

The other issue was Dermot Gallagher's refereeing of the Arsenal v Chelsea Premier League match yesterday where, according to most reporters and commentators, he had allowed far too much violent play and had failed to send Steve Bould off when, early in the game, he committed a foul which prevented an obvious goal-scoring opportunity. It was personally disappointing to hear this as I have always respected Dermot hugely. Ironically, last week I spoke to him at length when he phoned me after the announcement that Paul Durkin was going to the World Cup. Dermot had wondered then where he stood and I explained that there were doubts at the FA and in UEFA about his fitness and also a feeling that he was no longer a 'strong' referee and was ducking the necessary disciplinary actions. This had been confirmed in the minds of many at the recent Premier League referees' meeting where he continued to defend his decision not to dismiss a player for a foul which prevented an obvious goal-scoring opportunity even though everyone else was convinced it was a red-card offence.

When Dermot was working hard to become a top referee and get on the FIFA list I had told him (as he often reminds me) that the very best referees have to have that killer instinct, i.e. when really tough matches or decisions arise they can be utterly ruthless and do their job with clinical precision. Those referees who do not quite make it can, in that simile, commit manslaughter but not murder. I had felt for some time that Dermot had lost the killer instinct which had made him a fine referee and, two years ago, a real contender for the World Cup.

Tuesday 10 February

With my ankle back to apparent fitness and having trained sufficiently, I took my first steps back on to the field by refereeing the Harrow 1st XI match against Bedford School. It was a very straightforward game which Harrow won impressively 3–1, although all three Harrow goals were talking points afterwards. It was a good run out and the boys' behaviour was immaculate – in fact I wondered whether my presence had somewhat spoiled the game for them as they seemed to hold back in tackles and their conduct was almost too controlled and careful. My ankle twinged now and then and did not seem fully recovered but I was in desperate need of a match because I was feeling very lethargic. No matter how much training one does, the match situation, with its physical and mental demands, cannot be replicated.

When I got home there was an intriguing message on my answerphone from Sam Hamman, owner of Wimbledon, saying he wanted my advice on a non-refereeing matter. Over the years I have had my ups and downs with Wimbledon but, like most people in the game, have huge respect for the way Sam, Joe Kinnear and Vinnie Jones in particular kept the club in the Premier League and prominent in English football. I wondered if his call had anything to do with their plans to move to Ireland and play in Dublin.

Wednesday 11 February

I spent part of the morning being interviewed by someone from the University of Leicester who was doing research for a book about football. One of the questions I was pleased to answer was about the role of assistant referees. Many people do not understand why they so rarely flag for fouls they must have seen. The answer is that the referees give them instructions before the game as to what assistance they should give. In general, I ask them to flag only for fouls that I have *not* seen, as opposed to flagging for every offence they see; I ask them to flag only when I am out of position or the offence is on my blind side. Importantly, I ask them to tell me what decision I would have given had I seen the offence, given the way I am refereeing the game at the time. What they should not do is tell me what their decision would be if they were refereeing, as that might well be different from mine. Players and the crowd have a right to consistency within a match and that can only be achieved if the assistants get into the mind of the referee and officiate according to the referee's tolerance levels, which can of course vary during the game.

I also opened one of the most extraordinary letters I have ever received. It read as follows:

Dear Mr Elleray,
In April this year I am to be best man when my lifelong friend Mike marries Susan who is from the United States where the wedding is to be held followed by a blessing in this country.

Mike is a keen follower of Chesterfield FC and as such one of the happiest days of his life prior to this year was 13 April 1997, when Chesterfield came so close to reaching the FA Cup Final, a game in which you played a prominent role. You will probably be aware that since that day you have not been the most popular person in Chesterfield. However, in a spirit of reconciliation, I wondered if you could take a moment to reply with a message of congratulations to Mike and Susan, joining everyone in wishing them happiness in their future life together. I am sure you will agree with me in viewing such a gesture as a positive step towards healing last season's wound.

Thank you for taking the time to consider this rather unusual request.

How could I say no? It reminded me of a letter I received some time after the 1994 FA Cup Final from a vicar, requesting a photo of me because each year they put a famous face on their Guy Fawkes guy and they thought that I might be willing to be burned on the bonfire to cleanse my soul after the evil I had done in giving two penalties against Chelsea.

Thursday 12 February

I eventually made indirect contact with Sam Hamman, but by the time he got my message the matter he had wanted my advice on had been resolved and I was left intrigued as to what it was all about. As I went down to the fields to watch some soccer I was stunned to hear that Ruud Gullit had been sacked by Chelsea and replaced by Gianluca

Vialli. My few dealings with Mr Gullit had been interesting and had shown how the pressure of management changes people. Initially he had been very laid back and had an almost indifferent attitude to referees – Arsène Wenger had started the same way. However, as the pressure for success grew he became more animated and there were more frequent outbursts about referees, and opponents. I remembered his comments at Liverpool earlier this season but when I saw him again at Chelsea he was charm personified. Whatever the reason for his leaving, the Premier League would be poorer without him.

BBC Midlands TV called to ask for an interview following Jim Smith's comments that it was time to get rid of the small list of Premier League referees and return to the situation where a referee was at Derby one week and Darlington the next. This attitude seemed bizarre. Would he recommend that the best way to get high-class performances out of a player would be for him to be playing in the Premier League one week and in the Third Division the next? More significantly, the biggest gripe from managers used to be the lack of consistency among referees. Having only 19 gives us a far greater chance of a large measure of consistency than if there were a list of 40. Moreover, as the teams and referees meet frequently, the players get to know the referees better and vice versa, so there is less 'testing out' and a generally better rapport on the field. I really could not understand what Jim Smith was driving at.

I was interested to learn that the Premier League had written to Dermot Gallagher for his observations following last Sunday's match. Several Premier League colleagues had contacted me expressing their concern that, as one of them put it, 'Dermot has set refereeing back a long way by failing to do what every other Premier League referee would have done.'

Friday 13 February

An invitation arrived from John Barnwell of the League Managers Association for a group of Premier League referees and match observers to meet the six NW managers in March at Old Trafford. I discussed with Mike Foster of the Premier League which referees we would invite as we wanted sensible ones but who were also capable of holding their own against some rather forceful characters. We decided upon Steve Lodge, Gerald Ashby and Peter Jones. As I was due to be at Leeds v Blackburn the night before I thought I might also attend.

In the afternoon the Druries Torpid Seconders gained a convincing victory in their Harrow Football final. I umpired along with James Baron, House Master of our opponents, the Head Master's House. When I went up to teach at 5.15 p.m. the news of the appointment of three new House Masters had broken and I was delighted that I could officially comment on my pleasure that Peter Bieneman had been appointed to The Grove, Mel Mrowiec to Rendalls and Graham Dunbar to Bradbys. I am godfather to all four of Mel's daughters and to Peter's middle daughter Katie and was especially thrilled for them both.

In the evening I entertained some 30 people to dinner before we had House Songs. After Songs finished most of the guests stayed for drinks and coffee and there was much fun and plenty of conversation, the last ones not leaving until 3.30 a.m. I tidied up with the help of Daniel Hepher and Blair Abbiss and finally got to bed at 4 a.m.

Saturday 14 February

Today was Founder's Day – Old Boys' Day. I taught until 10.40 a.m. and then watched the Yearlings and Torpids Harrow Football Finals. Moretons were a little too big for us in the Yearlings and we lost 0–2 but we had a magnificent victory over the Knoll in the Torpids – 6–1. It was an excellent match enjoyed by all the Druries' supporters, and even Hugh Thompson, House Master of the Knoll, acknowledged that we were a strong team. Joe McKinney, master in charge of Harrow Football, believed we were the strongest Torpids team he had seen for a decade or more.

After lunch various Old Drurieans drifted back to the House to play Harrow Football against the House team. We had a fun afternoon with the current Drurieans winning 7–4. I always enjoy umpiring Harrow Football as it is one of the games which spawned soccer and rugby. The offside rule is basically that of rugby: if you are in front of the ball you are offside. In Harrow Football, if you catch the ball, which is larger and heavier than a modern football, when it has been kicked in the air you shout 'Yards'. The umpire marks where you caught it with his stick and you then take a long run up and when you reach the stick you take the biggest three strides you possibly can. Where you land is where the defenders stand and that is called 'three running yards' and is approximately 10 yards. This is the origin of 10 yards in soccer and rugby.

We in Druries feel a particular affinity for soccer and especially the FA Cup, as the man who started it was an Old Drurian – Charles Alcock. He came to Druries in 1855 and when he became Secretary of the FA he set up the FA Cup and actually played for Wanderers in the first final, having a goal disallowed for handball. Wanderers, of whom he was Secretary, won the FA Cup three times and therefore won the right to keep the trophy outright, but Alcock in his capacity as Secretary of Wanderers gave the cup back to the FA Secretary (himself), on condition that no one could ever win it outright again. Few people realise that its official title is the FA Challenge Cup for, in the early days, there was a qualifying competition whose winners challenged the holders who were exempt until the final. Charles Alcock went on to referee several FA Cup Finals. When I refereed the FA Cup Final in 1994 I slept in Druries the night before and had a real sense of history having come full circle.

In the evening I gave a dinner for Mel and Vivien Mrowiec and Peter and Lynette Bieneman to celebrate the wonderful news of their appointment to Houses. The boys have gone home for half-term so all was quiet and we were undisturbed.

Sunday 15 February

I drove to Ely to stay with a former girlfriend of mine, Susan, who organised a super lunch party for several former colleagues and friends. I went to evening prayer in Ely Cathedral – an uplifting experience in a stunning building and with an excellent choir from Cambridge. We had time for a long walk and to catch up with the news, and I was particularly keen to follow the Test score on Ceefax.

Monday 16 February

I slept late and then had coffee with some friends in their amazing house next to the cathedral. The view from their kitchen window must turn washing up into a joy, although the ghost upstairs might make life a little spooky at times. Susan took me to her office where I worked for a few hours before driving home listening to the absorbing Test match. When I got back to Harrow I was not surprised to find my answerphone crammed with messages from people wanting to discuss the non-penalty decisions by Mike Riley (Manchester United v Barnsley) and Martin Bodenham (Arsenal v Crystal Palace). In both matches what appeared to be clear penalties were not awarded. Mike Riley's was easy to explain because his view of the incident was partly blocked by the players involved and he could not have been 100 per cent sure that there had been a foul so could not award Barnsley the penalty. With Martin, one incident had happened so quickly that everyone had thought the foul was outside the box, but TV had shown it to be inside, raising again the question of technology. In the second 'penalty' incident the Arsenal player over-reacted. Referees these days will not give a penalty unless they are absolutely certain, and if there is an over-reaction from the player fouled the referee is far less likely to penalise the tackle as he does not want to be shown to have been conned. In this respect players who exaggerate really do risk achieving the opposite of what they are after. I decided that I was on holiday, left the messages unanswered and went out to dinner.

Tuesday 17 February

I spent all day at my desk trying to write the executive summary of my vision for the future of Harrow for my submission to the governors. I spoke to Ken Ridden about the UEFA course I missed in Majorca. He updated me on its content and explained that the Referees' Committee would be delighted to welcome me back when I became available. We discussed recent refereeing controversies and he told me that I had been appointed to Liverpool v Arsenal and Leeds v Chelsea in April. I made a note of the dates and thought nothing more about it until later in the afternoon when I suddenly remembered that it was Chelsea v Leeds that had given Graham Poll so many problems in the 'Battle of Stamford Bridge' – two red cards and about eight yellows in the first half. I had been given the re-match.

Wednesday 18 February

I again spent most of the day at my desk – this time updating and rewriting my C.V. In the evening the boys came back from the (too) short half-term break. Peter Jones phoned to say he could not referee the Boodle and Dunthorne Independent Schools Cup Final, so I persuaded Steve Lodge to take the appointment. I telephoned him just after Middlesbrough and Chelsea had both won their Coca-Cola semi-finals. Given that Steve refereed Chelsea v Middlesbrough in the

FA Cup Final in 1997 I told him I was convinced that history would repeat itself and he would get them again in the Coca-Cola Final.

Thursday 19 February

I was very pleased to receive an invitation to the PFA awards dinner in the post today. I taught for most of the day and worked in the evening before having the victorious House ensemble team in for a celebration Big Mac. Unfortunately, I was pretty ill during the night, as were several of the boys.

Friday 20 February

As I read the paper in the bath this morning I saw that Samassi Abou of West Ham has been given an additional one-match ban and been fined £1,000 for grabbing hold of me at Spurs. I think he had got off pretty lightly and was disappointed that the FA had decided to take no action against him (or Patrick Vieira) for failing to leave the field of play immediately upon being shown the red card.

My day was then taken up with responding to the three Barnsley MPs who put down an Early Day Motion in the House of Commons condemning Mike Riley's non-penalty decision at Old Trafford on Sunday and suggesting that the Premier League referees were biased against Barnsley. I did several press and radio interviews but MPs are probably held in lower regard than referees, so the interviewers were always on my side and usually felt that the MPs should have better things to think about, as we appeared to be on the brink of war with Iraq. I knew Eric Illsley, one of the MPs, reasonably well through Steve Lodge so I phoned Steve and told him to give Eric a hard time.

Saturday 21 February

The last Saturday without a Premier League match so I refereed Harrow 2nd XI versus Wellington College – an excellent 2–2 draw with only three or four fouls and no dissent. Such a pleasure compared to the aggro I knew was in store for me in the coming weeks. I received notification that the Premier League had decided to withdraw Dermot Gallagher's next match following his refereeing of Arsenal v Chelsea. A few years ago, when the game was blighted by 'alternative referees' who would not conform to agreed practices, referees voted to give the

Premier League the authority to remove matches from referees, if they significantly underperformed. It had happened only rarely, although Rodger Gifford from Wales had been so treated a few years ago. At a time when there was concern that referees are not accountable it was a positive move to show that we are dealt with if we do not perform to the required standard. I felt sorry for Dermot but I had warned him before that match that there was concern at the FA and in UEFA about his refereeing.

In the evening I had a working supper with Mel Mrowiec explaining Harrow's entry procedure while he helped me with my submission to the governors.

Sunday 22 February

A very interesting piece from Patrick Barclay in the *Sunday Telegraph* encapsulated what many of us think about some of the TV commentators and so-called experts. Commenting on Chelsea v Arsenal in midweek he wrote,

> my enjoyment was rather spoilt by one aspect of the commentary. Alan Parry criticised the referee, Graham Poll, for doing no more than caution players who asked for it. Meanwhile, the normally admirable and instructive Andy Gray began by endorsing bookings then ridiculing them as they mounted up. And we are told that referees are inconsistent.

We had noticed the same problem with Andy Gray when Steve Lodge admirably refereed the Chelsea v Manchester United FA Cup-tie, and you sometimes feel the same about managers who want their players protected but then complain that there are too many yellow cards in the game. Of course Alan Parry is a notorious referee-hater and has been disciplined in the past for outbursts at referees after matches at Wycombe Wanderers. He is the only broadcaster who makes a point of not even extending the usual courtesies to referees when you pass him in the corridor at matches where he is commentating.

Barclay went on to say,

> with the exception of Patrick Vieira's first yellow card – unfortunate in that his second led to dismissal – every punishment was not only justified but necessary, given the recent history of

aggravation between the teams . . . Poll should have been praised for his control. The question of why players and managers so often get away with their mistakes whilst referees are attacked for good judgement is one that testifies to the game's increasing madness.

No more comment needed and thank goodness there are still a few sane and respected reporters to point out how the game is developing these days.

I was disappointed that I was unable to referee the Old Harrovians v the Harrow 1st XI at Roehampton, not least because it was the first match after injury for Blair Abbiss, the Drurian captain of the team. He was desperate to play as his brother Justin had come over from Hong Kong to play. In the event the match was an excellent 3–3 draw and Blair played without further injury for the last 10 minutes and his brother scored a cracking goal, watched by their parents Linda and John, great friends of mine. Peter Leaver, Chief Executive of the Premier League, refereed; he regularly officiates for the Old Harrovians even though he is an Old Etonian.

In the afternoon I watched the Yearlings convincingly beat the Park 3–1 in the first group match of their cup competition. In the evening I dined with George Attenborough and Peter Hunter. I was celebrating having almost finished my submission.

Monday 23 February

An interesting letter arrived from *Time* magazine asking if I would write an article of 800–1,000 words about the World Cup for their June issue. The importance of an event I was still feeling pain about missing was brought home to me in the letter which said, 'Eagerly anticipating the World Cup (along with the rest of the planet), *Time* is planning a special issue in advance of the finals in France . . .'

In the same post arrived the latest copy of *FIFA News* with some interesting points about refereeing including a 'Referees' Prayer' from Michel Vautrot, a Frenchman on the FIFA Referees' Committee who famously sent two players off in the 1990 World Cup Finals when Cameroon beat Argentina. He once told me that that match made him so famous in Africa that he even had an African turn up at his home asking him for help as he was the only European whom he had heard of. The prayer was:

1. Protect the game, the players and the occasion.
2. Be taken seriously, but don't take yourself too seriously.
3. Don't confuse authority with authoritarianism.
4. Always put the spirit of the game before the letter of the Law and never forget the unwritten Law 18, calling for common sense and intelligence.
5. Football was not invented for referees.

There was much wisdom in those words, not least the second and fifth points. Law 18 does not exist but expresses the philosophy that referees should always try to referee in the way which is best for the game itself. We often say that people who know the Laws backwards do not always make good referees, rather like passing your driving test does not necessarily make you a good driver.

I had an interesting phone call from Steve Lodge who was reserve referee for Gary Willard at Newcastle v Leeds yesterday. At half-time Steve was walking out with Terry McDermott and Kenny Dalglish, who asked him whether he was paid the same as the referee. They were amazed that a referee in the Premier League is paid only £375 and the assistant referees £175. They thought it should be at least £800 and Kenny simply said that he would not do it for £1,000 a match and could not believe how poorly we were paid for all the hassle and pressure. The difficulty of being the reserve referee was brought home to Steve by the arrival after half-time of George Graham, who shouted at Steve every time a decision went against Leeds. In the end Steve told him to be quiet, or if he had to shout he should direct it at the referee as his decisions were not Steve's fault. Graham then started swearing at a female police superintendent who Steve was hoping would take action against him but nothing happened.

I was amused to hear that I was blamed on David Mellor's 606 radio programme for the penalty given against Barnsley at Coventry by Alan Wilkie. Alan and I do have somewhat similar hair-styles, but it is bad enough being abused for my own decisions without being blamed for other people's.

Tuesday 24 February

I awoke this morning to read in the *Daily Telegraph* the official news that the Premier League had taken Dermot Gallagher off the Blackburn v Leicester match this Saturday, following the Arsenal v Chelsea game.

As I went up to teach for the morning I knew that the day would be hectic once the news went around the media. I was not wrong!

I spent almost the entire afternoon taking calls from the newspapers and then doing a live interview for Radio Five. In the early evening I went into Sky News' studios to talk to Mark Saggers and Alan Mullery about the pressures on referees. I think the media were somewhat surprised that Dermot accepted his punishment and that I was supporting the Premier League, so a real controversy did not develop. I wanted to make it clear that Dermot had been withdrawn from his match not because of one incident (the failure to send off Steve Bould) but because of his overall performance for which the match observer had given him a grade D, the lowest possible and the only one awarded so far this season. I believe it is important for referees to be seen to be accountable but to be punished only on the basis of the match observer's report and then only for overall performance. We have to accept that referees make mistakes and it would be wrong to suspend people left right and centre so that they were fearful of every decision. However, it had become clear that Dermot was not refereeing as he should and, probably subconsciously, had eased off. This was a good reminder to him and the rest of us that we have to apply the Laws and mandatory instructions whether we like it or not. I spoke to Dermot at length and he was very sensible and accepted the situation, not least because he, like the rest of us, has enormous respect for Philip Don, the match observer.

Wednesday 25 February

Further refereeing controversy for me to deal with when it emerged that the Swedish referee, Leif Sudnell, while on a referees' course in Spain went to watch Real Betis play a Spanish League match and was entertained by the home team in the directors' box. This would have been all right had Sundell not been due to referee Real Betis against Chelsea next week in the Cup Winners' Cup. He had been quite professional going to get a feel of the ground and watch the team but he had been foolish to accept hospitality. I checked the facts with Ken Ridden before commenting to the press but I had no doubt that UEFA would take him off the game as they would wish everything to be above board. It just shows how thin the line between success and failure is and how a moment's lack of thought and sense can bring a whole heap of trouble and disappointment.

Thursday 26 February

I was delighted to learn that Peter Jones from Loughborough had been appointed to referee the Chelsea v Middlesbrough Coca-Cola Cup Final. I had expected Steve Lodge to be appointed but was thrilled for Peter as he is a really honest, kind and decent man. He refereed the Charity Shield with distinction at the start of the season and had certainly earned a return to the twin towers.

I received a nice letter from Doug Insole about the Oxford v Cambridge Varsity match I had been appointed to referee. I also had a letter from the Cambridge University AFC President asking me if I would write something for the match programme.

Friday 27 February

Woke up this morning feeling very negative about tomorrow's match – Crystal Palace v Coventry. I am not sure whether it was the prospect of another encounter with Gordon Strachan or just that I enjoyed the break so much that I was fearful of returning to the spotlight and the inevitable pressure and possible abuse. Since I lost the chance to go to the World Cup I had noticed a perceptible change in my attitude; my hunger for refereeing had been waning and I was thinking more and more about retiring. I was also distracted because the week of the House play was getting closer.

Saturday 28 February

I drove to the match with a heavy heart and sense of foreboding. In the event all went well and I had a really enjoyable afternoon. My assistants were Pete Walton and Phil Sharp and Alan Robinson, a tireless worker for the Referees' Association, was the match observer. It was Gary Pendrey who brought in the team sheet for Coventry, so I asked with a big smile where 'my friend' was. Gary replied in jocular vein and the air seemed to clear.

The match was relatively straightforward, especially as Coventry scored after about 45 seconds and went on to win 3–0 without extending themselves too much. Both sets of players were friendly and co-operative. I am sure that this was an excellent example of how a manager can really influence the behaviour of his players. I have no doubt in my mind that the Coventry lads had been told not to give me any trouble – they were probably assuming that I was out to settle a few scores. Consequently, they behaved sensibly and we ended up getting on well, with respect enhanced on all sides. There were four yellow cards, two for each team, mainly for fouls which were late or tactical rather than nasty. It was somewhat ironic that the first player to shake hands at the end of the game was Gordon Strachan's son, although his father did not appear afterwards. It's strange how they are quick to come and talk if they want to complain.

Driving home I felt positive and good. I had enjoyed the physical exertion and there had been no controversy. If all matches were like that, then refereeing would be so much more enjoyable. Perhaps I had been too hasty to want to retire, after all.

March 1998

Sunday 1 March

I was up early as a group of boys in the House were going on the Countryside march to London. They had to leave early to get back in time for the afternoon rehearsals for the House play – *Amadeus* – which they were going to perform later in the week. I spent most of the day in and out of the theatre checking the rehearsals and then going back to Druries to try to work on my submission to the governors.

No comments on yesterday's match in the papers which was pleasing.

Monday 2 March

Most of the School were busy with the CCF night exercise and Field Day but I had pulled all of Druries out so they could get on with their work and with the play. I taught in the morning and then got ready for the arrival of the five young boys who were coming to sit the Harrow Entrance Scholarship.

Tuesday 3 March

A hectic day teaching, watching school soccer and looking after the scholarship boys while also keeping an eye on the play's dress rehearsal. I sent off a Premier League referee's shirt to PC Bogle of the Metropolitan Police for a charity draw. I also persuaded the boys in the House that we should 'adopt' an overseas child through a charity. I felt it would be something very positive for the boys to do and they would see a direct return for their donations rather than the money just disappearing into some large pot. They were very keen on the idea.

Wednesday 4 March

The first night of *Amadeus*. The school's Ryan Theatre was almost full with about 380 people in the audience and the play went exceptionally well. I was most impressed with all the boys, especially Charlie Hollway as Mozart and Alex Ward as Salieri. Poor Alex, who was on stage for almost the entire play, had started the first act wanting to go to the loo and had been stuck for almost an hour. It was ironic that the first act closes with his character saying that he had bladder problems and an interval was needed.

After the performance people were lavish in their praise of the boys both onstage and backstage and I was enormously proud of them all. Two years ago we had, as a House, staged *The Madness of George III*, which had generally been regarded as the best House play for many years. *Amadeus* looked like improving on that achievement.

Thursday 5 March

The word around the School this morning was that the play had been excellent, and as Harrovians are not quick to compliment this was pleasing for all the boys involved. There were lots of nice letters from various people, which I pinned on the boys' door. The scholarship boys finished their last exams and went home and at lunchtime I told the House that they now had a really difficult task ahead of them as tonight's audience would be expecting excellence, so the pressure was on. If the boys thought that everything would automatically go well it would be a disaster, so I tried to motivate them to improve on last night's performance. I felt a little like a football manager.

I spent the afternoon preparing for parents coming to dinner and getting things ready for the post-play party. In the early evening I was reminded of how magnificent life at Harrow can be. I had parents for drinks in my beautiful drawing room and then it was off for supper in the equally impressive masters' dining room. This was followed by the play in our theatre. The boys were superb and acted even better than last night. Woody Stileman as Mozart's wife was so stunningly good, one forgot that he was a boy. Afterwards the compliments flew and many adults commented that it was better than a lot of productions in the West End and could not believe that all the actors were from one House. Again I felt really proud. We had a good party back in

Druries and made presentations to matron, who had worked so hard, and to Al Boag, who had directed the play with such sensitivity and care. He had earned the genuine respect and affection of all the House and had clearly enjoyed his involvement with Druries.

Friday 6 March

In addition to lots of kind cards and notes about the play, I had an interesting mailbag this morning, including something from a group calling themselves World Soccer Supporters Club. They were aiming to set up a club through the Internet and wanted me to be involved in the international press meeting and to write a short article and raise questions for the Internet page, which they would then like me to update every month or so. I wrote back saying I was happy, in principle, to take part. Even more extraordinary was a letter from a theatre company who were putting on a play about Chesterfield's run in last year's FA Cup. They wanted me to write some notes for the programme about the three matches I refereed: Chesterfield v Nottingham Forest and the two semi-finals against Middlesbrough. They even offered me free tickets for the play and the use of a professional make-up artist so I could attend in disguise.

Saturday 7 March

Mixed weather on the drive down to Southampton was reflected in the match later in the afternoon. I have never been hugely popular with Everton or Southampton so I was expecting a 'warm' welcome from both sets of fans and, as the game turned out, I had them on my back at different times.

The early stages of the match were very easy. I am always somewhat apprehensive if the early stages of a game are quiet for, no matter what one's reputation is, it is always useful to have a few opportunities to establish control and imprint one's authority on the game. In the 36th minute Everton knocked a ball through the home defence, and although the Everton forward appeared offside, there was no flag from my assistant, Kevin Pike. The forward was in the penalty area when he was tugged down by Ken Monkou so it was a clear penalty and a red card for denying an obvious goal-scoring opportunity. Poor Ken sat with his head in his hands before trudging off. Jason Dodds asked if I could avoid sending him off, as there was a player on the goal line. I explained that this made no difference as there is often the goalkeeper on the line and it is a goal-scoring opportunity that determines the punishment, not the certainty that a goal would be scored. With the home fans howling, the goalkeeper saved the penalty. The game livened up then and I looked for, and found, an opportunity for a yellow card to calm tempers. After any major incident the temperature of the game always rises and it is important as a referee to establish one's authority quickly and firmly. The usual technique is to penalise every foul, no matter how minor, and effectively kill the game until tempers calm down. A yellow card is equally helpful provided it is reasonable, but any offence in this period is likely to be penalised strongly. We left the field at half-time to a cacophony of boos for the assistant who had failed to flag offside.

During the half-time interval I discussed with Kevin how he was coping with the pressure and whether he wanted to change sides with Phil Sharp and get away from the crowd and the trainers' benches. I was pleased that he decided not to take this easy option, not least because it would have left him with the Southampton defence and we might have had another contentious offside. The second half was an almost mirror image of the first with, this time, Slaven Bilic of Everton bringing down a Southampton player in the penalty area, earning a penalty and a red card. I know that some would say that I was evening up my decision of the first half, but I was simply being consistent and there could be few complaints. Again, the few minutes after the penalty were lively and I produced the yellow card a couple of times. In the end Southampton won 2-1 and Dennis Hughes, the match observer, seemed very happy with our control of the game.

Returning to our cars after the match, we were met with a mixture of autograph hunters and those wanting to hurl abuse. When some home fans complained about the Southampton sending off our security escort told them that Ken Monkou himself had agreed that he deserved to be sent off and that seemed to stop the moans.

I had a good drive home and then had friends to supper, which meant that I missed *Match of the Day*.

Sunday 8 March

A quiet day. There was nothing in the papers following yesterday's match – the two dismissals seem to have been accepted by everyone and were not even talking points. I intended to work hard but was tired after last week and had a peaceful day, much of it spent on the rugby fields as Harrow was hosting the prep schools tournament. Roger Uttley and I chatted to parents and at times were swamped by autograph hunters. I had an excellent lunch with my god-daughter, Katie, and her family. Later we had a parents' evening so I was busy for a couple of hours with them.

Monday 9 March

Nothing much in the papers except that the *Daily Mail* launched a berserk attack on me – it seems that my fitness has crashed since last week and the man who writes the referee watch column was cross that I had not given up my Sunday to talk to him.

I had an interesting call from the *Daily Express* wanting to know why I was not available for UEFA matches until June. I explained that I was busy at Harrow and that, following my withdrawal from selection for the World Cup, I had decided to spend more time at School. The reporter wanted to know if I had been forced to withdraw by the school or parents but I put him straight on that.

Tuesday 10 March

This morning I foolishly agreed to referee the Harrow v Westminster School under-15 match at Harrow. It was foolish because by the time kick-off came around it was freezing cold and pouring with rain. Nevertheless, it was an excellent game and both teams played wholeheartedly, Harrow winning 3-1. There were hardly any disputes although I did have to point out to one of the masters that a player cannot be offside from a goal-kick.

When I got back home there were messages from Sky News and the Press Association wanting to talk about the various announcements from FIFA about how referees would officiate in the World Cup. There was particular excitement that the tackle from behind was being outlawed and would be punished by a red card. My understanding was different, that FIFA had only restated their view that severe tackles from behind would be given a red card. As I did not have the text to hand I felt it would be wrong to make any pronouncements.

It always seems strange that FIFA bring in new interpretations for the World Cup Finals, when it would be more logical to introduce them when the qualifying matches begin. Perhaps they feel that the World Cup is such a big stage that this is the best way to disseminate new procedures throughout the world. They are also obviously keen that the skilful and exciting players should dominate the competition; historically, this has not always been the case. Indeed the Brazilians felt that Pelé was literally kicked out of the 1966 World Cup. For that reason no English referee officiated with the Brazilian national team for the next 30 years, and I had the honour of breaking that 'ban' when I refereed South Africa v Brazil in Johannesburg in 1996 in the Mandela Trophy match.

Wednesday 11 March

A small piece in the *Daily Express* announced that I had opted out of both the World Cup and European duties because I could not spare the time from my work as House Master. The piece mentioned that I refereed yesterday's School's match as a warm-up for this evening's Leeds v Blackburn fixture.

I had a good journey to Leeds and the match was excellent. There were four very impressive goals from Leeds but the most pleasing aspect was that I went almost an entire game without a yellow card. Both sets of players responded really well to my chatting to them, and as there was no undercurrent of nastiness, when there was the occasional foul I could talk rather than caution. Although offences like the bad tackle from behind have mandatory punishments, there still exist areas where the referee can use his discretion and decide what action to take on the basis of the seriousness of the offence and the nature of the game. I have always believed that yellow cards should be used to maintain control rather than as a measure to try to regain control. In this match control was never threatened so I could talk much more and use the private, and not so private, rebuke.

I got to the 88th minute and was almost being overtaken by the excitement of not having shown a card – a rarity these days for most Premier League referees. Then Chris Sutton was guilty of a late, bad tackle in the centre circle but as Leeds kept possession I applied the advantage clause. George Graham was up off his bench shouting for action and berating the assistant referee (Peter Walton) because I had missed the foul. Fortunately, there was the perfect response – Leeds continued with their possession and scored their fourth goal and I then went back and showed Chris the yellow card. Even George had to admit, grudgingly, that I had done the right thing.

After the game Alan Sutton, one of the Leeds physios, kindly came in and presented me with the green shirt which I had worn for the second half of the Leeds v Newcastle match as my kit had clashed with Newcastle's. He had kept it in a drawer for me and the gesture was typical of the kindness he shows to the Premier League officials.

It was a long drive home. When people say that the money is not bad for 90 minutes' refereeing, they forget that for a match like this I leave home at two o'clock in the afternoon and get in at about two in the morning – a long 12 hours.

Thursday 12 March

Not quite the hectic day I had originally planned as I had decided not to go to the meeting with some Premier League managers in Manchester because I would not be back in time for an evening function. It was the Lady Bourchier Reading Prize and I had two of the eight finalists. Beforehand I had dinner with the Head Master and his wife, Gilly, along with the adjudicator, Miss Prunella Scales. We had all been expecting a real-life Sybil Fawlty, but she was nothing like that and was good company at dinner. However, her adjudication was somewhat controversial, in part because she mixed up the boys' names and did not pick the two boys who everyone else thought were the best. Ah well, that is the beauty of outside adjudicators and it reminded me of a comment I once made to Tony Adams of Arsenal that we may be useless but we aren't biased.

Earlier in the day I had been somewhat thrown when Sandy Smith, another House Master, told me that *The Times* was saying that I was the most hated referee in football. It turned out that I was 'feared' rather than 'hated', but I was disappointed that the *Times Diary* had some gossip about me and the appointment of the new Head Master of Harrow. The item read:

Home Win?
The most feared referee in football, David Elleray, a housemaster at Harrow, has a clash of fixtures which will prevent him brandishing his cards at this year's World Cup. Elleray insists that 'supervisory duties' at Harrow prevent him from travelling to France. But I learn of more pressing business in Harrow. Nicholas Bomford, headmaster, is retiring and interviews for the post begin in July. Elleray is a prime candidate.

I did not regard this as particularly helpful, especially as it came out on the very day that my application was being delivered to the clerk of the governors. I was concerned that the governors might think that I was orchestrating a press campaign – which could not be further from the truth. There was nothing I could do about it and I hoped that the governors would see from the inaccuracy of the date of the interviews that this was just gossip and speculation and that the information had not come from me.

Friday 13 March

Real pleasure and excitement today when I got a phone call from the FA to say that the German Football Federation had invited me to referee their forthcoming friendly with Brazil. This match, a warm-up to the World Cup, would be played in Stuttgart between the World Cup holders, Brazil, and the winners of Euro '96. For me it would complete a unique double as I had already refereed Brazil when they played South Africa, the African champions, in 1996. After discussions with the FA it was agreed that Graham Barber would go with me as senior assistant and Phil Sharp as the other official.

In the evening I went to Moretons, where I used to be the resident House Tutor, for House Songs. It was an excellent evening as I taught a number of the senior boys, who were socially confident and easy to talk to. The sketches were fun and mainly portrayed the Moretons House Master, Simon Berry and I battling it out to be top dog. I was flattered when a parent told me that the reputation of Druries in Norfolk was that I took only one in every 80 applicants and that it was the House that everyone wanted to get their sons into. It was another late night and I got to bed about two in the morning.

Saturday 14 March

It was strange to have no Premier League match again but it meant that I could devote the morning to teaching. Afterwards I interviewed twin brothers for places in Druries in September. In the afternoon I refereed a Junior Colts match and very much regretted having volunteered as the weather was diabolical – wind, rain – but the boys played well and there were few problems. In the evening the Sixth Form in my House held a Finds Dinner, entertaining a number of masters to a spectacular meal in my dining room. Everything was properly done from the written invitations through to dinner jackets, Latin grace, Loyal toast – a thoroughly enjoyable affair which ended some time after three.

Sunday 15 March

The morning was spent cleaning up after last night's Finds Dinner. In the afternoon I watched the Shell athletics and was delighted that we came second overall. There had been much debate in the papers about FIFA's decision to outlaw the tackle from behind, with the British press going mad. They had interpreted the FIFA comments as meaning that every tackle from behind in the World Cup would result in a red card. The situation was that FIFA had reaffirmed their decision to require referees to be very strict with tackles from behind. It is perfectly possible to tackle cleanly from behind but there should be no contact with the opponent before the ball is played. However, if the challenge is so forceful that contact with the opponent takes place simultaneously or is inevitable and potentially dangerous then the referee should give a yellow card at least. Any tackle from behind which 'endangers the safety of an opponent' should receive a red card. While people were protesting that they do not pay good money to see players sent off, they needed reminding that they want to see skilful players and we want no more situations like that of Marco van Basten who was forced out of the game by injury from violent play.

Monday 16 March

I received a letter from a student in his final year of a media production degree course at Farnborough's College of Technology. He wanted to come and film me at a match and do an interview as part of a 30-minute video documentary. I explained that he would have to get Premier League permission to film me at a match but that I was happy to be interviewed at Harrow early next term. The day was dominated by House soccer matches. The Yearlings won their group game and tense matches for Torpids and House teams ensured that we had a chance of being in all three semi-finals. In the evening I hosted the School 1st XI soccer dinner.

Tuesday 17 March

This afternoon the Yearlings won their semi-final while the House and Torpid teams qualified for their semi-finals. The evening was dominated by a stunning choral society performance of Mozart's *Requiem* with the Speech Room jam-packed – a memorable occasion.

Wednesday 18 March

This afternoon saw the inter-House drill competition and the culmination of weeks of practice and preparation of the uniforms. There were two sections – the inspection and the drill – and we came second in both, but only by a whisker. These scores were added to the ones from last term's assault course and meant that we emerged victorious as the top CCF House and thus retained the coveted Ansell Bowl.

The Ansell Bowl is one of the major Inter-House trophies. The CCF competitions epitomise the excellent team work that can be developed by the boys over a whole range of skills and challenges and emphasises that boys at boarding school gain much more than just an academic education.

After supper I had a quick drinks party to celebrate and we drank champagne out of the silver Ansell Bowl. I then went across the road to the Head Master's House for Songs.

Thursday 19 March

This afternoon we lost the House soccer semi-final but it was a really wonderful match of exciting football and thrilling end-to-end action with scarcely a foul or word of complaint – just as football should be played. Fortunately, the Yearlings and the Torpids both won their semi-finals so the House was in good spirits when I took them all to the cinema followed by a trip to McDonald's. However, as I was going to be pushed to write all my end of term reports because I would be away at the weekend, I checked the boys into the cinema and then popped back to the House to write reports for an hour and a half before returning at the end of the film. They were none the wiser that I had not been in the cinema.

Friday 20 March

The last full day of term so the morning was filled with the usual routine administration and meetings. In the afternoon we emerged as joint winners of the Yearlings final (0–0 after extra-time) but won the Torpids final 1–0 against our old rivals, Elmfield. This gave us revenge for their victory in last term's rugby final and meant that we had won the Torpid soccer competition for the fourth year running. We had drinks to celebrate before the end-of-term supper. After this we had the presentation of the bicentenary awards to the top performing boys in the House and they, not surprisingly, went to the actors from *Amadeus* – Alex Ward, Charlie Hollway and Woody Stileman. The House then watched videos but one or two had caught the party mood too much and I was up until late dealing with a junior who had drunk illicit beer and another who decided that he would smoke a cigarette out of his friend's window. As ever, the end of term is a time when everyone is a little tired and irritable and these incidents took on a greater significance with the boys than they would usually have done, but they were resolved sensibly in the end.

Saturday 21 March

Having been up late dealing with various misbehaving boys I felt very tired. After clearing up the House and sending the boys off on their Easter holidays I spent the rest of the morning and the afternoon writing end-of-term reports. About five o'clock Gary Willard and Martin Bodenham arrived to drive me to Moor Hall for the Premier League referees' meeting. Before dinner the news broke that Paul Durkin had been appointed to referee the Cup Final with Graham Barber as reserve referee. I was particularly pleased for Graham, as he had been one of my linesmen in the 1994 Final. It gave him the real possibility of becoming the first person to have a hat-trick of finals

as linesman, reserve and ultimately, referee. The usual evening meal
went well until Paul Durkin and Paul Alcock announced that they
wanted an emergency meeting of all the referees tomorrow morning
to talk about next season's fees; and they did not want Ken Ridden
or Mike Foster to attend. I agreed but a number of colleagues were
cross that a meeting should be called at such short notice.

Sunday 22 March

The emergency meeting did not amount to much as several colleagues,
who had been vociferous in the bar yesterday evening, had lost some
of their fire. Some wanted much more money and I explained that
more money would mean extra commitment and, at present, we
were in a happy position of being paid pretty well but being able
to maintain a full-time job. If the fees were to increase significantly
then the Premier League would, understandably, want more of our
time, and many of the Premier League referees could not afford to be
available at the drop of a hat throughout the season. Reason prevailed
in the end and we did agree that I should tackle the FA about the lack
of support referees were receiving when they were either threatened
on the field or verbally attacked by players and managers.

The main part of the morning was again spent looking at video
clips with a particular focus on penalty-kicks and whether the
correct disciplinary sanctions were being applied when penalties
were awarded. Players, managers and spectators often feel that if
a penalty is given then it is sufficient punishment and there should
be no red or yellow cards. What they fail to appreciate is that the
penalty-kick is the *team*'s punishment while the red or yellow card
is the *individual*'s punishment. The second part of the morning was a
very interesting talk on food, nutrition and health and this made lunch
a rather sombre affair with very few risking the chocolate pudding and
almost all going for the fruit salad.

Monday 23 March

As I was going away to Germany the following day I spent the
whole day writing reports, doing the House accounts and composing
the House newsletter. I received an extraordinary nine-page letter
from a fan about 'The Performance of Referees' which discussed in
exceptional detail the perceived effects of Dermot Gallagher's removal

from a Premier League match. The letter had been copied to all sorts of people and rambled on and on in an illogical manner. I try to reply to all such correspondence without being drawn into huge debates; but it does show how much people care about the game. In the evening I had dinner in London with parents of a boy in the House.

Tuesday 24 March

By mid-morning I had finished all my paperwork and felt as though the holidays were at last here. I travelled to Heathrow and met up with Graham Barber and Peter Walton and we had the usual friendly greeting from security. After a good flight we were met at Stuttgart airport by Horst Maier, an official of the Stuttgart club, and Marcus Schmidt, a young German referee. We were disappointed to find that the hotel had been changed but this often happens in international as opposed to club matches with the match officials not being particularly well treated. We were taken out for a fine meal, however, and our German hosts introduced us to people at a nearby table as curling players, so that we were not disturbed by questions about the match.

Wednesday 25 March

Mid-morning we went to Hotel Graf Zeppelin to organise match details and found out that the game was being televised live to 122 countries and there would be a press corps of in excess of 400 at the match. We were invited to the official luncheon which turned out to be something of a pain because we were in a smoke-filled room until 3 p.m. when we would rather have been back in the hotel resting. During the official speeches Egidius Braun, President of the German Football Federation and the man tipped to be the next UEFA President, had several sly digs at us about the battle between Germany and England to host the 2006 World Cup. We sat and smiled diplomatically and left as soon as we could.

After a sleep and some tea we went to the stunning Stuttgart Stadium, and before the game watched some youngsters playing exhibition matches on the pitch. Our dressing rooms were fine and we had a cheery welcome from Jürgen Klinsmann when he arrived. The German fourth official (a dentist) was excellent and sorted out all the pre-match administration for us.

Walking out in front of the teams I had a real sense of anticipation and excitement, and a few butterflies in the stomach. I was immensely proud to have been put in charge of such a prestigious match. I was hoping that I would be able to sit back and let the game flow and only have to intervene here and there; unfortunately, I had not read the newspapers and did not realise that the Germans were determined to get a victory and gain a major psychological advantage over one of their main World Cup rivals.

This game, between the top two footballing countries in the world, started rather slowly and there was a distinct lack of atmosphere in the stadium. However, the Germans were really fired up and in the 6th and 7th minutes, I had to give yellow cards to Ziege and Hamaan for foul tackles. The Brazilians over-reacted and came rushing up on each occasion saying 'FIFA rules – red card'. In the 9th minute the Brazilian captain, Dunga, went into a challenge with his foot high and I cautioned him. This so-called friendship match had produced three yellow cards in the first nine minutes.

Refereeing competition matches poses few problems as there are strict regulations and guidelines but no one really expects referees to be over-strict and officious in friendlies. However, I did not want to let the game get out of hand and I was conscious that there were millions watching throughout the world. This would be the most important and most watched international match before the World Cup and I was aware that it would be seen by some as an indication of how strict the referees would be in France. I was also very conscious that all the World Cup referees and assistant referees were meeting in Paris this week for their pre-World Cup briefing and would almost certainly all be watching the match. We have no sterner critics than our fellow colleagues.

Matters calmed a little until the 34th minute when Jürgen Kohler committed one of the worst fouls I have seen on a football field, catching the Brazilian late and high. I gave him an instant red card and he walked off with little protest, indeed he apologised to the Brazil bench on his way to the dressing room, but his manager ignored him completely. There was little reaction from the crowd. Soon after Brazil scored and at half-time they were still leading 1–0 and I had cautioned a second Brazilian, Denilson. As we walked off I braced myself for a negative crowd reaction and protests from players and officials but none came.

When we emerged after half-time one of the Brazilian coaches came to chat and reminded me that we had met in Tokyo when he was with the Gremio team in the World Club Championship. It obviously helped that they remembered me from that match. The second half was rather like the first. I gave yellow cards to Junior Baiano and Caesar Sampaio in the 50th and 51st minutes, and in the 57th minute I sent off the Brazilian captain, Dunga, for a second bookable offence. He was not very happy as he trudged off and through my mind flashed immediately the thought that I would never be able to set foot in Brazil now that I had dismissed the national captain. Still, it was a clear yellow card offence and I had reached for the cards before I had had time to think – such decisions are born of years of experience and there is a gut reaction which instinctively has you making the decision and taking action without having to review in your mind what has happened. It is these sorts of decisions which lie easily on the conscience because you know instantly what needs to be done.

Then the Germans equalised. The match was simmering and I really was not enjoying myself at all. I had expected a fine exhibition game with some of the best players in the world on display but I was reduced to praying for the final whistle and not wanting another red card. Somehow, two red cards is acceptable but once you get to three or more matters change and all I wanted was for the game to end. In fact, I have never wanted a game to end so much in my entire career.

Bebeto came on and was immediately friendly and chatty and as the game drifted towards a respectable 1–1 draw I hoped that all would be OK, although in the 75th minute Helme became the sixth player cautioned. Suddenly, like a flash, a ball was played through the German defence and Ronaldo was on to it like a hawk, but from what looked like an offside position. For a moment I thought the keeper would bring him down and it would be another red card but Ronaldo went past him and did what he does best – he scored. I expected mass protests to Peter Walton but there were none and a few moments later, with much relief, I blew the final whistle.

We were very low after the match, and even when we were told that there had been no offside on the final goal we hardly felt better. I had sent off two players and booked six and our misery stemmed from having had our expectations shattered. We had anticipated a wonderful match and we had refereed a very unpleasant encounter. We went upstairs for a meal and everyone was very pleasant, indeed we seemed to be the ones emerging with much credit.

Back at the hotel we were bought some champagne by the fourth official and were joined by the famous 'Statto' (Angus Loughran) and someone from the FIFA TV company. It had all been something of an anticlimax.

Thursday 26 March

Arriving at the airport I bumped into Patrick Barclay (*Sunday Telegraph*), Matt Dickinson (*The Times*), Shaun Custis (*Daily Express*) and Paul Weaver (*Guardian*). They had all been at the match and wanted my opinion of the teams and also what message the game had sent out for the World Cup. What was of particular interest was the reaction of the British press compared to the German and Brazilian reporters and also the reaction of the national coaches compared to a typical Premier League post-match press conference. In the German press my refereeing had simply been reported factually, and in the press conference 25 minutes had elapsed before anything about the refereeing was mentioned. Then both managers accepted that their players had deserved to be sent off. The British reporters I was speaking to were of the opinion that, in England, the headlines would have been about the cards and how the referee had ruined the game. Their point was emphasised when they told me that at the end of the game the *Sun* reporter had jumped up and declared with some pleasure that 'Elleray's the story'. Arriving at Heathrow we saw the *Sun* and, indeed, I was the headline and the report implied that my performance had eclipsed the two best teams in the world. To be fair they were not critical but it did emphasise the obsession that we have in this country with referees.

Ideally, I would have had the afternoon and evening to recover but I was committed to doing an interview with Patrick Barclay and then going up to Bedfordshire – in the rush-hour traffic – to give a lecture to a group of Class One referees. Though I was feeling ill, I managed to speak for an hour before returning and collapsing into bed.

Friday 27 March

I did lots of work at my desk before getting a train to Stoke for the

Premier League Young Referees' Seminar. I had planned to work on the train and write the opening lecture for the course but when I sat down the young man next to me was a presenter on Sky TV's *Nickelodeon* programme and a fervent Manchester City fan. We chatted about football and also about schools.

Arriving at Keele University I spent the afternoon organising the final details for the course with Ken Ridden and then we met the 34 young referees who had been invited. They were all young referees who had been identified as having potential for the future and whom we wished to train over a weekend both in their on-field performance and also their off-field manner and conduct. They were fresh-faced and eager and hung on every word that Ken Ridden and I said in the after-supper session. All were keen to learn and aware that they have the chance, in time, to get to the top. We were joined by Martin Bodenham, Steve Lodge and Mike Riley who would conduct the sessions the next day while I was away.

Saturday 28 March

I was up very early to catch a train back to London for the Oxford v Cambridge match. On my answerphone was a message from a Brazilian journalist, and I had to rush to Fulham to do a piece about the boat race for LWT.

The match itself was a joy to referee. Oxford won 4–0 but it was not as one-sided as that and Cambridge hit the woodwork on three occasions. The players conducted themselves very well in a most competitive game and I only had to have words with one or two players at the beginning and again near the end of the game. Several remarked that it was an easier game for me than Germany v Brazil which they had watched on TV in midweek. Having just done that match helped me enormously as it reminded them of the level that I usually officiate at and they seemed genuinely glad that I was doing the game. There were about 1,300 fans, many well oiled after the boat race, and they gave me lots of good-natured stick. There were frequent cries of 'Elleray, Elleray, give us a wave'. The trophy and medals were presented by Richard Faulkner of the Football Trust and all the players shook hands and were very pleasant afterwards. I chatted to Doug Insole, and one of the Cambridge officials came up and remarked that I must have done well as the losing side had declared afterwards that, 'Elleray was brilliant.'

As I drove to Watford for the train back to Stoke I heard the news about the death of a Fulham fan at Gillingham and that put everything into perspective. I was somewhat alarmed when I arrived to find the station surrounded by police, as there were drunken Northampton fans on their way back from the match at Watford. I put my cap on and pulled my collar up as I did not want to be recognised, as drunken fans are not always the most friendly or reasonable of people.

I arrived too late for supper but in time to watch *Match of the Day* with Ken Ridden and Steve Lodge. It was not a good evening for referees, with a variety of problems and some poor refereeing decisions in places. Mike Reed, having cautioned Chris Armstrong of Spurs when he turned down a penalty appeal, failed to send him off when he punched the ball into the net. Uri Rennie had sent off two players at Bolton, and Gary Willard had sent off three at Barnsley – all from the home team; there had been fans on the pitch and in the middle of it all Gary had walked off. And so it went on. I was glad I was not at home to deal with the press.

Sunday 29 March

We concluded the morning part of the course and Ken Ridden drove me home. We talked about the forthcoming developments in football and, in particular, the decision of the Premier League to appoint a referees' officer to run all refereeing matters as from next season. Ken thought I might be interested in the post but the interview would clash with the Harrow interviews and I would not be able to take the drop in salary the post would represent or give Harrow the necessary term's notice.

Back home my answerphone was full of messages and I spoke with Trevor Heylott of the *Independent* and also made contact with Gary Willard to give him moral support. He told me about the events and how he had stayed in the ground until 7.45 p.m., although the press had been told that he had left at 6.30 p.m. so that they would not hang around waiting for him. He seemed remarkably calm but was delighted that he was going abroad tomorrow, away from the furore about his refereeing. The most amusing aspect, and there is always some gallows humour on these occasions, was after the final Liverpool goal when, having already sent two home players off, he was called across by his assistant, Andy Martin. Mindful of what had already happened, Andy had been very apologetic and had said, 'I am very sorry to have to tell you this but a Barnsley player has just struck an opponent and you'll have to send him off. I am so sorry.' The tension was relieved by Neil Redfearn, the Barnsley captain, who after the red card had been shown to Sheridan said to Gary, 'Did he punch someone?' When Gary replied that he had Redfearn had remarked, 'Well, he's a prat then, isn't he!'

The other major talking point in the game was the fact that Gary and his two assistants had suddenly walked off the field in the middle of the second half, just after one or two spectators had invaded the pitch. Several players had intervened to protect them and the safety officer requested that they leave the pitch while public order was restored. No one communicated the decision or any explanation to the players or managers so there had been something of a hiatus until the crowd was quietened and Gary was advised he could return. Unfortunately, it looked as if the officials had suddenly decided to walk off of their own volition and this had raised unfair questions about Gary's ability to cope with the pressure. This diverted attention from the real problem which was the encroachment of a number of angry spectators on to the pitch.

After dealing with the press I had tea with my twin god-daughters as it was their birthday and I was keen to escape from the press again.

Monday 30 March

I began with an early morning interview with BBC Radio 5 Live about violence in football and whether referees were protected enough by stewards and the police. I reiterated my fears and praised the players, especially Jan Aage Fjortoft of Barnsley who had run 50 yards to intercept a Barnsley fan running to attack Gary Willard.

By good fortune there was a meeting this morning at the FA of the Technical Liaison Committee, which included Graham Kelly, Brendan Batson and Gordon Taylor of the PFA and John Barnwell of the LMA. I was annoyed at the start when I overheard Jimmy Armfield remark that he believed referees were biased in favour of the big clubs and were intimidated by the crowds. The meeting was positive and I was very pleased to receive a formal apology from Graham Kelly when I expressed the Premier League referees' disappointment that we had reported players for failing to leave the field of play immediately upon being shown a red and the FA had taken no action. Graham was cross that this had not been dealt with and accepted that their refusal to leave the field could cause crowd reaction and problems. He promised to look into the matter and ensure that action was taken in future.

The other major complaint was raised by Brendan Batson, who was disappointed that referees were cautioning players for diving and he cited Mike Reed's caution of Chris Armstrong in the Spurs match at Crystal Palace on Saturday when TV had shown that there had been contact. While unable to defend that incident, I pointed out that we only issue a yellow card when a player falls to the ground when there has been no contact, but we felt that we were right to take action on those occasions. Although Brendan did not totally agree, I said that it is a cancer in the game and that it is wrong that players should try to get fellow professionals into trouble by either diving, feigning injury or exaggerating the seriousness of a foul.

After lunch I went along to the Football Café off Piccadilly and sat through a recording of the 1970 FA Cup Final between Chelsea and Leeds United. The reporter wanted me to referee it according to 1998 directives and Laws and see how many would receive cards. It was incredible how much the referee on that day – Eric Jennings – let go; indeed his officiating was so lenient that thereafter the FA stopped giving the Cup Final to a referee as his last match. He booked only one player but under current refereeing standards, by the end of the match, there would have been six players sent off (three from each side) and another eleven would have received yellow cards. Of course, in reality, matters would have calmed down after the first few cards but it just shows how much was allowed in those days and how violent football was then compared with today. What was interesting was that the referee got very little stick, from the players or the fans, but it was also noticeable that several players' contributions were greatly restricted as a result of injuries caused by the bad fouls.

April 1998

Wednesday 1 April

On TV this evening I saw the most extraordinary incident while watching the Real Madrid v Borussia Dortmund Champions' League semi-final. Before the game some Spanish fans had been climbing on the perimeter fencing and swaying backwards and forwards. Unfortunately, the ropes holding the goal nets were tied to the fencing and by pulling it backwards the fans snapped the goal posts. They could not be repaired and there was a long delay until a spare set was brought from the training ground. This placed great pressure on the Dutch referee. Firstly, he had to decide whether the posts could be repaired quickly enough to keep the players on the field. Once he decided to take them off there must have been great pressure on him in the dressing rooms with the Germans complaining that the delay was disrupting their preparation. When the game eventually started all the tension that had built up during the delay could have erupted on the pitch but Mario van der Ende, who had refereed the Italy v England World Cup match so magnificently, was clearly up to the challenge. I was interested in how he would deal with the situation and it shows that you always have to be prepared for the unexpected.

Thursday 2 April

Another day with Martin Bodenham, but the main interest was meeting Gary Willard for lunch to discuss the Barnsley v Liverpool match. Gary was very worried that it looked as if he had left the field because he could not cope, when he had in fact been told to leave by a safety officer concerned for his well-being. We debated the role of the players in intercepting one or two fans as Gordon Taylor of the PFA had spoken against his members getting involved and physically endangering themselves. We felt the players deserved praise for behaving in such a responsible manner. I was also impressed to hear that Gary had been very well supported by George Courtney, the match observer, and that Barnsley FC had been really helpful and considerate after the game in providing a quiet room to write the reports in, plenty to eat and drink and also getting rid of the press and fans by saying that Gary had left the ground at 6.30 p.m. when he was there until well after eight o'clock. All this served to remind us that relations between players and referees and clubs and referees are much, much better than many people think.

What impressed me most was that Gary had coped with all this well and there were no signs of mental anguish or loss of confidence. Obviously, it had been very stressful but he had come through with his integrity and fortitude intact.

Friday 3 April

Even though the weather was poor I decided that I needed some exercise so I went for a long run along the coast at Ferring. Whenever I am running I always try to focus on a particular issue and today I was mulling over for how much longer I should continue refereeing. There is no doubt that, in the days before a match, the steady build up of anticipation and excitement is now tinged by a dread that there will be trouble in the game resulting in controversy, debate and the inevitable abuse and hate mail. The pressure at the highest level has increased exponentially since the creation of the Premier League and money is little compensation. I was aware that I was becoming weary with the process and yet, once a match starts, the adrenaline flows and the buzz of the occasion inspires me. If the game goes well and there is good football and much excitement for the crowd then it all seems worthwhile. My post-match feelings are often in stark contrast to the pre-match anxieties. I had adjusted to not going to the World Cup but felt that I had few goals left. My one regret was not having officiated in South America; it would be fantastic to referee in Brazil or Argentina and experience a country mad on football. However, the way that they treat some of their referees (injuries, shooting, etc.) makes the Barnsley outburst seem mild and restrained.

Saturday 4 April

During the day I travelled back from Ferring having declined the opportunity to watch Martin referee at Crystal Palace. Driving to

London I reflected on how much more enjoyable the season can be when I am on holiday from Harrow and do not have to juggle my time to fit everything in. I don't think that this affects my refereeing, but it means that I am generally more relaxed, not rushing from one engagement to another. However, I soon get bored with all the free time and certainly would not enjoy being a full-time referee. I well remember Philip Don saying that the time he spent in the USA in the 1994 World Cup was very boring, with training and watching videos of matches soon becoming tedious. I am sure that there are some people who would cope but I would find it most frustrating if I was kicking my heels for any length of time and I am sure that that frustration would affect my mood and thus my refereeing.

Sunday 5 April

I spent the day at my desk with the FA Cup semi-finals on in the background. In the evening I drove into London for the PFA awards dinner. During drinks beforehand I had a long conversation with Barry Horne (the new PFA Chairman) and Gary Mabbutt. Both expressed great admiration for referees and were absolutely sure that they would hate to referee when they finished playing. They believe that Premier League referees are fair and far better than anyone gives them credit for, and they expressed confidence in our ability and integrity. At dinner I sat with Denis Sygny, an outstanding writer for *The Times* and Tom (Tiny) Wharton, a huge man from Scotland, who was one of that country's finest referees. He told me that I would be sharing with him the distinction of being one of the best referees ever not to have officiated in a World Cup. During the dinner Brendan Batson came up to continue the discussion about Mike Reed's unfair yellow card for Chris Armstrong for diving at Selhurst Park, which Brendan had raised at a recent meeting. I was delighted to be able to tell him that the yellow card had not been for diving but for dissent when the penalty was not awarded. This clarified the matter for Brendan who was very cross about the amount of diving he had witnessed at Spurs yesterday, with Ginola being a prime culprit in Brendan's view. I felt that he was coming round to our perception that this is a matter that will need tackling before it spoils the English game. I was pleased to bump into Vinnie Jones, who was accompanied by a former pupil of mine from Harrow, David Manasseh, who is now an agent for a number of major sportsmen. It was a very pleasant evening mixing socially with players, administrators and sports writers and enjoying some very interesting debates. The gulf between us is not as great as is often portrayed.

Monday 6 April

I spent the morning at my desk before driving north to Barnsley, arriving in time to watch Blackburn v Manchester United which was being refereed by Gerald Ashby. This has always been a very difficult fixture and Gerald Ashby, Dermot Gallagher and I can all recall testing matches involving these clubs. I well remember the game in 1995 when I sent off Roy Keane for trying to win a penalty kick by going to ground before being tackled. I had already cautioned another player for a similar offence but I knew that this would be a second yellow card for Keane and therefore he would be off. As I walked over to him I replayed the incident in my mind – sometimes referees can summon up almost instant replays – as I knew that it would be a major controversy. In fact, TV later proved that I had been correct. It was the first time that a player had been sent off for such an offence (albeit a second caution) and it helped referees make an early stand against this sort of behaviour which was just beginning to creep into the game along with the arrival of a number of foreign players.

Tuesday 7 April

I drove up to Durham to stay with friends feeling somewhat concerned about the weather as there had been a lot of rain and the Leeds United pitch, where I was due to referee the following day, looked pretty wet at the weekend. I hoped that I was not going to be faced with the problems I had experienced at Maine Road some years ago when I had been forced to abandon a match after 35 minutes with Manchester City winning 2–0 and needing the points to avoid relegation.

Wednesday 8 April

I returned to Yorkshire and found the Elland Road pitch damp but perfectly playable. Before the game I discovered that Sky TV were very angry because the Premier League were going to restrict their access to us at half-time and after the match. The Premier League felt that we could do without the hassle at half-time and that we should not be commenting on incidents we had not yet had a chance to see on television. While we were changing Shirley Bassey was performing outside, and then the crowd gave an ecstatic welcome to the pilot whose heroics had saved the Leeds team from disaster in a plane crash a few days earlier.

Leeds were in good form but Chelsea fielded a somewhat weakened team. I felt that having refereed Leeds a few weeks earlier helped and the game went well with everyone in a cheerful mood. I even had a £10 bet with Dennis Wise that he would not score from a free-kick on the edge of the Leeds box. The only problem came with the third Leeds goal. In the Leeds v Blackburn game I had played an advantage when a Leeds player was fouled, a goal had resulted and after it I had returned and booked the offending player. On this occasion I tried the same thing when Mark Hughes was fouled. Unfortunately, although they had a good chance to attack, Chelsea lost possession and it was Leeds who quickly went on to score. The Chelsea players were unhappy, especially when I returned and cautioned the Leeds player for the original foul.

During the game I was lenient when players committed fouls because of the slippery pitch. At the end, Graham Le Saux sought me out and said that he would send me an Easter egg as I had been so understanding. Another player who benefited from my tolerance was young Ian Harte of Leeds; instead of brandishing the yellow card I told him, 'You owe me one.' Reflecting afterwards I was aware that I had given him the benefit of the doubt because in previous matches, and also in this one, whenever I spoke to him he listened, chatted pleasantly and accepted my decisions. Unlike players who think they can bully you, lads like Harte and Graham Le Saux actually get the benefit of the doubt in 50–50 situations because I am much more likely to be understanding towards someone who is pleasant rather than someone who is forever giving me a hard time.

Thursday 9 April

I travelled across Yorkshire to stay with Brian and Jane Raper who live in the Dales. I had long admired their daughter, Catherine, now a married mother in South Africa. I had also taught their three sons, John, Michael and Charlie – all exceptional sportsmen like their father. All three had played in my Soccer 1st XI at Harrow and I was a godfather to Michael.

Friday 10 April

A lazy day reading and then watching Manchester United v Liverpool on TV. The referee was Graham Poll and this meant that he and I had refereed all the Manchester United v Liverpool games for the last three seasons, although I usually referee the one at Old Trafford and he the one at Anfield. They are always very difficult matches and this was no exception, and the tension culminated in the sending off of Michael Owen not long after he had scored another excellent goal. I thought that it showed how soccer can build you up and then knock you down as only a few days earlier I had seen him receive the PFA Young Footballer of the Year award. Watching Graham referee reminded me of the very difficult role the referee has in such matches. You have to work hard at calming the players down and have to keep things in check by hitting a delicate balance. If you are too weak the game gets out of hand, but if you over-react the players lose confidence in you. After the game I was sure Graham would have been wondering what he could have done, if anything, to calm Michael Owen down and stop him from committing the unnecessary, nasty, second tackle which saw him sent off.

Saturday 11 April

I had a good drive back from the snows of Yorkshire, enjoying listening to matches on the radio. A few days' break had done me good and I was eager to get down to work and also to improve my fitness in readiness for the extra demands that the vital remaining matches would make on referees as well as players. I had a long session on the rowing machine and the bike and then worked at my desk until *Match of the Day*. Watching the Everton v Leeds match brought back forgotten memories when the red card was shown to Lucas Radebe while he was being carried off on a stretcher. A few years ago I refereed Manchester United v Aston Villa at Old Trafford and John Fashanu committed a very late bad foul on a Manchester United player, I think it was Ryan Giggs. John rolled around in agony and I thought he was trying to avoid the inevitable yellow card but he was badly hurt. I had to show the card as he was being carried off with the injury that finished his career. It was ironic that the last action of a hard man like him should be committing a foul and being booked. I have a lot of time for John as he is always the politest and most pleasant of people off the field. On the pitch it was a different matter – although he was always well spoken and correct, he was very, very tough.

Sunday 12 April

In the morning I travelled down to Kent for a family lunch to celebrate my father's 70th birthday. He was a useful sportsman himself when he was young and he has always been an avid follower of my refereeing career, religiously watching my matches on television and often coming to games when I am refereeing in London. My father and my mother, now thankfully better after a bout of ill health, have been a huge source of support and inspiration to me since I started refereeing at the age of 13 back in 1968. My achievements have, in a small way, repaid all their love and the sacrifices they had to make to send me to Oxford University, and they get real pleasure from my career. I had a heavy lunch so when I got back to Harrow I had another long workout on the rowing machine and the exercise bike.

Monday 13 April

The extraordinary weather continued and I was delighted not to be refereeing. I watched Martin Bodenham referee Blackburn v Arsenal on Sky TV. In the first half Arsenal played so well that I became convinced that the title was now theirs. In the second half the snow came down and at one point Martin called for an orange ball which was easier to see. However, I was aware that he could have to face the dilemma of whether or not to suspend play until the snow stopped. To many it might seem rather strange to hold up play just because it was snowing but if the referee, assistant referees and players have difficulty seeing then play should be halted. If the snow impairs the referee's vision he could make a vital mistake.

Tuesday 14 April

I had two telephone calls from South Africa from Errol Sweeney, a former FIFA referee. Apparently in a Premier League match there at the weekend a referee had ordered a manager from the dugout into the stand. The manager was now saying that because the referee did not show him the red card his dismissal was not valid. I explained to Errol that the Laws are clear that red and yellow cards can only be used for players and not for officials on the bench. In fact, the use of cards is somewhat restricted and referees cannot use them after the end of a match as a player cannot be booked or sent off once the final whistle has been blown. All that can happen is that the referee can report the player for his misconduct. This mistake was made in Turkey a few years ago when Eric Cantona spoke offensively to the Swiss referee Kurt Rothlisburger after a Champions' League match between Manchester United and Galatasaray and was shown the red card.

Technically, the cards should not even be used for offences by substitutes. However, in England it has been decided that they can be, so that if a sub has been booked while on the bench and then comes onto the field to play it is clear to everyone that if he commits another yellow card offence he will be sent off.

I was contacted by a law firm in the City who wanted me to join Pat Jennings and Alan Smith to talk to various football clients during the World Cup to help them appreciate what was happening on the field during matches.

In the evening the boys returned from their Easter holidays and I was soon back into the swing of things, catching up on their news, collecting tickets, passports and pocket money and getting ready to teach tomorrow morning.

Wednesday 15 April

The mail brought a letter appointing me as fourth official on Sunday 3 May to Gerald Ashby on the Arsenal v Everton match, his last match before retiring having reached the 48 age limit. He and I have been very good friends for many years as we go onto the FIFA list together and he was my fourth official in the FA Cup Final.

There is much debate when referees of Gerald's stature, who are still refereeing well, have to retire because they have reached a particular age. There are always complaints about the loss of top officials with so much experience, but if people do not retire then there is no room for the new young referees to make progress. I always remember Jack Taylor, who refereed the 1974 World Cup

Final, telling me that he has two newspaper cuttings. One said how dreadful it was that England's top referee, Reg Leafe, was being forced to retire and was being replaced by an unknown butcher, J. K. Taylor from Wolverhampton. The other complained that Jack Taylor was being forced to retire and was being replaced by an unknown teacher from Spennymoor – George Courtney. George went on to be one of England's best referees. I always feel linked to that story, as it was the compulsory retirement of George and Keith Hackett which allowed Philip Don and me to move onto the FIFA list of referees. Old has to give way to new.

Later on Jeff Winter phoned somewhat concerned that the press had been on to him because they had spotted that he had not refereed Manchester United this season. They were trying to suggest that this was because he had upset them at Southampton last season when he sent off Roy Keane and Manchester United lost quite heavily. Jeff pointed out that he was due to be the reserve referee for their last match of the season at Barnsley and could see nothing sinister in not having refereed them; he thought the reporter was trying to create a story from nothing.

Thursday 16 April

A wonderful day. In mid-morning the telephone rang and at the other end a voice said, 'This is FIFA. We are sending you to Brazil.' It was a Mr Raia, who explained that the Brazilian FA had contacted them and FIFA wanted me to go to São Paulo to referee their Championship Final on Sunday 3 May. I would have to fly out on the Thursday and return on the following Tuesday. I checked with the Head Master, who said that as I had been unable to go to the World Cup because of Harrow the least the School could do was to let me go to Brazil. Having been fortunate enough to referee throughout Europe and also in Asia and Africa my one remaining wish had been to referee in South America. To go to Brazil – the most passionate football country in the world – to referee one of their finals would be spectacular.

I contacted FIFA and confirmed that I would be able to go and then spoke to the Premier League and asked to be released from being fourth official to Gerald Ashby on Sunday 3 May. The dilemma I had with the Premier League was that I was due back on Tuesday 5th and the next day I was supposed to be refereeing Liverpool v Arsenal – a vital match which could easily decide the

Championship. I was desperate to do that game but felt that I would very likely have jet lag and it would be totally unprofessional to try to referee, so reluctantly I withdrew from that match as well. Overall, though, I could not have been happier and this invitation, if confirmed by the Brazilians, would pretty well complete all I have ever wanted to achieve in refereeing – the World Cup excepted, of course.

Friday 17 April

I had an angry phone call from Jeff Winter in the middle of the morning. The few comments he had made to the press earlier in the week had been blown up out of all proportion by the newspapers, who were suggesting that the fact that he had not refereed Manchester United since Alex Ferguson complained about him, showed that the big clubs could dictate who refereed them and who did not. I advised Jeff to speak with the Premier League and then put it down to experience. It is fabricated stories like these which make referees reluctant to talk to the media.

I also spoke with Dermot Gallagher who, along with Neale Barry and Peter Jones, had been to Derby yesterday for another of the regional meetings with Premier League and Football League managers. Dermot had been most interested in the attitude of Gordon Strachan, who had announced that if he behaved badly on the touchline he would take no notice of a Premier League official or a Premier League referee acting as fourth official telling him that he was in the wrong. The only person he would listen to would be someone from the LMA. Gordon had also said that referees should know who the dirty players were and should have their cards marked straight away – he did not believe that everyone should start with a clean sheet. Gordon felt that if the Vinnie Joneses of this world committed a foul early on they should be sorted out straight away because of their reputation and should not be allowed the same understanding as others. No one risked asking him whether, as a vociferous manager, he would be happy for this principle to be applied to him, so that as soon as he spoke from the touchline the referee would send him up to the stand out of the way.

Dermot had found Dave Bassett of Nottingham Forest and John Gregory of Aston Villa the most sensible. Overall, the meeting had been useful in getting a small number of managers and referees together around the table, beginning to understand each other's problems.

Saturday 18 April

Two red card 'ducks' were broken today with Manchester United having Solskjaer sent off and Martin Bodenham sending off Vega at Barnsley. It is strange how a referee or a club can go for a long period without a red card; it is rare for Martin as he has always had the reputation of being a referee who does not avoid major issues. I was disappointed to be told that Paul Durkin had allegedly been making somewhat disparaging comments about me to other Premier League officials although I could understand that he felt somewhat disappointed that his selection for the World Cup came because I was not available; I did write to congratulate him on his appointment and reminded him that if he had not been considered good enough he would not have been selected.

In the evening I entertained Blair Abbiss, Will Matthews and Jason Keen to supper. Cooking is a real relaxation for me and spending an evening with these three senior boys, who are only a month or two away from leaving, was hugely enjoyable. They have a fascinating perspective on life at Harrow and were able to assess the school with remarkable maturity. Jason I had got to know over the last few months since we talked at length one evening about his future. Will Matthews, a fine sportsman, needed a boost to his self-confidence as far as work was concerned and also needed an occasional escape from his House where, as Head of House, he was under a lot of pressure. Blair, from Druries, is a great friend of Jason's and a very talented young man who has blossomed at Harrow.

Sunday 19 April

The football world was saddened to learn of the death of Lord Howell, the former Denis Howell, who was both a minister in the Labour government and a Football League referee in the 1960s. He wrote an excellent book on refereeing which was a seminal work in my early days as a referee. It shows how much life has changed that these days it would be impossible to combine both jobs, as the demands made on referees in the late 1990s in terms of time, commitment and fitness are huge. That is not to decry what was done in the past but the pressures and the physical demands get greater and greater every season. I spent quite a lot of the day paying tribute to Lord Howell to various sections of the media.

I now found myself really feeling the weight of pressure of the Harrow Head Master application. It seemed to me that it would be a massive job and that I would need all my reserves if I was to make a real mark. I was aware of the tremendous support I had within the Masters' Room from the 'beaks', as they are known, and from boys, parents and OHs and this gave me tremendous confidence but today was one of those days when, rightly, I had been carefully questioning myself and making sure that I appreciated the enormity of the task. However, I was still convinced deep down that the Harrow governors would go for someone who was already a Head Master as this had always been the case in the past. My mood was, in part, affected by the weather which was so awful the School could play no cricket.

I spent a large part of the day teaching. I gave a three-hour extra revision session to my two A-level divisions combined with one or two boys from other forms who were in need of a boost to their academic morale. At this stage of the A-level campaign some boys require a fair degree of attention, not so much in terms of learning new information but being shown how to learn, remember and apply their knowledge.

Monday 20 April

I half expected to hear something from the governors today but there was no news; perhaps I would not even make the first shortlist. I wrote an article for *Time* magazine about the referees for the World Cup. I outlined the political nature of the appointments and the difficulty when a South American country plays a European one – where should the referee come from as both continents play rather different football and referees are more understanding of the football played in their own continent. There would also be political appointments, for example USA v Iran – a clear favourite for that game would be Urs Meier, from neutral Switzerland. I was reminded of Phil Don's World Cup experience in USA '94 when the quarter-final he was originally appointed to turned out to involve Argentina. Whether it was because of the 'Hand of God' or the Falklands War he never knew, but his match was changed; or was that just coincidence?

Tuesday 21 April

The morning began well with an early phone call from Peter Walton to say that he had been promoted to the referees' list of the Football League. Although I was sorry that he would no longer be in my team as an assistant I was glad that he had been so successful. I congratulated him on joining Rob Harris, Tony Bates and Matt Messias as former assistant referee members of my team who have quickly been promoted to the referees' list. I received a fax from the FA giving details of the match in Brazil, the first leg of their League Championship Final, to be played between São Paulo and Corinthians in the Morumbi Stadium.

Wednesday 22 April

No football today. I received confirmation in the post that I had been placed on the shortlist for the Harrow Head Master's post and was invited for interview on Saturday 10 May, just before the last day of the Premier League season. I spent the morning doing an interview for a young student as part of his degree course in media studies.

Thursday 23 April

I was pleased to receive a letter from Chesterfield thanking me for sending the wedding message. During the day I thought quite a lot about the championship race between Manchester United and Arsenal. I knew that I would not be able to referee Arsenal's game at Liverpool in the last week of the season as I would be jet lagged from the Brazil trip, and as I did not have Manchester United again this season I could let myself weigh up the merits of each team as a neutral. I found myself admiring what Manchester United had achieved but thinking that it would be good for football if someone else were to win the title. I had been very impressed with Arsenal's play and the way they had thrown away the 'boring' tag. Arsène Wenger's attitude to most aspects of the game is admirable; he is one of the most intelligent managers in the Premier League. I had no doubt that the injury to Ryan Giggs was a turning point for Manchester United to say nothing of the loss of Roy Keane for the entire season. However,

Arsenal had done remarkably well and I felt that Overmars had been their most underrated player.

Friday 24 April

I received an invitation to referee the Denmark v Cameroon World Cup warm-up match in Copenhagen on 5th June but I was not sure I could fit it into my schedule. However, the geography GCSE and A levels would be finished by then so I would have far less teaching. I decided to accept as I would greatly enjoy the experience of refereeing an African side and Cameroon have always seemed to me to be an exciting, if occasionally volatile, team. The press was very interested in an experiment involving the use of a fluorescent ball in the Everton v Sheffield Wednesday match tomorrow. Experts claimed that the ball would be easier for players and spectators to see. It recalled the change from white tennis balls implemented at Wimbledon some years ago. Today there are many, many new ideas to improve football and the authorities are at least prepared to countenance change and test the different suggestions. It came as no surprise today, that the FA, after delaying so long, let Gordon Strachan off with a warning for his comments about Steve Lodge. How unlike Scotland, where the SFA are strong with managers who abuse and insult referees.

Saturday 25 April

I taught for most of the morning and then rushed to Villa Park to referee Aston Villa v Bolton. One of my assistants was Lee Cable, who had just been promoted to the referees' list of the Football League and was still on cloud nine with excitement. While being happy for him I was also a little sorry as he undoubtedly would have been put on the FIFA assistant referees' list for 1999 had he remained an assistant. In my mental build-up to the game I was aware that it would be a keenly contested match with Bolton on edge, desperately in need of points to remain in the Premier League, and Villa wanting points to secure a place in Europe next season.

I have a standard pre-match routine and always get changed in the same order at very much the same time, as I am extremely superstitious. I get partly changed as soon as the managers have been in with their team sheets, about an hour before kick-off. I put on shorts, under socks, vest and a training top and slowly warm up, doing a few stretching exercises. I lay out my whistles and cards and then begin to tape up my toes to try to prevent the blisters to which I am very prone. About half an hour before kick-off I give my instructions to the assistants and massage my legs with 'deep heat' to loosen the muscles. I do some back-stretching exercises and put on my boots and referee's shirt. I take two black pea-less plastic whistles with me, which have a high pitch so they can be heard above the crowd noise. I have tie-ups for my socks and put two pencils down the top of my right sock. I use these to write on the cards. In the back pocket of my shorts I have a yellow card which I use for cautions, in the top pocket of my shirt I have a red card and a yellow card and a coin. I always carry this second yellow card because when a player is sent off for a second yellow card offence we have to show the yellow card immediately followed by the red and it is much quicker and tidier if I have both cards in the same pocket. I also regard it as a spare ever since I went out for the second half of a UEFA match between Auxerre and Tenerife in France and left my yellow card in the dressing room. A player was fouled, I reached for the card in my back pocket and it was not there. I had to call the trainer on to treat the player while I ran over to the fourth official, Paul Durkin, to borrow his card.

We entered a sunny Villa Park. Dwight Yorke, a player who is always charmingly polite and pleasant before the match and remains so during the game, came up to chat and told me he was astonished I was not going to the World Cup. The match did not prove as difficult as I had anticipated but there were a few talking points. I had yet another occasion when a player committed a foul and I played the advantage ready to show the card when play stopped. In this case the game did not stop for almost five minutes and during that time I could feel the pressure building up on me not to bother with the yellow card, as everyone would have forgotten the incident. However, when the ball did eventually go out of play and I showed the yellow card to Alan Thompson, no one murmured any disagreement. Midway through the first half there was some dispute as to whether a shot from Aston Villa had crossed the goal line for a goal. I was on the edge of the penalty area and in no position to judge but my assistant was close to the line and adamant that the whole of the ball had not crossed the whole of the line.

On the way up the tunnel at half-time I congratulated Colin Todd on the way his players were playing but asked him to get them to speed up the throw-ins and free-kicks as I did not want to have to start giving out yellow cards for time-wasting. As usual, Colin was courteous and receptive and the evidence of the second half suggested that he took note of what I had said and had passed the message on. At the beginning of the second half Villa wanted to make a substitution and as there was no one around to deal with it, John Gregory, their new manager, found the boards and showed them himself, muttering something about being a one-man army. Once in the second half, John Gregory clearly wanted play kept moving and he rushed onto the field to retrieve the ball and throw it to one of his players. I looked across with a glare and he bowed in contrition – one of those occasions when a facial gesture is enough to make the point. The game finished with a 1–3 victory for Bolton leaving the Villa fans unhappy but Bolton still with a chance of survival. There was only one caution and it was a most enjoyable match. Both teams were competitive but friendly and on a personal level I very much hoped that Bolton would stay up as I have always enjoyed refereeing their players and have much respect for Colin Todd.

I drove back to Harrow for a dinner party in a very good mood and spent the evening at a most enjoyable Finds Dinner in one of the other Houses, Moretons, where the senior boys entertained a number of masters to a splendid meal.

Sunday 26 April

Today I attended the Catholic confirmation of Henry Gates in Ealing Abbey, a service enriched by some quite outstanding choral music composed by Eustace Santa Barbara from Druries. Driving from the Abbey back to School I reflected on the run of incidents where I have played the advantage and delayed giving the yellow card until the ball went out of play as the referee cannot give a yellow card while play continues. I remembered an incident in 1986 when I penalised a Tranmere player for deliberate handball but before I could get the card out the Wolves forward had suddenly taken the free-kick so I had to delay until play stopped again. What would I have done if the same player had committed another bookable offence? Well, I would have had to send him off.

Back at Harrow I had to deal with a senior boy who had tripped and fallen under a bus while down in Harrow the previous evening and who was so bruised and shocked that his art A level in the coming week was in jeopardy. As ever, Rita Kent, the Druries matron, had been fantastic getting him comfortable and taking him off for X-rays. Like her predecessor, Shirley Porter, and Jean Ferguson-Davie, another matron, Rita is a wonderful woman who dedicates herself to the welfare of the boys and greatly enhances the quality of care they receive while at school.

Monday 27 April

It was a very hectic day today with meetings, an interview with the Head Master and a long Geography Department meeting. I spoke to Ken Ridden to confirm that I would be able to accept the Denmark appointment, provided I could fly back to England immediately after the game and thus not miss teaching on the Saturday morning or the Philosophy-Football-World Cup event I was involved with in the afternoon. This evening I had an hour and a half mock interview in preparation for my Head Master interview on Saturday – it was a challenging and very useful session and I enjoyed being under pressure.

Tuesday 28 April

At last the weather improved and we had the first cricket of the term. However, I was getting irritated because I had still received no flight details from Brazil and did not know if they had been able to change the flight to allow me to return a day earlier immediately after the match ends. It reminded me of the time in 1996 when I was invited to referee the Mandela Trophy game between South Africa and Brazil (African Champions versus World Champions) in Johannesburg and they kept changing the flight times. There are occasions when one appreciates just how lucky we are in this country to have Colin Downey and his secretary, Angela, at the FA to organise all our travel arrangements.

In the evening I took the House on a theatre trip and sitting on the coach going into London I pondered about the list of officials for the World Cup and wondered how I would now be feeling if I had been able to go. I was sure that the tension would have been slowly building up.

I had a letter from *The Times* asking me to write a weekly column about refereeing during the World Cup – a challenge I was pleased to accept as the more we can open the public's eyes to refereeing practices, pressures and issues the greater chance there is that we will receive a fair hearing from the sensible spectators.

Wednesday 29 April

The main topic of conversation today among boys and masters was whether I would be in danger when I went to Brazil. They seemed convinced that every referee in South America risks life and limb at each game and were adamant that I had been invited to referee this particular fixture only because the previous referees had all been shot. I had a query from the *People* about my non-availability with UEFA and FIFA and had to scotch rumours that I had been banned by UEFA for not attending the course in Majorca.

Thursday 30 April

I hurried into Harrow to get some travel insurance and at last received pleasing confirmation that they had changed my flight back to Sunday night so that I would be able to return to Harrow in time for the parents' evening on the Monday and would miss no teaching on Tuesday.

The day was taken up with media interviews following the controversy over Alan Shearer's alleged kick at an opponent's head at Leicester. After watching a video of the incident my judgement was that Shearer had been annoyed by the opponent's challenge and had kicked out, but not with the intention of catching him in the face. What I did stress was that in the World Cup any incident like that would certainly be a red card as FIFA had made it clear that any form of 'brutal' play would be dealt with severely. Amid all the press inquiries I had an amusing request: would I judge the two FA Cup Final songs? Now I am prepared to put my head on the block on many things but I have not got a musical ear (not that you need one for the FA Cup Final songs), so I declined.

May 1998

Friday 1 May

I awoke early from a dream that had me already in Brazil getting ready for the match. My two assistant referees were, somehow, Steve Lodge and Gerald Ashby and the dressing room facilities were appalling. As in most of my refereeing dreams I was having trouble getting ready on time and kept losing parts of my kit or whistles. It just showed how keyed up I was for the trip. The actual adventure started at five in the morning. I had to leave early to get round the M25 to Gatwick before it snarled up with the morning rush-hour traffic, and thus arrived at the airport about eight with little trouble. I felt remarkably calm and assured about the prospect of the next few days but aware that I was going to experience pressure the like of which I had rarely felt before. The flight with BA was long but excellent and I got a considerable amount of work done. I had a set of essays to correct and then a great amount of reading in preparation for the forthcoming interview with the governors. Towards the end of the 11-hour flight I was approached by one of the stewards who wondered whether I was doing a game in Brazil. As we chatted, one of the few fellow passengers in the Business Class area joined in the conversation. He was Brazilian and told us about the two teams. Corinthians were the 'poor people's' club with huge support, and São Paulo FC were the rich club, but with less fervent support. He warned me that São Paulo was not the nicest place to be and that I should not go out alone. This did little for the nerves.

At the airport I was met by Ilton José da Costa, a former FIFA referee, who was on the São Paulo Referees' Committee and was to be my guide and also the match observer for the game. On the drive into São Paulo he explained that in the semi-final stage of the competition the Argentinian referee had made a complete mess of the game. He had awarded two penalties and had allowed two goals, and TV replays had shown that the penalties were wrong and both goals were offside.

Naturally, there was considerable anger at his performance and it had fuelled the controversy within Brazil about the use of non-Brazilian referees. That I had come and was not even from South America had fanned the flames of debate even more among some clubs and referees. This was the start of a steady increase in pressure which would reach almost fever pitch by the time I actually got to the stadium.

When we arrived at the hotel it was midnight British time so Ilton left me and I had a relaxing sauna and a light meal before bed. I had taken the first step towards fulfilling one of my last ambitions – to referee in South America.

Saturday 2 May

I enjoyed an excellent night's sleep. Fortunately, I do not suffer from jet lag, partly because I follow all the 'rules' and do not drink any alcohol on the flight and as soon as I get onto the plane I set my watch to the time of the country of arrival and operate immediately in that time zone. I had a lazy breakfast and went for a brisk walk, although there was not a lot to see or do as I was staying in the financial centre.

At ten o'clock Ilton picked me up and we visited the municipal football stadium before driving to the south of the city to look at the Morumbi Stadium, the venue for the match. I always get confused with directions in the southern hemisphere, as the sun is the wrong way round – as you drive south it is behind you. At the stadium I was immediately struck by how compact it was for a ground that holds 100,000. Inside it was almost like a bullring and I was impressed by the measures to keep the fans at bay – high fences and a deep moat.

The pitch was in excellent condition but the most surprising feature was the security arrangements to keep the players and officials apart. The referees' dressing room had its own tunnel and entrance to the field, and each team had their own separate tunnel as well. In England the dressing rooms of both teams and the match officials are usually on the same corridor and we all meet beforehand to march out in procession onto the field. At half-time and full-time we return the same way, players often intermingling with the match officials. At times this can lead to heated discussions between opposing players or with the match officials but generally there are few problems. Clearly in Brazil everyone is separate and Ilton made it clear that I would have guards and there were several heavy iron-barred gates which would be shut and no one would have access to me. It was intimidating and comforting at the same time.

Inspecting the pitch and stadium helped prepare me for tomorrow's encounter. It is immensely valuable to visit the venue beforehand to have a mental picture of everything – like an actor familiarising himself with the stage upon which he is about to perform.

We returned to the centre of São Paulo, a sprawling industrial city of 16 million inhabitants, to a stunning large park with several lakes. It was rather like Hyde Park, a real oasis of greenery where the people of São Paulo can escape from the pollution that bedevils the city. With acres of grass, fountains, lakes and trees the air was clear and there were several thousand people walking, jogging, doing exercises, playing various sports and generally creating a happy and almost carnival mood.

As we walked Ilton gave me the history of the matches and the invitations to foreign officials. Brazil is such a large country that they do not have a national league as such but the main regions, especially those based on Rio de Janeiro and São Paulo, have their own league system. São Paulo's is known as the Campeonato Paulista and in the later stages is played as a two-league system followed by semi-finals and a two-legged final. Tomorrow's match would be the first leg of the final. The invitation to foreign referees causes upset among many of the Brazilian referees who feel they should be doing the plum games. I am sure the Premier League referees would also be outraged if a Brazilian came to referee a vital game between Manchestor United and Arsenal or the FA Cup Final. However, the Brazilian authorities, and especially those in São Paulo, feel that the Brazilian referees are too emotionally involved in football and that if there were any real controversy they would be in terrible trouble and possible danger. A foreigner, however, can come in, referee the game and then disappear. He is an objective referee who knows few of the players and none of the politics. He also does not have to live with the consequences.

Ilton explained that Castrilli, the Argentinian referee, had made such a mess of one of the semi-finals that the question of foreign referees had blown up again with the morning's papers reporting the coaches of the two teams saying that the English referee would have a real influence on the outcome of the game. There had also been much analysis of my refereeing style by a number of former top-flight FIFA Brazilian referees. As Ilton told me all this, and more, I could feel the pressure growing and I was becoming increasingly aware that a huge burden would be on me tomorrow. I would have to justify the decision of the authorities in inviting me, and would have to show that I was as good as they had said my refereeing of Germany v Brazil had suggested I was. I was also becoming truly aware of how passionate Brazilians are about their football. I had visions going through my mind of making a dreadful mistake and being hounded out of town. We then went to Ilton's flat to collect the match-day kit. It was a pretty unpleasant mid-blue colour sponsored by a firm called Penalty.

I returned to the hotel for lunch which was interrupted by the manager coming to tell me that Brazilian TV was in reception wanting an interview. I explained that I had been forbidden to talk to the media and they left. I then wandered around the streets soaking up the atmosphere of the country and trying to get the game and the people into my skin and, briefly, into my psyche. The more I could understand about the country the more chance I would have of being on á wavelength close to theirs and of refereeing successfully, although I would have to remember to be aloof and distant enough to preserve my authority. Walking past a newsstand I saw a paper with a photo of me showing the red card to Jürgen Kohler in the Germany v Brazil match. Those sort of images were helping to reinforce my reputation as a strong referee.

In the evening I had another relaxing sauna and then dinner with Ilton and one of the assistants for the game, José Carlos de Oliveira, who had flown in from Porto Alegre in the southern part of Brazil. This town was familiar to me as it is the home of Gremio, the team I refereed in Tokyo in the World Club Championship match against Ajax in 1995. Carlos is a large, well built, kindly man who was clearly thrilled to have been invited to São Paulo to take part in such an important match. As a FIFA assistant referee he has a lot of experience but, the translator told me, was almost overcome at the opportunity to officiate with a European referee. Joining us for dinner was Dario, a wheeler-dealer if ever I saw one, who seemed to have his fingers into every pie and who produced all manner of interesting items, from FIFA T-shirts to lapel badges. Of great interest to me was a set of red and yellow sticky labels which could be stuck onto my red and yellow cards. Each label had players' numbers from 1 to 30 listed with room to write in details of offence and time. I usually just use a plain sticker to write on when I caution or send off a player but these were an excellent improvement.

After supper I returned to the hotel. Somewhat disappointingly Carlos was in a different, and less good hotel, but that rather reflects the way assistant referees are treated overseas as lower class citizens compared to the referee, and it was not for me to interfere with their way of doing things.

Sunday 3 May

I had another good night's sleep (still no signs of jet lag), had a leisurely breakfast and then went off shopping to get T-shirts for my godchildren. I also bought myself a couple of Brazilian oil paintings as I always like a souvenir which would remind me of my visit. By the time I returned to the hotel the other assistant referee, Jorge Paulo de Oliveira Gomes, had arrived from Brasilia where he did a match last night. He had the Sunday papers with him and I was shocked to see one, the size of *The Times*, whose front page consisted of a very large photo of me and the headlines 'OLHALA, HEIN, MISTER ELLERAY' (*All eyes on Mr Elleray*).

Another declared 'Gringo referee faces difficult mission' and said that

> it is quite possible that the Englishman, David Elleray, will enter the pitch totally unaware of the uncomfortable legacy Castrilli left for his successor. No matter how impressive his curriculum, he will still be viewed with great suspicion. There is no denying that Elleray, who has in his favour the fact that he refereed Brazil v Germany in a totally unflappable way, will work today under the shadow of Castrilli's misbehaviour. Elleray cannot afford to make any mistakes and will have to show much firmness and tranquillity.

Over a light lunch we discussed the tactics for the game and I was keen to ensure that the two assistant referees, who spoke little English, would be able to communicate with me effectively if there was trouble behind my back and they wanted someone cautioned or sent off. I remembered something from a book written by Jack Taylor, who refereed the World Cup Final in 1974 with two non-English-speaking linesmen. I gave Carlos and Jorge a small piece of card divided into a section for yellow cards and one for red cards. If they wanted a player disciplined they were to write the player's number in the first column and then tick either the São Paulo or the Corinthians box and give it to me. They were intrigued by the instruction but pleased that they would be able to make contact if necessary.

I packed my bags and we headed off for the stadium. The rain had started to fall very heavily and it was one of those journeys that get the nerves jangling and make you wonder whether you will arrive in one piece. It was amazing that almost three hours before the kick-off the roads were packed with singing and dancing spectators and the traffic was so bad that our driver decided to drive on the wrong side of the road and simply force anything in his way onto the pavement. It was hair-raising in the extreme and by the time we reached the stadium I was literally shaking in my boots and my stomach was beginning to churn.

After we parked I bumped into a famous former FIFA Brazilian referee, Senhor Coelho, who had officiated in the 1986 World Cup. He is now a commentator and had written some very complimentary things about me in the newspapers, saying that I was a strong but very calm and assured referee. He wished me luck and we disappeared through the throngs into the stadium itself.

I do not think I have ever felt so much fear and excitement rolled into one as I walked along the corridor to the dressing room. I had to get control of myself and my emotions and I almost went into a form of autopilot. I held my head high, walked purposefully and tried desperately to ignore the appalling things that were going on in my stomach. I had not experienced such emotion for a very long time. The experience was, I imagine, almost like being on a drug. There was a rush of something in my veins which I wanted to get rid of and, at the same time, did not want to lose. I was wondering what on earth I was doing putting myself under such pressure, and at the same time I was almost overcome with anticipation, excitement and exhilaration.

We unpacked our kit and went to inspect the pitch. It was pouring with rain and there was a ladies match on. Although it was two o'clock and two hours before kick-off there were already about 80,000 people in the stadium. The crowd soon recognised us and we got a fairly hot reception as they had clearly been whipped up by the press to be, at best, sceptical about this foreign referee. Returning to the dressing room we passed through a group of scantily clad dancing girls who were incredibly attractive and reminded me of those who had danced the samba before the Germany v Brazil match in Stuttgart. They were a fleeting but welcome distraction from the football pressures. As soon as we got to our room six huge riot police appeared and each solemnly shook hands with my assistant referees and me. They wore large grey capes, white helmets and had body size riot shields and explained that they were my guards and would accompany me to and from the pitch. Moreover, if I felt under threat from the players I should use a special sign (rather like reaching up and pulling the communication cord in a train) and they would rush on the pitch and protect me. This did not do much to calm my nerves.

I began to get ready but was continually interrupted by a stream of visitors – presidents, vice-presidents, committee men etc. Unlike in the Premier League where virtually no one comes into the dressing room beforehand, there must have been about 30 visitors and, irritatingly, the majority remained. They probably wanted to stay out of the rain but it made my physical and mental preparations all that more difficult. Equally, unlike the Premier League, we were not insulated from the crowd and we could hear the noise of singing, chanting and sporadic fireworks (or was it the gunfire the boys had promised me?).

At last it was time to go out onto the pitch, up our own security tunnel and into a cacophony of noise, colour and excitement. The teams arrived separately and before I knew where I was we had kicked off. São Paulo were in black, white and red stripes and Corinthians were in white with black shorts. I was determined to impose myself in the opening stages and in the first few minutes I gave several free-kicks and ensured that I signalled dramatically and gestured theatrically at the players. I mentally and physically stood tall and did everything I could to impose myself on the game. I knew that I was there with the reputation of being strict and strong and calm and I wanted to enhance every one of those aspects as firmly as possible. I was conducting myself in a flamboyant style that would have irritated players and spectators alike in the Premier League but you have to adapt to some degree to the environment in which you are officiating. I was keen to find a yellow card as the next stage of the process of establishing myself and after 11 minutes the No. 8 of Corinthians was guilty of a relatively straightforward foul but as it was slightly from behind I brandished the card with all the authority I could muster. I was desperately keen to ensure that there was not the slightest indication that I was weak or indecisive for I knew that if I could win the battle of the first 20 minutes I would have a good chance of winning the 90-minute war.

A few minutes later Corinthians scored an excellent goal and their section of the crowd went wild. The players charged around celebrating like mad but stayed on the pitch and kept their shirts on so there was no need for any yellow cards. Almost immediately I gave a yellow card to the Corinthians No. 15 who jumped into a tackle. This upset the crowd and I just missed being hit by a lighter thrown from the crowd. Given that the fans were held back behind fences and a moat I felt relatively safe but always in the back of my mind was the possibility of being shot. In the 33rd minute I cautioned the São Paulo No. 21 for a foul but the game was well in my control and the players were showing me a great deal of respect. Decisions went largely unchallenged and I could increasingly referee as if I was back in the Premier League, allowing lots of advantage so the game pulsated from end to end. The crowd were in raptures, the sound was deafening and the atmosphere electric. It got even better when São Paulo equalised and suddenly, from behind the stadium, there was a huge eruption of fireworks. The equaliser meant that the tackles would become fiercer and I upped the tempo a little and gave a few free-kicks for offences I might previously have let go, or played an advantage on. Having wrestled the players under my control through a mixture of reputation and strong early refereeing I was not going to let matters slip now.

There had been no stoppages or injuries so no additional time and we came off soaking wet but I was happy. In fact, I was delighted with the first half and the two assistant referees were thrilled, as was Ilton. His only comment to me at half-time was 'Perfect – exactly the same again please.' I was desperate not to become complacent and repeated to myself a saying I sometimes use to gee up assistant referees, 'We've done the easy half, it's now time to do the difficult one.' That is very much a truism, for the mistakes you make in the first half can often be forgotten, those in the second cannot be as they tend to have a much more direct effect on the final result.

The second half began easily and after eight minutes I had only given one free kick. Play pulsated and about 15 minutes into the half Corinthians scored. I again upped the tempo and was now alert for any sign of time-wasting. In the 71st minute I cautioned the Corinthians captain for gently kicking the ball away when I penalised him for a foul. It was the second time in a minute that a Corinthians player had done this and it was essential that I nipped things in the bud. All continued well until the 80th minute when a

Corinthians player went into a tackle from behind and brought a São Paulo man down. I blew for the foul, reached into my back pocket and showed the yellow card. As I did so I thought the player looked familiar and suddenly realised that it was the No. 20, who I had cautioned in the first half. I instantly showed the red card and he trudged off. There were very few protests as it was a clear case of a second yellow card offence. With São Paulo desperate to score and Corinthians under pressure I had to keep a firm grip not so much on the fouls but on the time wasting by Corinthians. Indeed, in the last five minutes I gave a yellow card for a foul by the São Paulo captain and to the Corinthians No. 4 and No. 2 for time-wasting. I allowed four minutes for stoppages and time wasting and then blew the final whistle. Before I knew what was happening the riot police surrounded me and I was shepherded off the field with any player coming to shake hands being brusquely pushed aside. I learned later that often the losing team attacks the referee at the end of the game so the riot police try to be the first people to get to the referee when he blows the whistle.

Back in the dressing room the scenes were somewhat emotional and very Latin. Both assistant referees shook hands vigorously, then each clasped me in a huge bear hug. Big Carlos was overcome by the occasion and suddenly burst into tears. He said, in very broken English, that he was so proud to have been part of the team, that it was the best match he had ever been involved in and was the proudest moment of his refereeing career. Ilton arrived with others and the compliments flowed. I had a great sense of pride and satisfaction and really felt that I had been tested in the fire and emerged unscathed. It never stopped raining throughout the entire game and I thanked them for making me feel at home with the English weather. As I took off my dripping blue kit Ilton came over and said that the press were ecstatic about the way I had refereed the game and were giving me 10 out of 10. Much more than that, the press (who seem almost to control football there) and the São Paulo Federation desperately wanted to know if I could come back next Sunday and referee the second leg. They would not take no for an answer even when I explained that I would love to but had a Premier League match. Reluctantly, they accepted my polite but firm refusal. It was a wonderful compliment, nevertheless.

As we left I was besieged by people wanting to shake hands and congratulate me – something that never happens in the Premier League. I was stopped by a reporter and the Brazilian officials were so happy with everything that I was allowed the rare privilege of speaking to the press. To ensure our safe exit from the stadium we were accompanied by three of the largest security men I have ever seen. We drove away with the rain still pouring down but I felt really satisfied inside. The elation and fear that had accompanied me as I had approached the ground had now been replaced by an equally intense sense of achievement.

I bade a rather emotional farewell to Carlos and Jorge, the two assistant referees, and felt that, in them, I had made two new friends with whom I had forged a special bond. Ilton, Dario and I had dinner in a carvery where the meal was punctuated by requests for autographs and photos, culminating in the manager making a presentation and then having a group photo taken of me with all the waiters. Then it was off to the airport where the girl on the BA check-in desk recognised me and said that she was a Corinthians supporter. On the strength of that I managed to persuade her to upgrade me to First Class and thus the flight home was in the exquisite comfort of a seat that converted into a bed. It crowned one of the most memorable and rewarding days in my thirty years as a referee.

Monday 4 May

The midnight flight home went like a dream and I awoke at Gatwick refreshed and still on cloud nine. As I waited for my bags an elderly Scotsman who had been on my flight began to chat as he recognised me from watching the game on television. He said that wherever you were in São Paulo you knew if someone had scored because the cheers seemed to ring out from every flat and house as the entire city had been watching the game.

I returned to Harrow in time for a parents' evening and then back into the House where the boys seemed genuinely pleased to see me back. Most had clearly thought there was a real possibility that I might be shot as someone claimed to have heard that the previous three referees to do that particular fixture had indeed been shot. It is amazing how the school rumour factory works.

Tuesday 5 May

The first thing that struck me as I read the papers to catch up with the news was that Arsenal had become Premier League champions, having beaten Everton. I was delighted that their particular brand of exciting, open football had brought them success. I contacted the FA to let them know that I was safely back in the country and to thank Ken Ridden's secretary, Julie Stearn, for all her hard work on my behalf in tying up the details of the trip. Julie is a superb secretary who is admired by all the Premier League referees and who genuinely looks after us all. In every lesson I taught, the boys were desperate to hear about the game and I allowed the odd few minutes to give them the highlights.

In the afternoon it was back to normal school routine with inter-House cricket matches. I also had time to speak with the Premier League to discuss the end of season bonus payments paid to Premier League referees and to hear progress on the appointment of the Premier League referees' officer. It transpired that they were interviewing Philip Don later in the week and, indeed, he phoned me for advice in the evening. Knowing that he was a strong candidate I advised him to ask for a good salary as the FA have a reputation of not paying particularly well and the only real opportunity you have to get a decent wage is when you negotiate at the start.

Wednesday 6 May

The news that Alan Shearer had been charged by the FA had my phone humming for comment with ITN in particular wanting an interview. However, the main issue was whether Alan Shearer should be dealt with before the World Cup so that it was not hanging over him while he was in France. As with any high-profile player, the FA were in a difficult position. Do nothing and they risked being accused of allowing the top players to get away with things; take action and they risked being accused of only acting because it was a high-profile player.

I spoke to Martin Bodenham who had refereed his last Premier League match at the weekend and had been moved by the presentation made to him by Sheffield Wednesday afterwards. Few fans realise what a huge hole in his life there would be now that he was no longer a top referee; and I was sure that Gerald Ashby would be feeling the same. The hardest time for them will be at the start of next season when the excitement of the opening day is all around but they are no longer an active part of it.

Thursday 7 May

A busy day teaching and with meetings was punctuated by Sky Sports who came up to do an interview on the use of video replays for disciplinary matters in the light of the Shearer incident. I explained that there are three instances when video evidence may be used:

1. A referee of his own volition can look at a video of an incident and if he feels that he wrongly issued a red or yellow card he can ask the FA to rescind it.

2. If a player is sent off for an offence which carries a three-match ban (e.g. violent conduct or serious foul play) then the club can request that the FA ask the referee to look at the video.

3. If there is an incident (as with Shearer) which the referee or assistant referee does not see then the FA can initiate their own action.

Apparently the PFA were claiming that this was unfair but it seemed to me that there was an element of common sense and justice about it. Referees are the only ones who can overturn their own decisions and that has to be right as they have a better feel for the incident and the atmosphere than can be gained just from a video. Video evidence does not necessarily record the tension in the game nor any previous incidents between the players involved. For example, off camera one player may have verbally provoked another and a few minutes later he is badly fouled by this opponent. The referee, aware of the previous provocation, may well issue a red card because he was aware of the intent behind the challenge as he can relate it to what has gone on before; the video would not show all that. It must also be right that extreme violence or foul play not seen by the match officials should still be subject to action by the FA. We should do all we can to make sure that our game is free from violence and unpleasantness and if players know that they cannot get away with things behind the referee's back they are less likely to indulge in such behaviour.

In the evening I did some extra teaching with two senior boys in other Houses who needed some extra help with their approaching geography A level.

Friday 8 May

I had a number of engagements today which helped take my mind off tomorrow's interview. In the morning I was interviewed for the

Times Educational Supplement and in the afternoon I spent an hour at Watford FC standing on a box in my referee's kit being photographed for a meat pie advert. I had to blow onto the pie for these adverts, which would appear on great hoardings in the north of England during the World Cup, with the caption 'Blow, referee, blow.' I also did an interview for *Newsnight* on the pressures of refereeing in general and specifically in the World Cup, as I watched Druries thrash Bradbys in a House cricket match – somewhat ironic given that the last time I was interviewed for BBC TV was when I was watching Druries beat the same House at Harrow Football.

In the evening Philip Don phoned to tell me that he had been appointed referees' officer for the Premier League – excellent news for the future of top-level refereeing as Philip is someone who is widely admired and respected throughout the refereeing and football world. His appointment will take some of the pressure off Ken Ridden and will ensure that we approached the coming season in a professional manner – it will certainly mean that some referees will come under particular scrutiny in terms of fitness and quality of decision-making as Philip is a hard, but fair, task master.

Saturday 9 May

I was up early to focus on the interview ahead and had a morning briefing session from Nick Shryane, the Harrow bursar. I taught three lessons and carried on as if it was a normal day as very few people were aware that it was the first round of interviews for the next Head Master. I changed and, feeling remarkably calm, I took the tube into London, located the building where the interviews were being held, and went to a nearby park where I sat in the sun and tried to focus all my thoughts. I was preparing myself just as I do for a football match – slowly but carefully clearing my mind of everything but the task ahead. You become almost mentally blinkered and able to shut out so much of the extraneous noise and thoughts that try to intrude and invade your mind. I needed to be calm but with that little bit of fear and tension which would get the adrenaline flowing and make me be at my best. I have always been lucky in that I am someone who tends to rise to the big occasion rather than be crushed by it. There was no doubt that my experience of big-match situations helped me greatly in my mental preparations for one of the most important hours in my life so far.

By the time I entered the interview room to face the panel of seven I was as focused and ready as I possibly could be. The hour and a quarter flew by and I greatly enjoyed being tested and challenged by a panel of governors who were courteous but thorough. It was very hot as the air conditioning was not on and I think this left everyone a little dulled but I felt I had given a good account of myself. As I left the interview I instantly started analysing the one or two areas where I thought I could have given better answers. As with refereeing I was being super-critical of myself, as I am a perfectionist and my own harshest critic.

Back at School I went down to watch the cricket and it turned out to be an excellent day for the Drurieans in the School 1st XI with Sam Stevens getting six wickets and Dan Hepher, the captain, the other four in a crushing defeat of Epsom College. I returned to the House to see the Lower Sixth off to a dance at a girls' School, and spent the rest of the evening at my desk, trying to forget the interview and waiting to see what the official reaction would be.

Sunday 10 May

I was up early for the long drive to Blackburn for my last domestic game of the season. A certain circularity struck me as my first Premier League game of the season had also been at Ewood Park. I did not feel as positive about this game as last week, possibly because I was experiencing some deflation after yesterday's interview and also I was dreading the long drive home through the heavy Sunday traffic.

The journey went well and I thought a great deal about the challenges I had faced this season and the remarkable pressure I had been under at School with the Head Master application on top of everything else, plus the huge demands that refereeing had placed upon me. As usual, everyone at Blackburn was friendly and I was pleased that my assistants were Peter Walton and David Babski and that Adrian Titcombe from the FA was the match observer. In the pre-match briefing we were told that the Home Secretary, Jack Straw, would be at the game and there was a security alert as there was the possibility of him being an IRA target.

Waiting in the tunnel before the match I gave Tim Flowers a hard time for getting the red card for swearing at an assistant last week when he was substitute. Tim laughed and said that it was ridiculous and if he had spoken to me like that I would just have laughed at him and he'd have shut up. During the pre-match kick-about Alan Shearer came up and shook hands. I reminded him, not that he needed it I am sure, that the eyes of everyone would be on him not just because of the incident at Leicester but also because he left Blackburn to go to Newcastle.

The first half went well although there was an early attempt at a tackle from behind on Shearer by Colin Hendry which I had to think very carefully about before deciding not to give a yellow card as Shearer had jumped out of the way well before the tackle was made. I did not want to be seen to be giving him more protection than anyone else but it was one of those occasions involving a high-profile player when whatever you do risks criticism. One player who surprised me was David Batty, who was in a terribly bad mood and not his normal chirpy self. I can usually have a good laugh and chat with him but he was in a foul temper, moaning and groaning about everything, so I stopped trying to natter to him and just let him get on with his game. Although there was a bit of an undercurrent in the match, not helped by Shearer being called 'Judas' every time he got the ball, I got to half-time with no cautions and wondered if I was in for a repeat of the opening day when the entire match was caution free. That would turn out to be wishful thinking!

Before we kicked off for the second half I had Alan Shearer moaning at me for not giving Colin Hendry a yellow card for that early tackle and I asked David Batty if he was in better mood but the grunt I got suggested he was not. Fairly early on I gave a yellow card to Hendry for an offence which, in itself, was not quite a yellow card but given that I had given him the benefit of the doubt in the first half I felt that the two offences together merited a card and he accepted my decision. I was more than happy in my own mind that Shearer's intervention at the start of the half had not influenced me in the slightest. It is always important to bear in mind previous offences by players especially as you can give a yellow card for persistent misconduct when someone commits a series of relatively minor fouls. Soon after, Alan Shearer hit a shot miles wide and received a deluge of catcalls. He turned, smiled at me and shrugged and I smiled back. I thought that that showed the communication and empathy that can exist between players and referees especially when we 'team up' against the crowd.

The game was certainly much more competitive than in the first half. I cautioned Henchoz of Blackburn for a poor tackle in the 63rd minute and almost immediately David Batty and Gary Flitcroft slid strongly in to tackle for the ball. For no apparent reason Batty was livid and got up, chased Flitcroft and threw a punch at the back of his head. To Flitcroft's credit he hardly reacted but I had seen the offence and showed Batty the red card. Whether he connected or not was immaterial as the offence in Law is 'striking or attempting to strike an opponent'. Batty started to walk off but then turned back, said something and pushed me in the chest. I hardly noticed this as I was anxious to calm tempers as Albert and McKinlay were squaring up to each other. All my reserves of experience came into play and I knew that I had to establish order so I took a long time talking to people and then gave Albert and McKinlay a long lecture to take the heat out of the situation.

The game was lively for the next few minutes but everyone remained sensible and I had a useful conversation with Gary Speed when I explained that it did not matter whether Batty had connected or not. I asked Gary what was wrong with Batty and he said that these days he was always in a bad mood and was terrible company in training where he kept losing his temper and moaning. I was glad it wasn't just me.

Blackburn had a third yellow card – Dahlin – and then from a free-kick near the Newcastle penalty area Chris Sutton scored the only goal of the game to secure a place in Europe for Blackburn. At the final whistle most players came to shake hands and I wished the Newcastle players good luck for the FA Cup Final next Saturday. I was surprised that there was no sign of Kenny Dalglish as we came off the field but he was soon sending messages via the match observer, wanting to know whether Batty had connected and whether I would look at the video. To be fair there was a difference of opinion about the tackle which provided Batty's reaction. Mike Riley (who yesterday refereed for the first time at Wembley in the FA Vase Final) and I thought that there was nothing wrong with the tackle but Peter Walton, the assistant close to it, thought Flitcroft's challenge was worth a yellow card.

By the time we left the dressing room it was pouring with rain and I knew that I would have a long drive home. It would enable me to reflect on the season and what had happened in a most exciting and challenging eleven months.

My immediate thoughts were that the David Batty incident would be picked up by the press and there would be considerable attention on the pushing, especially given that Abou, Lomas and Petit had been disciplined during the season for laying hands on referees. I felt somewhat sorry for David as I have always got on extremely well with him and he is one of those players you can talk to during a game – although sometimes you have to give as good as you get verbally.

My thoughts then strayed ahead to forthcoming matches and beyond them to the World Cup. I was delighted to have the chance to see three of the main teams in action just before the tournament starts. I had been invited to Spain to referee the centrepiece of Athletic Bilbao's centenary celebrations, a match against Brazil. It seemed that my love affair with Brazil this season was continuing and it would be fascinating to see the World Champions in action 10 days before the competition began. A few days later I would be in Copenhagen to referee Denmark v Cameroon, a chance to see at close hand one of the most exciting African sides of recent years.

I cast my mind back over what had been a wonderful international season. I had some fantastic overseas matches, particularly the trip to Saudi Arabia and the UEFA Super Cup Final. Although there was the huge disappointment of declaring myself unavailable for the World Cup there were compensations in the appointment to referee Germany v Brazil which led directly to the unbelievable experience in Brazil. In the space of a few short months I had fulfilled two of my few remaining ambitions, officiating in the Middle East and in South America.

Domestically there were challenges and times when I had felt the pressure was almost too much – not the pressure of the matches and the decisions but the constant wearing away at my time trying to combine refereeing, my off-field commitments and my many responsibilities at Harrow. However, I enjoyed a very good season on the pitch and feel that I had improved my relationship with many of the Premier League players, and some, though not all, of the managers.

As I drove through Birmingham I realised I had many, many people to thank for yet another kaleidoscope of experiences: Ken Ridden for his tolerance and understanding of my restricted availability and his attempts to persuade me to keep the door open for the World Cup; my refereeing friends, who were such a support throughout the season, my colleagues and friends at school, particularly Glynn Jenkins, Mel Mrowiec, Peter Hunter, George Attenborough, Peter Bieneman, Hugh Thompson and Rita Kent, whose support, understanding and willingness to cover my absences were vital in allowing me to fulfil so many domestic and international appointments; the boys in my geography divisions, who put up with absences and rearranged lessons; Nick Shryane for his support and encouragement; and most of all the boys in Druries whose achievements, behaviour when I was away and genuine interest in my refereeing have made me so very proud to be their House Master.

Modern football is about pressure and success, but it is also about enjoyment. When the time comes and I look back over a season and am not filled with an overwhelming sense of enjoyment and pleasure then I shall hang up my whistle. Without a doubt the 1997/8 season had been wonderful and I was already looking forward to getting my break from football over and done with.

Roll on Saturday 15 August . . . but not those fitness tests!

World Cup

The build-up to the 1998 World Cup was dominated by FIFA's pronouncement that they required the referees to be very strict with tackling, and especially tackling from behind. Within FIFA there were disagreements as to whether tackling from behind should be abolished altogether. One group firmly, and rightly, believed that tackling is an important skill and that football should not be reduced to a non-tackling game of limited physical contact. However, it is widely recognised that the tackle from behind is potentially one of the most damaging and dangerous in the game. The back of the leg, and particularly the Achilles tendon, is unprotected (unlike the front of the leg which is now compulsorily guarded by a shin pad) and serious injury can result, often because the player is not fully prepared for an unseen tackle from behind.

Urged on by FIFA, the International Board (guardians of the Laws of the Game worldwide) declared in March that 'a tackle from behind which endangers the safety of an opponent must be sanctioned as serious foul play'. Serious foul play is a red card offence. Much debate ensued and concern was expressed that the World Cup would be a festival of red and yellow cards with the crowds deprived of seeing the best players because so many would be suspended. What many failed to appreciate was that the edict against tough tackling was designed to protect the skilful players, as had been achieved so successfully in the 1994 World Cup in the USA and subsequently in the Premier League. Quite rightly, the intention was to remove the sort of tackles which ended the career of the great Dutch player Marco Van Basten and which meant that Diego Maradona could rarely play without drugs to kill the pain in his ankles.

The 34 referees and 33 assistant referees chosen to officiate in the World Cup had assembled in March at the Manoir de Gressy, 30 km north of Paris and their responsibilities had been clearly laid down by the FIFA Referees' Committee. FIFA promised to produce a video which would identify foul tackles that were just free-kicks, those which would merit a yellow card and those requiring a red card. But as the weeks passed there was no sign of this video and national teams resorted to inviting top referees to training sessions to explain the interpretations to the players. Not surprisingly, the issue of tackling and refereeing would become a dominant one in the World Cup although not, certainly in the early stages, because the referees were being too strict.

Another purpose of the week-long meeting in March had been to establish fitness of the officials and prepare them for the mental and physical stresses that lay ahead. Most important, had been to attempt to establish a degree of consistency, not easy when you have referees from countries as diverse as Italy, Thailand, Australia, Mexico, Morocco and Russia. Not only do different continents have different attitudes and interpretations of the Laws but the range of experience is also immense. Italy's Pierluigi Collina who refereed the 1996 Olympic Final is vastly more experienced than someone like An-Yan Lim Ke Chong from Mauritius, simply because of the weekly pressure of refereeing in Serie A.

An early challenge for the Referees' Committee was the appointment of the referees for the group matches. FIFA had declared that, as a matter of principle, only one referee per country could be selected and, as they had decided to include referees from the smaller footballing nations, this meant that the 34 selected referees were not the best 34 in the world. Cynics would argue that referees from smaller countries were selected for political reasons. In reality, for refereeing standards to improve in those countries, needs their top referee to be involved and learn from the experience of a World Cup and then return home and help raise standards.

Even before a ball was kicked the appointment of officials was a potentially explosive problem for the administrators. Everything is fine when both teams are from the same continent as they have similar playing styles and attitudes, but what would happen when a hard, uncompromising European side played a skilful South American team unhappy with strong tackling? I came across this problem when I refereed Germany v Brazil in Stuttgart in March 1998 in a so-called 'friendship match' between the top two footballing countries in the world. Two red cards and six yellow cards were evidence of the clash of styles and temperaments.

The first set of appointments revealed that the Referees' Committee had done their homework. The opening game, Brazil v Scotland, was just the sort of match both teams would prefer a referee from their own continent. In the event, Spain's José Manuel Garcia Aranda was appointed – a European, but one whose domestic football is Latin in flavour and thus not unlike that of the Brazilians. The most political appointment of all was to the clash between USA and Iran – not two of the world's greatest footballing nations but in political terms a major match. It made many smile when FIFA announced as predicted that the referee would be Urs Meier from Switzerland – the most neutral country in the world.

A week before the tournament started the referees gathered in France to receive their final briefings and their new kit – red, yellow and black shirts specially designed for the tournament. In addition, the assistants were given their electronic flags.

FIFA issued them, and the teams, with seven directives on the Laws of the Game:

1.   Players should not to be treated on the field of play with the exception of a goalkeeper, or a goalkeeper and outfield player who had collided. Anyone with an open wound should leave the field immediately and if a trainer came onto the field then the player should leave either on a stretcher or under his own steam. Any player leaving the field could only return from the touchline during play or from any boundary line if play had stopped.
2.   Any violent tackle should be sanctioned with a red card.
3.   Any jewellery such as signet rings, chunky necklaces, bangles, bracelets and pendant earrings should be strictly prohibited.
4.   Any player taking a penalty must keep moving directly towards the ball without feigning or stopping.
5.   Any player not retreating 9.15 m (10 yards) immediately at a free-kick should be cautioned.
6.   Referees should be assiduous in adding on time lost for substitutions, injuries, etc.
7.   Referees should ensure that every player kept his shirt tucked in.

From this it was clear that FIFA expected the referees to deal with everything from the sublime to the ridiculous – from violent tackling to not having a shirt hanging out. One most welcome innovation was that in the closing minute, the reserve referee would hold up the electronic substitution board to show how many minutes of stoppage time should be added.

Everything was set for the opening match on 10 June. The Spanish referee would be under intense pressure to set the disciplinary standard for the tournament; if he was too strict the critics would be out for his blood, but if he was over-tolerant then problems would occur later in the tournament. Being appointed to one of the opening matches in any tournament is always a great honour but also a poisoned chalice. I well remember refereeing Germany v the Czech Republic on the opening day of Euro '96 when we had been instructed to go out and be strong. I issued 10 yellow cards and was roundly criticised by Berti Vogts, the German manager, and most of the British press for being over-strict, and yet the UEFA assessor criticised me for being too lenient and thought there should have been a couple of red cards.

In the event Garcia Aranda refereed with great sensitivity and care and received widespread praise. Early on he was sensible when Gordon Durie was slightly late with a tackle but he imposed his authority with a yellow card for Darren Jackson, soon followed by one for Brazil when he awarded Scotland a penalty for a push. This was a rather harsh yellow card, I thought, but in the 45th minute he cautioned Aldair from Brazil for a tackle from behind. If FIFA had told referees to be really strict on such tackles then this would have been a red card, so it seemed that the pre-tournament fears of excessively harsh refereeing were not to be realised. Indeed, there were signs that Garcia Aranda was somewhat lenient for Durie went uncarded for a nasty two-footed jump tackle in the 61st minute which merited at least a yellow card even had he not already been given the benefit of the doubt in the first half. This incident raised a nagging worry in my mind which was to grow as the first week of matches progressed – would referees deal with all bad tackles strongly (but not excessively) and would they deal with the persistent offenders who do not necessarily commit bad fouls but commit a significant number of petty offences and gain an advantage in so doing?

The opening match was notable for a lack of dissent and encroachment at free-kicks (although there was significant Brazilian encroachment at the penalty) and good use of stretchers to remove injured players. Jewellery was almost completely absent and everything was pleasing. The commentators and experts who like no controversy and a minimum of cards were delighted but one or two of my colleagues and I were surprised that the refereeing had been so low key.

The second match was Norway v Morocco, controlled by Pirom Un-Prasert from Thailand – an early test of the ability of a referee from a smaller footballing nation. He looked nervous early on and his performance was technically naive, revealing a poor understanding of positioning, especially at ceremonial free-kicks where he placed himself so wide he could not see or control the pulling and pushing in the defensive wall. It was a quiet game and he was hardly noticed although a very high foot from Saida Chiba of Morocco in the 40th minute merited a yellow card.

On Thursday 11th in the Italy v Chile match we saw the first really poor refereeing decision. The referee was from Niger – Lucien Bouchardeau – who, ironically, was only officiating in France because he had replaced Sidi Bekaye Magasse from Mali, who was struck off the list after a poor performance in the African Nations Cup. The decision in question was a second-half penalty to Italy when Baggio kicked the ball at close range against the hand of a Chilean defender who was just inside the penalty area. It was a clear case of 'ball to hand' and handball can only be penalised if the player deliberately handles the ball (i.e. if the hand moves towards the ball). In this case the player had obviously been trying to get his hand out of the way. Whether the referee gave it on his own or with the help of his assistant, who was facing the incident, was not clear, but it was a poor decision, even though some of the TV pundits agreed with it because 'it affected the play'. It crowned a poor overall performance from an official who failed to get a grip early on and let a lot of poor tackling pass unpunished. He also did not deal with the Chilean time-wasting, delaying tactics and dissent. My notes at the end of this match read: 'I think that a trend of not very strong refereeing is developing which will cost the competition dear in the later stages.'

The next few days did nothing to shake me from that belief and my frequent discussions with Philip Don revealed that his analysis matched mine. There was a clear absence of strong referees taking charge of the game and stopping all manner of poor tackling and persistent fouling. By the end of the first round of matches there had been 33 yellow cards and 3 red cards but there should have been many more of the latter.

The three dismissals were all different. The first player to be sent off was the Bulgarian Anatoli Nankov against Paraguay on 12 June. He was on a yellow card when he committed a poor tackle and was sent off. Most commentators thought it was for a second yellow card but it transpired that the tackle had been deemed worthy of a red card by the Saudi referee Abdul Rahman Al-Zeid. Naturally, it was greeted by a torrent of protest from the Bulgarian coach, who claimed that refereeing like that would destroy the competition.

The next day Ha Scok-Ju of South Korea was sent off 80 seconds after he had given his team a 1–0 lead against Mexico and his indiscipline was to cost his team dear; he also entered the history books as the first player since Brazil's Garrincha in 1962 to be sent off in the World Cup Finals after scoring a goal. There was little doubt that Gunter Benkoe of Austria had been firm, fair and entirely in line with FIFA's edicts when he brought out the red card instantly to punish the South Korean player for jumping into a tackle from behind which could easily have broken the Mexican's leg.

Later that day Holland's Patrick Kluivert was sent off following an off-the-ball incident which was spotted by one of the assistant referees. There was an exchange between Kluivert and Staelens of Belgium and suddenly Kluivert elbowed the Belgian firmly in the chest. The assistant drew the attention of the disappointingly off-colour Italian referee Collina and Kluivert was shown the red card – a harsh but perfectly proper decision. The distasteful aspect was that the Belgian player fell to the ground clutching his face even though he had been struck in the chest. While FIFA upheld the decision and gave Kluivert a two- rather than one-match ban, it was a pity action was not taken against the Belgian for his clear exaggeration of the offence.

The tolerant refereeing continued, and it reached something of a nadir in the second half of the England v Tunisia game on 15 June, a match refereed by Masayoshi Okada from Japan. In the early stages of the game he allowed the Tunisian goalkeeper to take an inordinate amount of time with goal-kicks and the Tunisians slowed the game down at every opportunity. Tackles flew in and there were several incidents which should have brought yellow cards for players of both teams. However, it was the second half that revealed Okada's weakness and lack of understanding of the game. On two occasions England players were brought to the ground by tackles from behind but no yellow cards were shown. Towards the end of the match Sol Campbell committed a very poor tackle, Okada rightly played an advantage and returned with a yellow card which might have been red. However, in the first half there had been one or possibly two tackles by Campbell which were yellow card offences and if Okada had done his job on either of these occasions then this final tackle would have seen Campbell sent off. What was most disturbing was that Okada allowed the Tunisians to foul England's forwards, and Shearer in particular, in a low-key but persistent and destructive way. Three times Shearer was dragged to the ground or pushed over and on each occasion the foul was deliberately committed to stop his attacking move. The aim of the Tunisian player was to halt the attack so the award of a free-kick was no punishment. An aware referee would have yellow carded each offence for its cynical intent. There was certainly a strong case against the Tunisian captain and another defender for a yellow card for persistent infringements.

With all this slack refereeing, and an even more inept display later in the day by the Mauritius referee in the Romania v Colombia match, it came as no surprise that the newly elected FIFA President, Sepp Blatter, spoke out strongly on the morning of 16 June – the start of the second phase of group matches. Blatter hit out at 'too soft' referees and was quoted as saying, 'They are not applying the ban on tackles from behind. It's not up to them to decide how fouls should be interpreted. There have been tackles from behind so far that deserved red cards.' He was also unhappy about time-wasting by goalkeepers and that referees had not penalised the worst excesses including the Moroccan goalkeeper El-Ouaer, who in the first half of the match against Norway had held the ball for over 20 seconds. The problem was one of interpretation since the six-second law only applies to the goalkeeper holding the ball in his hands, once he drops it to the ground it is there for everyone to play and he cannot pick it up again.

The first match after Blatter's outburst was Scotland v Norway which was very well refereed by Lazlo Vagner from Hungary – included in the World Cup list in part because the 1994 World Cup Final referee, Sandor Puhl, had been suspended by FIFA and UEFA for failing to deal strongly with bad tackles in UEFA matches. Vagner is an excellent referee and responded well to Blatter's words without going over the top, cautioning a number of players of both sides for bad tackles. However, he could still be criticised for being rather lenient.

The improvement was short-lived and in the evening Nikolai Levnikov from Russia gave an inept performance in Brazil's 3–0 win over Morocco. He allowed the Africans to commit all manner of assaults on the Brazilians and in the first half, when Said Chiba caught Ronaldo on the upper thigh leaving a six-inch wound, not a card was in sight. It was a wonder no one was sent off, especially as Michel Platini had declared earlier in the day that any referee failing to do his duty would be on the first available flight home. I wondered whether Aeroflot had an extra passenger on the morning of 17 June – had Platini given his first red card?

There was little doubt that the referees would feel pressurised by these very public statements, as well as the private meetings at the referees' base with members of the Referees' Committee and FIFA officials. The acid test would be whether there would be an over-reaction and the pendulum would swing too far the other way. On Thursday 18 June it appeared it had when two matches produced five red cards. The excitable Colombian referee John Jairo Toro Rendon sent off three players when Denmark played South Africa, while later that evening the Mexican referee Arturo Brizio Carter, a man with a strong reputation from the last World Cup, sent off two in the France v Saudi Arabia game in St-Denis. Needless to say, the five dismissals provoked great discussion and managers, players and pundits naturally took issue with most of them.

In the afternoon game the Colombian referee gave a poor performance, over-reacting and losing control of himself. He issued red and yellow cards by marching up to the player, standing as tall as he could and thrusting the card high into the air. It was all too dramatic and served to provoke players rather than calm them down. He sent off three. Denmark's Miklos Molnar's dismissal was a mystery. I was unsure whether it was for a foul or because Toro Rendon thought he saw Molnar stamp on his opponent. In a World Cup dominated by players over-reacting to the slightest incident, the fact that both players moved away from this clash preparing to deal with a throw-in suggested that they thought nothing had happened. But the Colombian brandished the red card. By doing this he set himself a very high standard, so when South African midfielder Alfred Phiri raised him arm in a challenge the Danes rushed to the referee demanding a red card and the Colombian had to send him off to be consistent. However, there can be little sympathy for Phiri as the referees had shown themselves to be strong on the use of the arm as a weapon. Later in the game Morten Wieghorst of Denmark committed a straightforward yellow card tackle from behind but by this stage Toro Rendon had lost his composure to such an extent that his judgement had gone and to everyone and no one's amazement the red card appeared. At each match a special camera was being trained on the referee; footage of this official would be very useful in showing how a referee's body language can portray his emotions and affect the players.

This match increased the pressure on Arturo Brizio Carter from Mexico as he prepared to referee the host nation's match against Saudi Arabia but he put in one of the better performances of the tournament to book himself a place in the latter stages. He was firm but calm and steadily won the respect and confidence of the players. He sent off two players. The Saudi defender Al-Khilaiwi jumped two-footed into a tackle and although he only clipped Bixente Lizarazu, if the Frenchman had not taken avoiding action his leg could easily have been broken. It was just the type of tackle that strict referees should punish strongly to protect players. Later on Ziredine Zidane of France reacted to a tackle and stamped, not violently but certainly deliberately, on Amin Fuad Anwar, the Saudi captain. Aimé Jacquet, the French coach, agreed afterwards that Zidane deserved to be sent off. I hoped that Brizio Carter's firm but astute officiating would set the standard for the remainder of the World Cup.

A few days later the refereeing of Marc Batta of France shone out like a beacon in England's disappointing defeat by Romania. He took control of the game right from the start and yellow carded Gheorghe Hagi Romania after he committed two fouls in quick succession. Batta then made it very clear that he, and not Hagi, was going to referee the game. One feature of this match that really did disappoint was in the first half when Paul Scholes threw himself to the ground having lost possession in the Romanian penalty area. It was yet another example of the attempts to con the referees that dominated this World Cup. The media and the experts were, quite rightly, beginning to rail against the appalling practice of players increasingly miming the showing of a card in an attempt to persuade referees to book or dismiss opponents. One professional trying to get another into trouble by diving, over-exaggerating or gesticulating in this manner is distasteful and such actions need stamping out before they become endemic in football throughout the world.

Paul Durkin's first appearance as a referee was on 23 June. Italy v Austria would be an opportunity to shine, as a game between two European teams would not throw up some of the problems that a European v South American match might pose. It was a tense and difficult game and Paul seemed somewhat remote and not quite the ebullient referee we are used to seeing. After the match there was criticism from both teams, the Italians feeling they had not been protected and the Austrians claiming they had been denied at least one penalty. Colleagues who watched the game felt that Paul Durkin had been less than strict with one or two tackles and, a few days later, I was concerned to learn that the FIFA referees delegate had been unhappy with Paul's performance. Indeed, the post-match inquest was such that Paul had indicated to his local newspaper that he did not expect to get another game.

The final set of group matches saw 12 referees receive a second appointment including the impressive Mexican, Brizio Carter, and also Mario van der Ende of Holland, who I felt was in with a real chance of the Final. Brizio Carter was exceptionally good in England's triumph over Colombia, a match marked by a free-kick goal of sheer genius from David Beckham which reminded me of a similar one he scored against Liverpool when I refereed Manchester United at Anfield last autumn. The completion of the group games was not without incident, especially in the Chile v Cameroon game where Vagner of Hungary sent off two Africans. The Cameroon contingent departed for home muttering about conspiracies. In Scotland's final game Craig Burley was sent off by Al Bujsaim, the referee from the UAE, for a bad tackle.

When the eight referees for the first round of knock-out matches were announced seven were from Europe, and Castrilli from Argentina was the eighth. It was noticeable that referees from some of the major footballing nations (Argentina, Germany, France, Denmark) were being used as FIFA would persist with its policy of sending home at the quarter-final stage any referee whose home country was still in the competition.

The talking point of this round of matches was the officiating of Kim Milton Nielsen from Denmark in the England v Argentina game. Prior to the game there had been much talk about past encounters and Maradona's 'Hand of God' and I was disappointed that Glenn Hoddle, who had played in that match, was critical not of Maradona for handling the ball but of the Tunisian referee for not spotting it, even though Hoddle admitted that several England players had also missed the offence. It was rather like suggesting that if someone is mugged it is not the fault of the mugger but of the police. His comments reflect a modern-day paradox in football – when a player cons a referee there is greater criticism of the referee for being deceived than condemnation of the player for cheating.

The match was largely devoid of the brutality and gamesmanship which had marred past encounters between the two countries and this was in no small measure due to Nielsen's accurate decision-making, imposing physical presence and calm refereeing. Although everyone tried for days afterwards to blame him for England's defeat, his performance was exceptional and when normal video frames threw some of his decisions into doubt the close-up replays showed that he was right – for example, in disallowing Campbell's goal because Alan Shearer elbowed Carlos Roa, the Argentinian goalkeeper, in the head as the cross came over. Possibly Nielsen's only mistake came after he had ruled out this goal. He allowed Argentina to take the free-kick quickly from the wrong position and England were very nearly caught out.

Nielsen awarded two penalties, one against Seaman. The goalkeeper came out to meet Diego Simeone, the Argentinian midfielder, who pushed the ball wide and Seaman's momentum brought him down. Any challenge where contact is made with an opponent without the ball being played is a direct free-kick, and in the area that means a penalty. Later on Roberto Ayala tried to avoid making contact with Michael Owen who was on an electrifying run into the penalty area but the Argentinian blocked his path and down Owen went. Neither penalty was an intentional foul but they checked the progress of an opponent without the ball being played. The match also contained two handball incidents. In the first half the ball struck Tony Adam's hand in the penalty area but it was a clear case of ball to hand and there was no intent, an essential requirement for handball to be penalised. In the second half José Chamot challenged for the ball with his arms high and again there was contact but, again rightly, Nielsen decided there had been no intent.

I was saddened, but not surprised by David Beckham's sending off. We had already seen with the dismissals of Patrick Kuhvert of Holland and Zinedine Zidane of France that if a player retaliated using an arm or foot as a weapon then, regardless of the force used, he would be sent off. Beckham was fouled by Diego Simeone, who was about to be shown the yellow card and a free kick had been given. As Beckham lay on the floor he suddenly kicked out and caught the Argentinian. It was a moment of madness. Although it was a sneaky little kick and Simeone over-reacted, Nielsen had no option but to show the red card and Beckham's reaction was clear: he went straight off (unlike the Argentinian Rattin in 1966 who held up the game for 15 minutes arguing with the German referee). He didn't protest and nor did his team-mates. For days everyone debated Beckham's crime. How did I feel? Part of me was angry and frustrated at his childish behaviour. However, few of us have not, in a split second, done something foolish that we instantly regretted. I could feel sympathy for him as he would be playing the incident over and over in his mind and just wishing that he could turn the clock back and be rid of the awful sick feeling in his stomach. His action may have cost England the game but was it worse than whoever allowed David Batty to take a penalty in the shootout when he had never taken one before?

After that match there was a reception for the World Cup referees and assistant referees before 24 of the referees went home. Unfortunately, Nielsen was one who had to leave as Denmark had qualified for the quarter-finals. Yet again the World Cup would lose some of its best referees as most of the major nations had qualified. Thus Collina of Italy, van der Ende of Holland and Batta of France would take no further part in the tournament. This is a difficult matter. While sending home referees from the qualifying countries ensures complete neutrality, it does deprive the competition of many excellent officials. England's defeat made Paul Durkin's earlier flight home all the more disappointing as, if he had performed well in his match, he would have had a great chance of perhaps featuring in the semi-finals or final. The good news for Britain was that Mark Warren, the English assistant, and Hugh Dallas, the Scottish referee, had been retained. The other European referees retained were from Spain, Norway and Switzerland as were six more from Mexico, Paraguay, Saudi Arabia, Morocco, UAE and Egypt – none from Africa, or the Far East or Australia.

The first two quarter-final matches on 3 July were largely uneventful. Hugh Dallas refereed Italy v France very competently, using his cards judiciously to stamp out any signs of niggle, but allowing the game to flow – an essential ingredient as it was a poor spectacle, eventually decided on penalties. Equally, Gamal Ghandour from Egypt controlled the pulsating Denmark v Brazil game with a quiet authority, ably supported by two assistants from Tunisia and Mali showing that we should not be too dismissive in our attitude to officials from 'lesser' footballing countries.

However, it was the second set of quarter-finals the following day which provided the talking points, not because of errors but because strong refereeing preserved both matches as exciting spectacles. Brizio

Carter of Mexico was at his strong best in Holland v Argentina. He sent off Arthur Numan of Holland for two yellow card offences: the second was a clear foul but the six rolls executed by Diego Simeone of Argentina were a touch unnecessary. Late in the game, Ariel Ortega ran into the Dutch penalty area and threw himself over a defender's leg to try to gain a penalty. As Brizio Carter marched over, yellow card in hand to caution him for cheating, the Argentinian got up and head-butted Van der Sar, the Dutch keeper. The yellow turned instantly to red. That evening Rune Pedersen, the relaxed but firm Norwegian referee, controlled the potentially volatile Germany v Croatia game with care, trying to avoid a repetition of their notorious battle in Euro '96. He rightly dismissed Christian Worns of Germany for a very bad tackle and this helped set the scene for Croatia's shock 3–0 victory.

The quarter-finals were marked by good, firm officiating and if all matches in the early stages had been refereed like this the tournament would have been much better. Unfortunately, though, none of the referees showed any real sign of getting to grips with the inordinate amount of shirt-pulling and shirt-holding which was a negative feature of this World Cup, as was the widespread blocking and holding at corners.

Semi-finals

The semi-finals saw Al Bujsaim of the UAE appointed to Brazil v Holland and José Maria Garcia Aranda to France v Croatia. The first match went well and there were few disputes or problems. Al Bujsaim was ably assisted by his colleagues from Tunisia and Oman giving the third team a real North African and Middle Eastern flavour. Indeed the game posed few challenges to him and although I expected trouble to flare at any moment there was none – just the huge disappointment of the Dutch in losing on penalties. The only talking point was when Holland's Pierre van Hooijdonk appeared to be pulled to the ground just inside the Brazilian penalty area towards the end of normal time. Al Bujsaim was following the flight of the ball and when the players came into view all he saw was van Hooijdonk falling dramatically to the ground. Having not seen the shirt-pulling that led up to this the referee assumed that it was another case of a player simulating an offence and gave the Dutchman a yellow card – in many people's view a double injustice.

In the France v Croatia match the Spanish referee officiated in the style that had been so widely praised when he refereed the opening game between Scotland and Brazil. He was not over-strict, indeed somewhat lenient with some tackles, but generated a good atmosphere among the players despite the huge amount of shirt pulling and blocking at corners, which finally flared late in the second half. As the players jockeyed for position at a French free-kick, Le Blanc reacted to being held by Croatian Slaven Bilic by pushing him, with an open hand, in the face. In an over-dramatic reaction Bilic fell to the ground clutching the upper part of his head – nowhere near where contact had been made. Garcia Aranda sent off Le Blanc, he had no other choice given the attitude to such aggressive acts throughout this World Cup, but Bilic's reaction brought widespread condemnation. Indeed, this one incident highlighted and captured in a few seconds the appalling cheating and over-reacting that plagued World Cup 1998. Let us hope that this stark example of one player getting another into trouble will be the catalyst for such behaviour to be eradicated from the game, probably by FIFA using video evidence to punish players who simulate offences or over-react.

The Final

In the days leading up to the Final there was much debate about who would be chosen to referee. Would it be one of the quarter final referees, in which case Brius Carter of Mexico or Hugh Dallas of Scotland would have a good chance or would FIFA use one of the ten who had not featured in the quarter- or semi-finals? In the event Said Beloqola of Morocco was chosen along with Mark Warren of England and Achmat Salie of South Africa as assistants and Abdul Rahman Al Zeid of Saudi Arabia (who had been our guide for Saudi Arabia and China) as the reserve referee. It was the first time an African had been appointed to a World Cup Final and flew in the face of those who believe that only the top footballing nations produce the best referees. He refereed the game with a quiet authority and showed himself to be extremely fit and able to sprint as quickly as the players even in the final minutes, although some of his positioning was somewhat naïve. He read the attempt to win free-kicks very well and was strong, but not over-strict. In the second half when the Frenchman Marcel Desailly, who had already received a yellow card, committed a bad late tackle the player was already walking off before Beloqola could get the yellow and red cards out of his pocket.

At the end of the game no one was talking about the referee which to the vast majority meant that he had done well. He had avoided the controversy that had plagued the 1974 and 1990 Finals. In 1974 England's Jack Taylor awarded an early penalty to Holland before Germany had even touched the ball and later one to Germany. He also showed Johan Cruyff the yellow card at half-time for dissent. The most controversial World Cup Final referee of recent times was Elgardo Codesa who sent off two Argentinians in the 1990 Final and awarded a dubious penalty to Germany. His appointment had been contentious as he was the son-in-law of the Chairman of FIFA's Referees' Committee. In 1994 there had been a general expectation that Peter Mikkelsen of Denmark would referee the Final but Sandor Puhl was appointed and the ructions that followed saw three European members of the FIFA Referees' Committee removed at the end of the tournament.

The greatest pleasure for me, and very many others, was that Mark Warren was appointed as the No. 1 assistant: a just reward for his excellent lining career. We had all hoped that he might gain football's highest honour as he had performed very well in the FIFA under Championships in Malaysia in 1997 and had been the only European assistant to go to Burkina Faso to officiate in the African Nations Cup. I could not have been more delighted for Mark, and his performance on the night fully justified the faith FIFA had shown in him. I was very proud to be an English referee as I watched him perform in his usual low-key, unflappable manner.

Lessons for the Future

Throughout the competition there was, as expected, much debate about the standard of refereeing and whether full-time referees would raise standards. The emergence of good referees from smaller footballing nations seemed to reinforce the view that it is the person himself, and not whether he is full-time or part-time, which is most important. If so-called professional referees are so good why do Brazil (where the top referees have been professional for many years) import referees to do their top matches? I have no doubt that we will move towards more referees becoming full-time but the best solution for referees have a part-time job and be 'employed' by the national FA for part of the week to allow sufficient time for training and match preparation. This is currently being tried in countries like Norway.

In the end, no matter how much referees are paid or how full-time they become they are human beings who will make mistakes, just as players don't always score with every shot or time every tackle or pass to perfection.

Several points emerged which football and referees need to address. On the positive side the fourth official using the electronic board after 45 minutes to show how much time remains in each half worked well, and there was little on-field treatment of players. Indeed, the feigning of injury to hold up the game for tactical advantage has largely been eliminated by the removal of players from the field if they need or want treatment. The ten-yard enforcement at free-kicks was good and there was little dissent, especially when players were given red or yellow cards.

Few serious injuries occurred suggesting that the clampdown on violent tackles was successful. I can't think of one player who was kicked out of the World Cup and unable to compete because of an injury sustained from a foul challenge. The benefits of the strict refereeing were probably best exemplified by Michael Owen's wonder goal against Argentina when he was able to run at speed and score, whereas in 1990 or before he would probably have been chopped down before he reached the penalty area. Those who worry that strict refereeing means that good players will not be seen because they have been suspended should realise that if players are protected then attacking football and skilful play will flourish.

There were a number of negative areas. Shirt-holding and shirt-pulling reached almost epidemic proportions and became the problem that tackling from behind used to be. Associated with this was the considerable blocking, holding and checking that took place at corners and attacking free-kicks which was almost impossible for the referee to deal with as so many players were involved each time. What was needed was for referees to delay the free-kick at corner and speak to the players. If this had been done the Le Blanc-Bilic incident in the semi-final might have been prevented.

The issue of diving and over-reacting, basically cheating, needs to be quickly eradicated, probably using video technology. Where else should technology be used? Decisions of fact such as whether the ball crossed the line for a goal would seem to be clear-cut examples of where we could use cameras without undermining the authority of the referee or holding up the game too much. Beyond that there is a danger that what is essentially a non-stop sport could become punctuated with stoppages as decisions are reviewed either by the referee or someone in a replay control room. Not until we are satisfied that we want more hold-ups and the technology exists so every camera angle is available (remember Brazil v Norway where TV purported to show that the referee had wrongly given a penalty but the following day the internet had an image showing a clear shirt-pull on Tore Andre Flo) should we allow it to intrude into the game. Human error by players, managers and referees is part of football and some of the enjoyment for the spectators is post-match debate over decisions and controversies. Let us not destroy this wonderful game with the quest for perfect decision-making.

As ever the World Cup provided much enjoyment, much emotion and much discussion. It was the world's greatest sporting event. If only I had been able to be there. . .

Epilogue

I reached the final round of interviews for the Harrow Head Master's post. I was very close to being appointed but, as I had always anticipated, the governors chose an existing Head Master. For a brief period I was deeply disappointed but the tremendous support I received from colleagues, friends, parents and boys helped greatly and I was soon getting ready for the new season and making plans for the future.